Detective Work

Detective Work

A Study of Criminal Investigations

William B. Sanders

THE FREE PRESS

A Division of Macmillan Publishing Co., Inc.

NEW YORK

Collier Macmillan Publishers

LONDON

The Free Press
A Division of Macmillan Publishing Co., Inc.
866 Third Avenue, New York, N.Y. 10022

Collier Macmillan Canada, Ltd.

Library of Congress Catalog Card Number: 77–72687

Printed in the United States of America

printing number

1 2 3 4 5 6 7 8 9 10

Library of Congress Cataloging in Publication Data

Sanders, William B
    Detective work.

    Bibliography: p.
    Includes index.
    1. Criminal investigation. 2. Detectives.
I. Title.
HV8073.S228   364.12   77-72687
ISBN 0-02-927660-8

To my wife, Eli

Contents

Acknowledgments

In an extensive examination of studies on the police, Peter Manning found that a disproportionate number of these studies were based on participant-observation methods. At the same time, the findings of the researchers almost uniformly point to massive suspicion, clannishness, and cynicism among police. The irony of these two observations is that participant-observation research requires a good deal of trust and understanding on the part of the party being observed, and that, more than most occupational groups, the police have opened their doors to researchers who have come to live with them during their working hours, underfoot and often a source of embarrassment. Without their cooperation, trust, and assistance, none of these studies would have been possible, and the one reported in this book would have been unthinkable. To the detectives of the "Mountainbeach County Sheriff's Office" I owe my most profound gratitude for making this study possible.

Don Zimmerman, Donald Cressey, and D. Lawrence Wieder served as prime movers in stimulating my interest, opening doors to the research setting and helping to organize the ideas. Their efforts enabled me to make something out of observations that would otherwise have been mere descriptions. Howard Daudistel and Mike Williams were co-researchers with whom I shared ideas, work, and adventures, and I am grateful to them for their many and varied contributions.

For the European data I was able to accumulate, I owe much to Professor Albert Hess of the New York State University College at Brockport, who provided introductions to both the

German and Dutch police. Schutzpolizeidirektor Johann Gebert
of the Münster Police Academy was extremely helpful in explaining German police organization, education, and methods,
and Inspector Monstor of The Hague police was equally helpful
in explaining the Dutch police. Mr. Stanley Green of Scotland
Yard made possible an extremely fruitful interview with Detective Inspectors Gordon and Coote. The University of California,
Santa Barbara, provided support through a Patent Fund Grant
making the study in Europe possible.

Professors Edward Sagarin and Marvin Scott offered valuable advice on organization and style of the book. They, along
with Gladys Topkis of The Free Press, are responsible for
clarifying and demystifying much of what I had to say. Brenda
Stoney typed the near-final draft of the manuscript and enabled
me to turn everything over to my publisher more or less on time.

Finally, my wife, Eli, and sons, Billy and David, put up with
me while I was conducting research at all hours of the day and
night in all sorts of strange places, and later when I was writing
it all down. Their toleration, understanding, and support were
much needed and appreciated.

William B. Sanders
February 1977

Detective Work

Introduction

The idea of doing a study of detectives grew out of my interest in the sociology of mental illness. In research on various forms of mental illness, I have always been especially interested in one psychiatric classification—the paranoid. The paranoid is characterized by what is an abnormal amount of distrust. I believed that if I could learn about distrust, I could learn about trust, which plays so important a role in social interaction.

One of the key elements in the characterization of the paranoid is that his distrust is delusional. However, after coming to know a few paranoids in mental hospitals, I became aware that many of their feelings of persecution had some grounding in reality. For the most part the paranoids were obnoxious individuals, and no one particularly liked them. I have little doubt that others did do things to them that were harmful, so the paranoids' beliefs that they were being persecuted were in some cases true.

This realization led me to further questions. What is real and what is not? This question once again involved the issue of trust, since trust is based on the assumption that others will not harm us and will more or less play by the rules of the game. Together, these matters led me to an inquiry into the nature of information: How do social actors go about gathering and assessing information? And how is a sense of information constructed? The former question, derived from the work of Erving Goffman, was directed at uncovering how information functions in social interaction. The latter centered around the works of Harold Garfinkel and the ethnomethodologists.

1

As my interest came to be focused on information, I looked for a subject to study that would reveal something about information. Since police detectives are information gatherers, and because they, like other police officers, have been characterized as paranoid, they seemed a good choice (Symonds, 1976, pp. 73). In this way what began as an interest in mental illness resulted in a study of detectives.

THE STUDY AND THE SETTING

In order to learn about detectives and information work, I spent a year in participant-observation research in the detective bureau of a county sheriff's office. The details of the methodology are provided in Chapter 9, and the organization of the department where the study was conducted is described in Chapter 2. Here I should like to say something about the county and town where the study was done to provide context for the findings.

The county, here called "Mountainbeach," is located, as the name implies, between a coastal range of mountains and the ocean. Founded by Spanish missionaries, Mountainbeach today has a thriving tourist business, owing to its temperate climate and its unspoiled setting, and is free from most of the indignities of urban blight. However, it is not a cozy seaside resort with total dependence on tourism. The total county population is 266,000, including 147,000 living in the city of Mountainbeach and its suburbs located along the southern coast of the county. In the northern part of the county are an inland city of 33,000 with an agricultural economic base, a few small towns, a federal prison, and a military installation. South of the city of Mountainbeach there is an incorporated "beach town" of 7,000.

The city of Mountainbeach is under the jurisdiction of the city police; the Sheriff's Office is responsible for all unincorporated areas in the county. Two sheriff sub-stations, one located 70 miles north of the city of Mountainbeach and the other about 30 miles inland to the northeast, provide services for the outlying rural districts. The remaining unincorporated area of the county is supervised through the main Sheriff's Office, which was located in the city at the beginning of the study and moved just outside city limits during the study. There was also a small foot-patrol office in the university community, directly supervised by the main office.

Most of the study was conducted in three areas around the city of Mountainbeach, for very few investigations took the detectives from the main office to the outlying parts of the county. (The sub-stations handled most investigations in the rural areas; only occasionally did an investigation initiated in the main office take the detectives there.)

One of the three areas where most of the research took place was "Beachcliff," a community of about 15,000 population located adjacent to a state university. Most residents of Beachcliff were students, but the community was also a haven for runaways and hangers-on to the campus scene. It had the highest burglary rate in the county, and the rate of bicycle and surfboard theft was also extremely high.

The second area, The Valley, was a middle-class residential area that began at the city limits and extended in a strip between the mountains and the ocean about five miles up the coast. At one time The Valley was mainly agricultural, with orange, lemon, and avocado groves.

As suburban growth rapidly increased after World War II, The Valley was engulfed by shopping centers and housing developments, and only a few scattered citrus and avocado groves remained. In addition to several large shopping centers and discount houses, The Valley housed a number of light industries, particularly small electronic manufacturing plants. As in the rest of the area, including the city, there was no heavy industry.

The third main area, Little Mountain, was located on the opposite side of the city from The Valley. Little Mountain was populated by upper-middle and upper classes. It was not affected by urban sprawl to the same extent or in the same way as The Valley, and as a result Little Mountain changed very little over the years. There was a village of Little Mountain, with some small businesses and professional offices as well as a single small shopping center. Little Mountain was patrolled by a private security force serving to keep away outsiders. Although there were a number of burglaries in the area, and a spectacular double homicide during the time of the study, it had the lowest crime rate of the three areas.

Between The Valley and Little Mountain was a transitional

area, The Canyon, running north of the city and populated by a combination of middle- and upper-middle-class families. The Canyon was not so distinct as either The Valley or Little Mountain and has not been included as a separate area. It was important, though, in that it served as a buffer zone between The Valley and Little Mountain.

Mountainbeach and the adjacent county to the north made up a Standard Metropolitian Statistical Area (SMSA) in the 1970 census. The northern county of the SMSA was far more rural than Mountainbeach, and as a result the census data may show Mountainbeach to be somewhat more rural than it actually is. However, we can still see some of the unique features of the area from the census figures. The statewide percentage of those whose occupation was listed as "professional, technical, and kindred workers" was 17.4; the figure for the Mountainbeach SMSA was 20.8 (Bureau of the Census, 1972). Typical blue-collar occupations, on the other hand, were underrepresented in the Mountainbeach SMSA. Statewide, 10.3 percent of the labor force was employed as "operative except transport" (e.g., assemblers, machine operative, welders); in Mountainbeach the figure was 7.9 percent (Bureau of Census, 1972). Thus, Mountainbeach can be characterized as a middle- and upper-middle-class community in relationship to most other communities in the state.

The ethnic makeup of the Mountainbeach SMSA was predominately white, with a sizable Chicano minority population and small black population. The census identified 28,987 people (11 percent of the population) as having Spanish as a mother tongue, of whom 5,774 were born in Mexico. Of the Mexican-born, only 1,504 were naturalized citizens; the rest were identified as alien, and many of this group were farm laborers in the northern county of the SMSA. The nonwhite population (mainly blacks) was only 5,663 (2 percent of the population).

Most of the minorities lived within the city limits of Mountainbeach. Except for a few Chicano enclaves, there were no "ghettos" of poor blacks or Chicanos in the county. Most of the blacks and Chicanos who lived in the area where the study was done were either students at the State University or middle-class families living in The Valley.

More could be said about the texture of life in the Mountainbeach area, but for the purposes of this book it is sufficient to note that it is a small- to moderate-sized city with a large unincorporated suburban fringe and a state university with an accompanying student community. Mountainbeach is atypical in that it is underrepresented in minorities and working-class members. However, the suburban areas around the city where the study was conducted do approach typicality in makeup since most suburbs are composed heavily of middle- and upper-middle-class whites. Moreover, the student community is fairly typical of most areas adjacent to universities, and the makeup of the student body is no different from that of other state universities.

As we will see, the socioeconomic composition of the community has little direct bearing on the investigative practices and information development which are the main focus of this study. It is important to know something about the community, for the detectives were essentially responding to citizens' requests for police services, and the nature of their responses cannot be divorced from the nature of the community. Nevertheless, it should be kept in mind that we are dealing with the generic features of information and its development, and the findings of this study dealing with the detectives of Mountainbeach can tell us about how people in general deal with information in social interaction.

1

Detectives and the Study of Information

Regrettably, empirical studies of detectives are nowhere to be found. As with most of the specialized units, hypotheses about decision-making are made . . . , but with very little evidence in the literature as foundation (Pepinsky, 1975, p. 27).

This book is a study of detectives and how they go about developing information. As a study of detectives it focuses on the routine, everyday work detectives do in investigating crimes, from making decisions to filling out report forms. This entails a good deal of ethnographic description and analysis to bring out the nuances of detective work.

As a study of information the book looks at the processes involved in gathering data. Since detectives are essentially information gatherers, detective work is a form of information work, and detectives provide a resource for understanding information in a generic sense. That is, the book uses the detective's methods of gathering information to show how information *in general* is made available and used in social interaction.

INFORMATION AND INTERACTION

As a background for studying detectives and information, it will be useful to consider and elaborate the conception of social interaction put forth by Erving Goffman. For Goffman (1959),

6

social interaction is essentially grounded in the information interactants have about one another. Social actors monitor one another's behavior for cues or signs, given intentionally or given off more or less unwittingly, which are taken as informative about the other's social status, interaction role, and intentions. Knowledge of one another acquired through the information supplied in these signs makes it possible for interactants to carry on sustained face-to-face contact in a fashion that is consistent with shared understandings of each social actor's performance. A working consensus is established between interactants as to what role the other plays in terms of the interaction situation, and it is through this working consensus that stable, orderly interaction is possible.

What an individual presents in social interaction that may be taken as informative about his identity has a promissory character in that it is expected to be an actual representation of his identity. That is, whatever signs, cues, gestures, or other informative materials or acts are presented constitute a promise, in most situations, that the actor can back up the implicit claims of his presentations with credentials or performances. For example, if a man "comes on" as a surgeon, we expect that he not only has the necessary degrees and training to be a legitimate surgeon, but also that he can perform certain kinds of operations. The promissory character of the presentation obligates the actor to back up his claims if challenged and, at the same time, obligates others to acknowledge the claims. Because of this promissory element, interactants can typically assume that the other is in fact what he presents himself to be, and they can respond appropriately on the basis of the presented information.

However, one cannot assume in all social situations that the other is presenting himself honestly. The con man is the prime example of a person who typically misrepresents himself, and the con game exemplifies a situation of misrepresentation. Whether in a con game or on a blind date, information is problematic, and social actors therefore examine carefully whatever is presented. For the sociologist, such situations are important, for they permit him to discern the activities and processes whereby social actors consciously deal with information. Moreover, it is in situations where information is problematic that the entire notion of what information consists of and how it is used in social interaction can be explored most usefully.

Concepts of Information

As a point of departure, we will examine some conceptions of information from the interactionist point of view. Goffman (1971, pp. 303–4; 1974, pp. 133–34) refers to information as what the social actor knows about the other's intentions. More generally, Scott (1968, p. 1) defines information as what the social actor knows about the situation. Glaser and Strauss (1967, p. 430) treat information in social interaction in terms of actors' "awareness contexts." Scheff (1970, p. 6) refines and reconceptualizes the Glaser-Strauss position by specifying awareness on the levels of understanding, agreement, and realization. All these conceptions of information, despite their differences, refer in some way to what one social actor knows about the other.

Note that Goffman's treatment of information assumes that some *factual* or *real* state of affairs exists independent of interpretive work. For example, in his work on strategic interaction he notes that a spy seeking to pass unnoticed in an enemy country may present the proper attire, gestures, and habits, but this presentation is a faked one. The reality behind this facade is his intention to gather military secrets. The extent to which enemy counterintelligence units are aware of the spy's intentions points to their having "real" information about the spy. Similarly, normal appearances may mask a psychotic killer, an undercover agent, or any other sort of person seeking to conceal his intentions (Goffman, 1971, pp. 283–309). For Goffman, as soon as one is aware of the other's "actual" intentions, one has information about the situation.

It might be argued that Goffman is dealing with interpretations of information, for the actor must consider the possible meanings any presentation may have, including the possibility of misrepresentation. However, Goffman clearly points out that interpretations or "definitions of the situation" play only a marginal role in his analysis:

> Defining situations as real certainly has consequences but these may contribute very marginally to the events in progress; in some cases only a slight embarrassment flits across the scene in mild concern for those who tried to define the situation wrongly . . . , presumably, a "definition of the situation" is almost always to be found, but those who are in the situation ordinarily do not *create* this definition, even though their

society can be said to do so; ordinarily, all they do is to assess correctly what the situation ought to be for them and then act accordingly (Goffman, 1974, pp. 1–2).

What Goffman appears to be saying is that there is real information if only we can get to it. We will learn of a misrepresentation if we have access to the information that will reveal the actor's true intentions. Thus, Goffman points to "real" information and "fabricated" information that exist independent of massive interpretive work.

Glaser and Strauss (1967) hold similar assumptions. In situations where a dying patient is attempting to assess what the doctors "really" believe about his chances of survival, these authors equate awareness of the doctors' opinion with having accurate information, or "being informed." Here again, we can see that to these authors information is a "thing in the world" depending on access rather than interpretation. Likewise, Scott (1968) treats knowledge of a trainer's opinion of his horse's chance of winning a race as access to information instead of as interpretation of something as informative. A bettor's knowledge that the trainer thinks his horse can win a particular race is information; how the sense of the fact developed is uninteresting to Scott. The bettor's strategies for getting to the information is the social point. Making sense out of ambiguous information is a relevant concern, but none of these writers centers his attention on the interpretive practices for constructing and formulating phenomena as information.

In addition to treating information as factual, these writers stress the ambiguity of information—that is, the fact that information may have more than one possible interpretation. For example, hearty laughter at a derisive homosexual joke may mask homosexuality on the part of the laughter (Goffman, 1963, p. 87); the most authentic-looking Frenchman may in fact be a British agent (Goffman, 1971, pp. 256–68); or any given appearance can be employed to belie the opposite intent (Goffman, 1969, p. 12). Knowledge that false fronts may be presented to shield intentions and identity leads the social actor to believe that presentations are subject to more than a single interpretation. However, the *fact* of the informative presentation, even though subject to more than one interpretation, is not treated as interesting.

A second source of ambiguity occurs in situations where no

fabrication of information is believed to exist. Scott (1968, p. 2) describes a situation in which racetrack gamblers are confronted with the information that a horse has dropped in class. Such information can be interpreted to mean that the horse has a good chance of beating horses of a lower class; on the other hand, the bettor may conclude from the same information that the horse has become unsound and doesn't stand a chance of winning. Thus, we can see that both unfabricated and fabricated information may be ambiguous.

A final feature of information related to factualness and ambiguity is the assumption of completeness. When one is confronted with ambiguity, the obvious practical remedy is to seek further information to "complete" what information one has. In the previous example, the bettor may attempt to find out whether the horse's owner needs money urgently; if he does so discover, he may take this new information to mean that the horse was deliberately dropped to give it a better chance to win. With this "more complete" information, the bettor sees himself in a position to make the correct betting decision. Scott (1968, p. 2) points out that social actors are generally limited by incomplete information and usually have to make their decisions on the basis of what can be inferred from the information available. He implies, however, that complete information *is* available if only one has the resources for gathering it.

The point of showing how interactionists deal with different aspects of information is that while interactionists demonstrate that information is being interpreted in the face of ambiguity and incompleteness, there is an underlying assumption that there is a "real" or "factual" state of affairs behind appearances. Thus, instead of dealing with the process of interpretation, interactionists tend to examine the conditions under which social actors make decisions, given ambigious and incomplete information. They tend to assume that if an actor has all the facts, there would be no need for interpretive work.

The Development of Information

In contrast to the studies of information cited above, this book will examine how information is *constructed* by social actors, along the lines suggested by Garfinkel (1967). Rather than examine information as a "social fact" (Durkheim, 1933, p.

60) in the world independent of interpretive work, we will ask how a sense of information is developed, how a given datum comes to be formulated as information. Specifically, we will examine the process whereby a sense of consensus is accomplished between social actors in interaction, for if, as Goffman (1959) notes, social interaction is based on such consensus, and if consensus is developed through comonitoring (i.e., mutual assessment of signs), then an understanding of how these signs are formulated as informative about an individual or situation is necessary for an understanding of social interaction.

When discussing the development of information, it is easy to confuse two different processes. We can examine an information search from the actor's point of view and discuss the development of information as a piecing together of the facts, treating each fact as an object free of interpretation. On the other hand, we can try to see how the sense of anything is developed as being informative, as a fact of a certain kind. The latter is the approach followed in this book. Thus, we will be examining the methods used in making sense out of people, things, and events. Because these methods involve interpretive work, we will refer to them as "interpretive practices." When we discuss the detectives' development of information, then, we are talking about the development of the *sense* of information through interpretive practices.

In looking at how detectives develop their primary forms of information—leads and evidence—it is important to understand some of the basic assumptions of ethnomethodology. Since facts are to be treated as the product of interpretive work, our discussion will deal with those moments when actors formulate facts. Thus, we will be talking about "situated" and "occasioned" facts in order to stress the idea that the facts are developed in specific situations and on specific occasions (Zimmerman and Pollner, 1970, pp. 94–95), rather than being independent of the situations in which they are formulated and the interpretive work in these formulations. For instance, in a case where a woman was cut with a knife, a bloodstained knife found at the crime scene was photographed as evidence. The sense of the knife's evidentiary character was situated by the understanding of the case (the situation) as involving a knife. In contrast, a bloody knife would probably not be considered a lead or possible evidence in a forgery case, but other things would be developed as evidence instead. Anything else that is formulated to be evidence is situated in the same way, and even though some things may appear to be obviously relevant to a case, it is only an understanding of the assumptions social actors have about a situation that makes them "obvious."

The central method of making interpretations is the documentary method, described by Garfinkel (1967, p. 78) as

> . . . treating an actual appearance as the "document of," as "pointing to," as "standing on behalf of" a presupposed underlying pattern. Not only is the pattern derived from its individual documentary evidences, but the individual documentary evidences, in their turn, are interpreted on the basis of "what is known" about the underlying pattern. Each is used to elaborate the other.

The documentary method of interpretation is an ongoing process. An underlying scheme is used to elaborate the specific sense of any appearance. The interpretive scheme is not inherently tied to the appearance; different schemes can be employed to interpret a given appearance. At the same time that the interpretive scheme tells the actor what he is looking at specifically, the scheme itself is validated by the appearance (the documentary evidence). For example, in burglary cases detectives look for signs of entry, such as indentations in window- and doorsills; any indentations they may find are treated as possible leads and evidence. The appearance of an indentation would be treated as a document of a burglary (the presupposed underlying pattern). At the same time, the assumption of a burglary would *make* the indentation on a door- or windowsill *sensible* as a sign of breaking in. Thus, the indentation "points to" a burglary, and the interpretive scheme of a burglary explains the indentation.

DETECTIVE WORK AND INFORMATION

The detective's task is to gather, organize, and use information about social behavior. Assuming that basic practices of developing information are the same for detectives as for others, we can treat detectives as generic examples of people developing information; the only difference is that what detectives do explicitly is done implicitly by most others.

Further, in situations where information is problematic, social actors are more likely to think about it, verbalize, and behave in other ways that reveal how something comes to be treated as informative. Since the detective's information work is routinely problematic, it is more highly visible then most others' and therefore researchable. Thus the police are a natural source for studying information, and detectives, whose work centers on information development, are the most useful resource within the police organization.

In order to understand the detective's position in relation to information work, we need to understand his role in the context of police organization (see chapter 2). The basic line organization of a police department consists of uniformed patrol and nonuniformed detectives. The uniformed patrol officer's job is to walk or otherwise patrol a beat, alert to anything that may require his attention in terms of assistance, order maintenance, or law enforcement (Reiss, 1971; Cumming, Cumming, and Edell, 1965; Manning, 1971). Detectives, on the other hand, investigate two different kinds of crimes. Some crimes are reported by victims and are handled by detectives who are known to all parties concerned to be police officers. For such crimes as theft, burglary, robbery, rape, assault, and homicide, detectives can be considered "reactive" investigators (cf. Reiss and Bordua, 1967; Reiss, 1971). Detectives also investigate crimes such as drug addiction, which have no victims (cf. Schur, 1965) or in which the victims do not see themselves as victims. Illicit drug use, prostitution, gambling, and homosexual activity are usually investigated by undercover detectives who are not generally known to be with the police. They are essentially "proactive" investigators (Skolnick, 1966; Skolnick and Woodworth, 1967) in that they do not as a rule act in response to a citizen's complaint. This study will deal with information generated in a detective bureau that was organizationally "reactive."

In developing information, detectives encounter sources they take to be possibly unreliable. They meet people who intentionally lie about themselves or others (Goffman, 1969, p. 7). This, they believe, is to be expected since the lies may enable the teller to avoid legal sanctions. However, the police believe that they can overcome this problem by interrogating suspects and witnesses, by checking their stories against available evidence, and by locating inconsistencies among various accounts. This belief that a "real world" or the "true story" lies behind contrived stories postulates some stable reference point that is independent of interpretive work. Instead of questioning the methods they use to develop a sense of information, the police see their questioning in terms of getting at information that is already there.

Further, detectives believe that even well-meaning witnesses tend to be inaccurate in their descriptions of people, things, and events. They complain that automobiles described by witnesses as black are sometimes green, that suspects described as clean shaven in fact often are bearded, and that the same event is described in so many different ways by people who believe that they are accurate that it is often impossible to find out what actually happened. This mistrust of information, however, does not question the belief that factual information does exist, for it is assumed that if people were better observers and more honest reporters the real facts would be found. What is suspect to detectives, then, is not the existence of a stable, concrete world of things and events, but rather the accuracy and honesty of accounts of things and events.

Complete Information

An underlying assumption of detectives in their attempts to unravel contradictory stories, expose liars, and solve cases is that it is possible to have complete information. At some point in accumulating information there is an end, and when one reaches this end, the information can be said to be complete; until that time the information state is incomplete. For example, in situations where two people are telling stories that are diametrically opposed, the detective regards the information he has (in this case the two different stories) as incomplete, for if he had access to further information he would be able to tell whom to believe. Not until the detective can determine who is telling the truth and who is lying is the information deemed complete.

Complete information in a case conceivably could mean *all* the facts that could be gathered about the case and the people involved in it; but this would involve an infinite number of facts. For all practical purposes, "completeness" is synonymous with "sufficiency," and when there is a sense that there is enough information it is considered complete for the time being. At the time that he identifies a suspect, decides to close the case, or makes any other practical decision, the detective's information is incomplete, but it is typically considered to be enough to "get by on." Incompleteness does not mean inconclusiveness. From the detective's point of view, when he can confidently decide that one story is false and the other true, his information has a *sense of completeness.* The notion that he is finally in possession of conclusive information appears invariably to be a retrospective realization. At the point where the information appears no longer to be ambiguous, for all practical purposes it is complete; at the same time, the sense of completeness serves to resolve the ambiguity.

To illustrate the moment-by-moment inconclusive character of information, let us consider a case in which a clue indicative of lying was the key element in the investigation. In attempting to arrive at a decision about the truthfulness of a suspect or witness, such manifestations as perspiration and trembling hands are taken as indicators of possible lying (Goffman, 1971, p. 261), whereas calmness and steady hands are taken to be signs of honesty. However, these readings are not always conclusive.

In a case I observed, a woman said that an acquaintance had stolen one of her checks and signed her name to it. The complainant seemed unusually nervous when she reported the crime at the detective's office. Upon interviewing the suspect identified by the nervous victim, the detective was told that the suspect had had the victim's permission to sign her name to the check and that therefore the act was legal. At this point the detective tentatively interpreted the complainant's nervousness as a sign that she had indeed been lying. Upon reinterviewing her in her home, he noticed that she had bitten her nails down almost to the quick. He also learned that she had previously been under psychiatric care. In view of this information, her nervousness was seen as a normal condition for the woman. Additionally, the detective pointed out that such a person would be a good victim for a criminal since, if the case went to court, it would be unlikely that she could hold up under the examination of a competent defense attorney. In this case the detective was dealing with what he saw as "incomplete" information, for he did not know at first how to read the signs suggesting lying. The "information" was in an inconclusive state in his mind, and through further digging he attempted to reduce the ambiguity. In such circumstances, which are not rare in detective work, the inability to have complete information sometimes causes the detective to put aside the case and go on to others. Only by fiat can information in these circumstances be "made" to be anything other than ambigious and incomplete.

Inconsistency and Incongruity

In virtually every case investigated by detectives during the period of my observation there was more than a single *possible* interpretation for the information at hand. Usually, if the detective thinks he has a good idea of what a given case is and who is involved, he does not entertain alternative interpretations, but in cases that are ambigious from the detective's point of view, he will attempt to get more information. However, it is not always possible to obtain the additional information required, and sometimes additional information merely serves to increase the ambiguity as new interpretations arise when the new information is considered.

Another way detectives attempt to reduce ambiguity is by testing information for consistency and congruency. In the case of the nervous victim, the consistency of her nervousness was taken as an indication that the complainant had emotional problems, and not that she was lying. Similarly, a Juvenile detective found that a suspect had won several athletic awards, and on this basis justified his belief in the youth's innocence. In this detective's view, juvenile involvement in athletics was inconsistent and incongruent with delinquent behavior. Sacks (1972, p. 283) points out that police use an "incongruity procedure" to locate potential troublemakers and criminals. Thus, because robbers sometimes wear long coats to conceal guns, the police view with suspicion anyone attired in a way that is incongruent with the weather (e.g., long sleeves on a hot day). For their part, as Wambaugh (1973) has noted, criminals are aware of the necessity to act and appear in a way consistent with the setting and weather and prefer the dark and foul weather, which conceals their intentions.

However, seeing consistency and congruency does not always eliminate ambiguity. In the business of espionage and counterespionage, the participants are aware that the other side is attempting to present a consistent appearance and to locate inconsistencies in *their* appearance (Cookridge, 1966). During the Nazi occupation of France the British went so far as to make sure that agents who were sent to France had the buttons sewed on their clothes using typical French stitching patterns. The Gestapo was equally aware that the British agents were well trained and appeared to be anything but British. If the Gestapo stopped someone who was every bit a Frenchman with the exception of wearing a jacket with the buttons attached in the English manner, such information could be employed in two entirely different ways. It might be taken as indicating that the person was not a British agent, for agents know better than to be caught with such incriminating evidence. On the other hand, it might point to an agent who made a mistake. Goffman (1969, p. 69) describes the ambiguity of such situations:

> In unimportant situations there is a comforting continuum with valid appearances at one end and obviously faked ones at the other—the only difference being with cases in the middle. But in matters of significance, matters likely to arouse sharply opposed interests, the end of the continuum can come together to form a terrible loop. When the situation seems to be exactly what it appears to be, the closest likely alternative is that the situation has been completely faked; when fakery seems extremely evident, the most probable possibility is that nothing fake is present.

It is this type of situation with which the detective is most often faced, since a smart criminal has enough sense not to present himself as a criminal. As one successful burglar explained, a cloth cap, a striped shirt, and an eye-mask do not constitute appropriate working attire:

> I used to get a kick out of driving into nice neighborhoods to watch the cops push the greasy long-haired kids around. . . . I generally drove a Cadillac because it looked right for the neighborhood I liked to hit. I didn't want to overdo it, so I usually bought one a couple of years old. Another thing was my appearance—you never would have found me without a shave and a white shirt and tie on.
>
> So when I saw a couple of policemen talking to a carload of suspicious-looking kids, I would always lower my window and wave to them. Give them a little smile to let them know that I, as a citizen, appreciated what they were doing. Then I would

> find myself a big, beautiful home with the husband away at
> work and the wife away at bridge club, and I'd go in and get a
> few thousand dollars' worth of stuff (Younger, 1973, p. 41).

As can be seen from this example, the burglar attends to the
same features of his appearance as do the police. He manages his
appearance so that he will be overlooked by anyone in search of
"suspicious-looking" characters. His appearance is congruent
with the normal appearances of legitimate others who live in the
neighborhoods he burglarizes.

To the extent that the police and detectives are aware that
some criminals are smart enough to blend with the setting when
they commit their crimes, the incongruity procedure is of little
use in reducing the sense of ambiguity in information. The
"terrible loop" described by Goffman comes together to fog the
degree of confidence one can give to information. The "obvious" suspect in a wealthy neighborhood turns out to be an
innocent gardner, and the man in the chauffeured limousine
who is never suspected by the police is later found to be a
sophisticated burglar.

But if establishing a sense of congruency and consistency,
while clearly not an infallible method, is taken to be a way of
reducing ambiguity, it is important to examine how some sense
of consistency is established in the first place. Goffman (1959,
pp. 22–25) points out that social actors construct "fronts"
consisting of an appearance, a manner, and a setting which they
expect to be accepted as legitimate. It is easy to identify styles,
habits, and other aspects of social actors that either "fit" a
situation or fail to do so; for instance, we can see the incongruity
of a skid-row derelict sitting down at a white-tie dinner, but it is
not so easy to explain what is meant when we say that something
is or is not congruent with other aspects of the setting. We may
know intuitively what seems to be in place or out of place or
what things seem to go together "naturally," and still not know
why.

A possible point of reference in examining what goes with
what is a "theme" (Gurwitsch, 1964, p. 340). The word is used
here in a broad sense, to include not only the topical backdrop of
appearances but also the context of an appearance. Thus, when
police officers see an old car parked in the driveway of a mansion
or a expensive new car parked next to a shack, they become

suspicious, since the car is incongruous with the theme provided by the understanding of the setting.

Not all themes are as apparently "automatic" as we might first assume, for a given setting or context can be formulated into different themes depending on the assumptions the social actors bring to the situation. For example, one may assume that a mansion is a boarding house and, under the thematic assumptions that go with "boarding house," consider certain objects and events congruent that would be considered incongruent in the thematic field of a mansion. Therefore, it is critical to consider the construction of a theme used to evaluate the congruency of appearances. In our examination of detectives we will be pointing out these constructions and their uses.

Ambiguity and Games

Goffman (1969; 1971) and Lyman and Scott (1970) take ambiguity to be a feature of information in certain situations where two or more actors are in competition. In these situations, which they characterize in terms of a game framework, social actors are viewed as rational players attempting to defeat their opponents (Schelling, 1963). In information games, one side attempts to conceal information and the other side attempts to uncover it (Lyman and Scott, 1970, p. 58). Deception is employed by both sides. Those attempting to conceal information (as criminals are from detectives) present false information and hide valid information; those who are trying to uncover information, (as detectives are) attempt to present a nonthreatening, disinterested appearance to deceive those from or about whom they wish to gain information. Detectives and criminals constitute a generic example of such encounters. If the detective identifies the criminal through information given off by the criminal, the detective wins; if the criminal prevents damaging information from becoming available to the detective, the criminal wins. The play consists of the detective's tracking down clues, disguising his interest in incriminating information, and offering explanations which will allow the criminal to give up and lose the game without losing face. The criminal plays the game by covering up any information useful to the detective and presenting false information designed to lead the detective on a false trail, or at least on one that diverts him from the criminal.

In this context of suspicion and deception, neither side can rely on ordinary understandings of appearance or the promissory character appearances normally have. Since neither side is expected to present itself for what it is, the exact meaning of any appearance is always in doubt. Thus an unwitting move by an innocent suspect may be taken by a detective as a move employed by the "criminal" to improve his position. Similarily, the criminal may begin to suspect that anyone who is at all friendly toward him may be a detective in disguise. Awareness of what normally "goes with" a given display is no longer a reliable resource for interpreting appearances (Schutz, 1971, p. 299). The more aware either player is of this state of affairs, or the more he interprets a state of affairs in this way, the less likely he is to trust anything as conclusively informative. But a radical distrust of all appearances leaves the detective with no stable reference point on which to ground any decision. This means that he must suspend distrust in order to carry out his investigation. This is not so much a means of coping with reality as it is a way of *establishing a reality* from which to operate. The alternative is a spiral into paranoia and radical cynicism, a path taken by many in police work (Symonds, 1976, p. 73).

For Goffman (1959), social interaction is made possible by the moral obligation to present a genuine appearance and the assumptions about appearances that interactants make in order to respond properly in social situations. Social interaction would begin to break down if these assumptions were brought into doubt. In some situations where identities are routinely fabricated and are not expected to bear any resemblance to actual identities, as is the case to some extent in bars (Cavan, 1966), social interaction is not threatened because none of the participants seriously expects a relationship between appearances and actuality. However, in more consequential situations there is a very real need for assurance that standard expectations about appearances will be maintained. As urbanites barricade themselves from the man on the street and old people go to collect their social-security checks only in protective caravans, we can see that what appearances convey is becoming increasingly ambiguous and consequential. Moreover, as Goffman (1971, p. 331) notes, the consequentiality makes for further ambiguity:

The vulnerability of public life is what we are coming more and more to see, if only because we are becoming more aware of the areas and intricacies of mutual trust presupposed in public order. Certainly circumstances can arise which undermine the ease that individuals have within their *Umwelt** Some of these circumstances are currently found in the semi-public places within slum-housing developments and slum neighborhoods, and there is no intrinsic reason why some of these sources of alarm (as well as some additional ones) cannot come to be found in the residential community of respectable classes, causing the fragile character of domestic settings to be evident there too. Certainly the great public forums of our society, the downtown area of our cities can come to be uneasy places. Militantly sustained antagonisms between diffusely intermingled major population segments—young and old, male and female, white and black, impoverished and well-off—can cause those in public gatherings to distrust (and to fear they are distrusted by) the persons standing next to them.

Thus, what is otherwise a study of a very special form of interaction, the "game" between detectives and criminals, can be generalized to public interaction in urban life.

RECOGNIZING AND GATHERING INFORMATION

In order for information to be of use to detectives, they must somehow learn to recognize and gather it. Here we will examine how detectives talked about and understood their methods of recognizing and gathering information, and we will begin to see that, while they were able to reconstruct their methods, they were never able to explain abstractly how information is gathered and recognized.

Evidence and Leads

The most familiar kind of information associated with detectives is commonly known as "evidence." The legal-technical understanding of evidence is the information presented at a trial to a judge or jury to be used in determining the truth about questions of fact (Stukey, 1968, p. 20). However, we will discuss evidence here in terms of its commonsense usage by detectives (i.e., how it is used in investigations).

*Goffman defines *Umwelt* as an individual's surround within which potential sources of alarm are found.

A second form of information developed by detectives is known as a "lead" or "clue." In general, a lead is defined by detectives as information that gives direction to an investigation. The notion of a lead has a prospective sense in that it suggests what to do next in a case and provides an interpretive scheme for aspects that are considered to be possibly relevant. In contrast, evidence has a retrospective sense in that what is good or solid evidence is not known until the end of the case. When detectives are looking for an unknown suspect, information that suggests who might be involved or might have further information is referred to as a "lead"; once a suspect has been identified, whatever is collected up to that point to suggest that the suspect is guilty is referred to as "evidence." A case that is inactivated without producing a suspect is labeled "CASE INACTIVE DUE TO LACK OF INVESTIGATIVE LEADS," while in a report of a case in which a suspect was identified but later released, the closing-out notation would say "CASE CLOSED DUE TO LACK OF EVIDENCE." Finally, what is initially taken to be a lead, such as a tire track or a fingerprint, may later be seen as evidence once a suspect has been identified and apprehended.

Recognizing Clues

The process of recognizing leads or evidence, while a routine activity among detectives (as well as in everyday life), is difficult to describe. In the literature dealing with criminal evidence, only one source was found that attempted to describe the recognition of information, and this one was vague. For example:

> Any serious discussion of the recognition of physical evidence at a crime scene must consider widely different capabilities among individual investigators. In departments where the laboratory staff personally examines the crime scene, the only important limitation is rooted in the branch of scientific education, resourcefulness, and imagination of the person conducting the search. A police chief has the right to expect that the laboratory man know where any physical evidence may be sent for examination if it is beyond the equipment of the laboratory or scientific training of the staff to handle.
>
> Sophistication in the recognition of physical evidence can be achieved only through *education and experience.* At present,

many chiefs place most reliance on the experience factor. No doubt much can be learned in due course through actual crime-scene search work; however, the possibility for the loss of some physical evidence will always exist because its recognition, in terms of laboratory potential, is not learned through on-the-job training alone. This experience must be supplemented or, better, preceded by formal scientific training if an examination of the crime scene is to be of maximum investigative value.

On the other hand, any experienced, practical investigator is not likely to overlook obvious clue materials. Blood, spent bullets or cartridges, paint chips, fingerprints, and the like are sufficiently well known even to detectives of limited training. More likely to be overlooked are odorless accelerants at arson crime scenes, glass slivers present in trouser cuffs or imbedded in rubber heels, fibers and other debris present on clothing, evidence to determine the direction of the impacting force that broke a window glass, evidence to determine if a lock was picked, and other more esoteric clue materials.

To insure the recognition of physical evidence, though experience is helpful, there is no substitute for scientific education. This does not imply that all investigators must be scientists. Rather it suggests that each department should have some scientifically trained personnel available who can assume responsibility for the crime-scene search at least in major cases (Osterburg, 1967, pp. 7–8).

Note that Osterburg does not lay out a program for recognizing evidence but rather suggests some things that can be subjected to laboratory analysis. He does not specify how to separate useless information from information that will lead to the solution of a crime—that is, evidence from nonevidence. His examples (glass slivers, fibers, and other physical artifacts) are not necessarily evidence, and Osterburg would no doubt agree that these things may lead nowhere in an investigation. Anyone's shoes have traces of dirt and other materials which can be analyzed in a crime laboratory, but this does not mean that these materials are necessarily informative. Only by placing something at a crime scene in an interpretive context can it be developed as evidence, vaguely at first and perhaps more clearly later on. Nothing by itself, independent of interpretive work, is recognizable as information, and the "facts" *do not* speak for themselves.

Criminal laboratory personnel explained in interviews that anything foreign to a crime scene is routinely collected as possible evidence. Thus in an otherwise neat and tidy home, dirt on a rug would be considered "foreign." Such "evidence" does not "stand out" in the same way in a messy house. Recognition of evidence in this kind of setting was accounted for as "just something learned through experience." Similarly, in discussing the recognition of leads, the explanation detectives gave most often was that "through experience" one came to know what to look for in a crime investigation.

It should be pointed out that for something to be seen as incongruous, out of place, or out of order, there must initially be some assumed idea of order. The detectives' conception of social organization allows them to talk about an appearance as being incongruous with their expectations in terms of that organization. Much of our discussion of the information work done by detectives will therefore reveal their working conception of social organization and order.

Another way of describing how evidence is recognized is through the developing aspects of the case. Detectives say that it is necessary to "wait and see" in order to recognize whether or not something is a lead or evidence. In talking to a detective about a case he had solved, I asked how he had recognized the initial lead. He said that "by keeping this and keeping that, not knowing whether it was important or not," he was able to preserve some things that later proved to be important. The practice of keeping everything that might be important was explained in an interview as follows:

> Anything can be a lead, and it's a matter of, you have to know how to recognize a lead when you see it. It can be a material thing. A lead can be something that would be, y'know, that tells you, well, look in this direction. . . . Or there's a possibility exists, 'cause you start out looking for a burglary suspect or something like that, you have just the scene itself if the guy's gone, and you start from there, and everything that you can compile from there will point to one direction, and if it doesn't you're out to lunch . . . and you have to start looking, you gotta find a point in which to go. . . .
>
> The majority of crime you don't have leads to go, and in some crimes you have so goddamned many leads that it just, y'know, it just mushrooms out, and you can go out and you start

off a lead and that lead will lead to another lead that will lead to another lead, and you spend a week and all of the sudden you run into a dead end and find out that wasn't the lead, and you turn back to the beginning. Like in those puzzles you go through. You get stuck, and you go all the way back, right, and start over again. . . . It's a matter of sitting down and analyzing what you have.

The detective must "wait and see" where the information will go, but, once having arrived, he will somehow know whether he is in the right or wrong place. Sometimes he must "wait and see" what is information; only by having more information can he make sense of the information in hand.

Thus far we have seen that detectives discuss leads in terms of special skills for developing information, while at the same time treating them as showing the way to the solution of a crime. Skill in recognizing information, however, is not discussed in the same way that a botanist would describe how to recognize different types of plants. That is, it is not described in terms of features or criterial attributes. The skill developed by detectives appears, rather, to be akin to the ability developed by a jigsaw-puzzle master. However, whereas the puzzle-doer is given a jumble of pieces which he knows are parts of a single puzzle, and he also knows what the puzzle is supposed to look like on completion, the detective at the outset of a case has numerous pieces but does not know which pieces fit which puzzle or, indeed, whether any of them belong in any puzzle at all. As more and more pieces are put into place, not only does the picture itself become clearer, but it is easier to recognize pieces as belonging or not belonging to the puzzle. Furthermore, pieces that were not identified at the outset are seen retrospectively to be a part of the puzzle and understandable in terms of the puzzle.

Detectives often explained that a good investigator "keeps everything" from a crime scene since he never knows until other facts are developed what will be useful as evidence and what will not. Photographs are taken so as to "preserve everything" in the crime scene as it was when the crime was discovered, and other phenomena, such as noticable odors and the temperature, are recorded. It is not so much that "everything" from a crime scene is in fact preserved, or that "everything" of possible informational value is recorded for later evaluation, but, rather, it is the *belief* that "everything" should be kept that is important. If it is true that all leads and evidence are recognizable by an experienced detective, just as various plants are recognizable by a botanist, then why is it necessary to keep "everything"? Why couldn't an "experienced and educated" detective, to use Osterburg's terms, simply preserve leads and evidence and not bother with the rest?

These questions of recognition kept cropping up in the research. During one case where the detectives were investigating the stabbing of a deputy, a set of circumstances developed that illustrated the need for preserving "everything":

CASE 58*

I arrived in the first detective unit sent to the crime scene after 11–99 [officer needs help] had been put out. There was mass confusion since the detectives had just moved into new offices the previous day, and there were still some bugs in the communication center. Every available unit from the sheriff's office, police department, university police, and highway patrol—over 25 patrol cars—was in the area, and there was no one coordinating the search for the suspect.

When the arrest was made, the suspect asked how the stabbed deputy was doing, so there was little doubt that they had the right man. Nevertheless, the detectives wanted to find the knife used in the stabbing as well as any other evidence that would connect the suspect with the crime. For the rest of the day a search of the crime scene and of the area between the crime scene and where the suspect was caught progressed. When the ID team arrived, the entire yard and house were photographed, and much of the house was dusted for fingerprints. The yard around the house was searched in an attempt to locate the knife or anything else that would connect the suspect with the crime.

During the search, an old plastic bleach bottle was seen lying in the yard by just about everyone involved in the search, but it was not considered important. The bleach bottle had been torn apart and was thought to be a stray piece of trash. Later, however, the suspect's belongings were found to

*Each case was numbered in the order it was encountered in the research, and the identification numbers used throughout the book reflect this sequence and not the sequence they appear in the book.

contain some pieces of plastic—thin pieces that burglars use to slip locks. Someone remembered the old plastic bleach bottle in the yard and pointed out that if the pieces of plastic found on the suspect matched the pieces torn from the bottle the suspect could be linked to the crime scene. Now, instead of being a discarded bleach bottle of little interest, the bottle was seen to be a piece of evidence.

In subsequent discussions the detectives frequently cited the bleach bottle as an example of why "everything" had to be kept. Since it is unknown at the outset what will and will not crop up in an investigation, what is or is not informative is also unknown; therefore, "everything" is potential information. The detective's recognition of leads and evidence can be seen to be an unfolding process. There was a retrospective sense that it was important to keep "keepables," against the possibility that they might subsequently be found useful.

INFORMATION AND DECISION MAKING

In his preface to an anthology of studies of decision making in criminal justice, Gottfredson (1975, p. vii) points out three components of a decision. First is the *goal* that is to be achieved by the decision, second is the availability of *alternatives,* and third is *information.* In this book information as it affects decisions is the main focus of attention, even though goals and alternatives will be discussed implicitly. Here we shall briefly examine the relationship between information and decisions, which will be developed and elaborated in the rest of the book.

Burnham (1975, pp. 94–95) notes that it is important to distinguish between "data" and "information." The former are potentially informative things that come to one's attention; the latter is anything that reduces uncertainty. Thus, what is at one point data may later be seen as information. Burnham also distinguishes between "noise" and "information." What is useful information in terms of a specific decision depends on its ability to reduce uncertainty in that context. Information is the uncertainty reducer, and the other data are residually defined as "noise." Information in one context can be noise in another, and vice versa. As Burnham states: "No datum is ever one thing or the other by virtue of any intrinsic quality; only the use to which it is put determines its status for that moment." For example, in a homicide investigation a spent cartridge is typically treated as informative; however, if detectives are investigating a burglary at a gun club, spent cartridges would be found all over the place and would not be seen as informative. In looking at information in decisions, it is important that we pay close attention to the situation in which the decision is made and the context surrounding the data taken as informative.

This leads to a second consideration that has not been discussed in the literature on decision making: how data are formulated to be information. We have suggested that information is not independent of interpretive work but must be constructed. This will be drawn out analytically throughout our discussion, and we will see that information is developed rather than merely "found."

A third and final consideration regarding decision making and information is the interrelation between the development of the information and the decision. If the decision is directly linked to the information developed in the context of a situation, we may find that the decision relates not to the situation itself but, instead, to the development of the information. For example, in deciding whether to work a case (investigate a case), detectives assess whether or not the patrol report warrants investigative action. If the data in the report are taken to be indicative of a serious crime, then the case will be investigated. Therefore, the characterization of the patrol report by the detectives determines whether or not the case will be investigated, and the decision is part of the characterization of the data, not independent of it. Furthermore, the decision action warrants whatever characterization is made, making the characterization and decision mutually determinative. This shifts the emphasis from the decision itself to the interpretive work of the detectives in constructing something as informative. Therefore, rather than emphasize the decision based on information, we will focus on the ways in which information is developed.

OVERVIEW OF THE BOOK

In order to examine detective work and information, it will be necessary to understand detective work in the context of the police organization. In chapter 2 we will look at the overall organization of a county sheriff's office and the detectives' position vis-à-vis the other components of the department. In chapter 3 we will examine how information is organized by detectives and the sheriff's office. In addition, we will discuss how information is organized in society and the strategies employed to "get at" and develop this information.

Beginning in chapter 4, we will analyze the process through which information is developed and decisions are made in criminal investigations. The issue of "detective discretion" will be introduced, and we will see how discretion is reflexively tied to information. In chapter 5 we will continue with our examination of how detectives develop information, concentrating on how they identify, locate, and "cop out" criminal suspects. In chapters 6 through 8 we will look at the different organizational units—Juvenile, Burglary, and Major Crimes—and the informational resources and strategies unique to each.

Finally, in chapter 9 we will discuss how the data were collected for this study, including the methodological tools developed and used in the course of the research. Along with the problems normally encountered in participant-observer studies of the police, this study had the unusual problem of examining methods with the use of the same methods that were being examined.

2

Detectives in the Police Organization

Just about every day some detective would complain about the quality of the reports sent by patrol. Usually the complaints had to do with some little thing the patrol officer forgot to include in the report. Burglary detectives were often given only the home address of a victim, not his or her work address. This was a minor matter, but it was exasperating to the detectives, for it sometimes took them a good deal of time to locate the victim. For this reason, detectives often held patrol officers in contempt and regarded them as generally uninformed about detective work. Those patrolmen who did complete their reports were treated with extra courtesy and respect, and if one of them was being considered for transfer to the detective division, he was given strong recommendations.

In an attempt to improve relations among the staff, the sheriff initiated a temporary duty (TDY) program requiring patrolmen to work in the detective office as detectives for two weeks. Whenever one of these temporary detectives complained about a poorly written patrol report, the detectives would remind him of the extra work he had caused them by similar reports that he himself had written. The program appeared to work in that after their TDY with the detectives, the patrolmen seemed to appreciate the detectives' problems. Rarely did a patrolman who had been a temporary detective write an incomplete report after his experience.

THE STRUCTURE OF A SHERIFF'S OFFICE

The Mountainbeach County Sheriff's Office (MCSO) was organized as are most police bureaucracies. The basic line organizations were patrol and investigations, with a supporting staff of administrative and technical services (Munro, 1974, pp. 67–86) and a division for detention and corrections (figure 2–1).

Special Investigations consisted of the Narcotics/Vice Detail and Intelligence/Organized Crime. The former detail handled mainly narcotic violations. With the help of a government grant, a county-wide narcotic task force had been developed which cooperated with the city police department and other local law-enforcement agencies. Most of the efforts of this detail at the time of the study were devoted to curbing heroin traffic, but it also worked on violations involving psychedelics, cocaine, amphetamines, barbituates, and marijuana. The Intelligence/Organized Crime Detail was responsible for information about radical political groups, such as SDS and the rightwing Minutemen, and also for any organized crime in the county (mainly bookmakers). The Special Investigations unit can be characterized as purely "proactive" (Skolnick, 1966) in that its work was directed toward meeting generalized demands for controlling criminal and political activities and in most cases did not involve direct requests from citizens. (None of the research reported in this study was carried out in the Special Investigations unit; its activities are presented here only to show its role in the organization and its use as an information resource.)

The Investigations unit of the Sheriff's office, called the Detective Bureau, comprised the Juvenile, Burglary, and Major Crimes Details. The work of these details sometimes overlapped; in particular, cases involving juveniles were sometimes investigated by Burglary or Major Crimes detectives. However, each detail typically investigated only certain kinds of crime. The Juvenile Detail's top priority went to investigating runaway juveniles (601 WIC),* then to crimes that generally involve

*The numbered sections of the various legal codes are presented here since they are used as a reference in any criminal investigation. The letters following the numbers indicate the California legal section to which the number refers. WIC indicates "Welfare and Institutions Code," PC "Penal

Figure 2-1 Organization of the Sheriff's Office

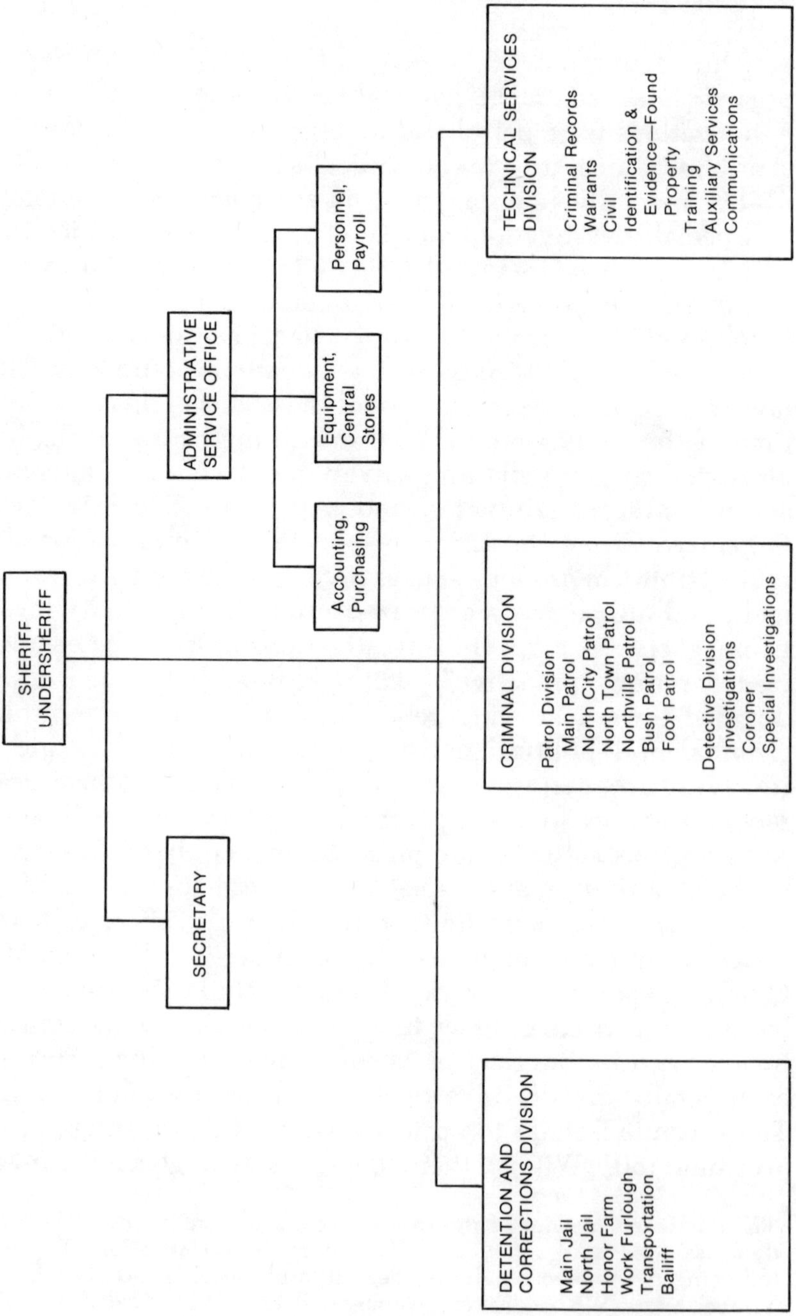

SHERIFF
UNDERSHERIFF

SECRETARY

ADMINISTRATIVE
SERVICE OFFICE

Accounting,
Purchasing

Equipment,
Central
Stores

Personnel,
Payroll

TECHNICAL SERVICES
DIVISION

Criminal Records
Warrants
Civil
Identification &
  Evidence—Found
  Property
Training
Auxiliary Services
Communications

CRIMINAL DIVISION

Patrol Division
Main Patrol
North City Patrol
North Town Patrol
Northville Patrol
Bush Patrol
Foot Patrol

Detective Division
Investigations
Coroner
Special Investigations

DETENTION AND
CORRECTIONS DIVISION

Main Jail
North Jail
Honor Farm
Work Furlough
Transportation
Bailiff

juveniles, such as bicycle and surfboard theft (488 PC and 487 PC) and malicious mischief (594 PC). The Burglary Detail handled mainly burglaries (459 PC), but one detective in the detail was assigned to handle bad-check cases (470 PC). The Major Crimes Detail was responsible for a large variety of offenses, but those typically pulled (i.e., taken from the batch of incoming reports for review and possible investigation) included disturbing the peace (415 PC), battery (242 PC), assault (245 PC), arson (447a PC), annoying phone calls (653m PC), rape (261 PC), robbery (211 PC), and homicide (187 PC). During the course of the research, the coroner-detective was reassigned to the Major Crimes Detail to investigate any deaths in suspicious circumstances. Mainly this involved deaths from drug overdoses and suicides, but his work also included homicides.

Figure 2–2 outlines the organization of the Detective Division of the MCSO, including the hierarchy of command and the number of personnal assigned to each detail.

Several works on police organization have pointed to the quasi-military and bureaucratic structure typical of modern urban police departments (Bittner, 1970, pp. 52–62). Others have argued that the police are not military or even quasi-military in their operations since the command structure is bypassed in communications and police officers operate individually or in teams of two instead of in platoons, squads, companies, and other military units (J. Wilson, 1968, pp. 79–80). Nevertheless, there is a militaristic style in their orientation, as witness the uniform, trappings, training, discipline, emphasis on spit and polish, and military designations in ranking. At the same time, police organizations have been characterized as bureaucracies in that they have specialized training, division of labor, and massive written records of their activities. Bordua and Reiss (1966) also make the point that the bureaucratization of police has taken them out of the political sphere, where they must be highly responsive to popular sentiment. Since they frequently have to enforce unpopular laws (e.g., traffic laws,

---

Code," HS "Health and Safety," VC "Vehicle Code." The most commonly used sections were from the Penal Code, except for the Juvenile Detail, which generally dealt with Welfare and Institutions, since all juvenile cases are adjudicated under this code, even though most of the specific charges were under the Penal Code.

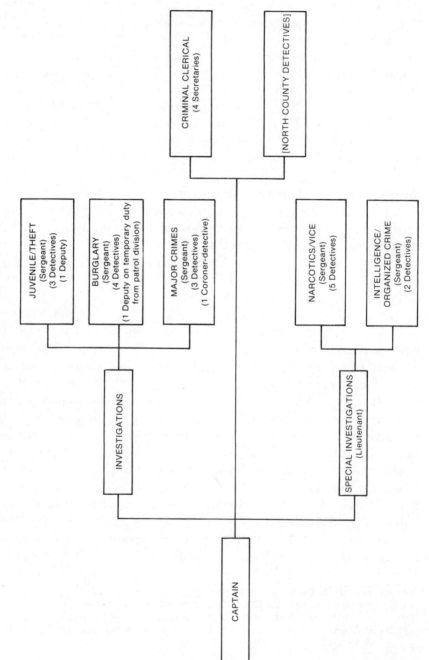

Figure 2-2 The Detective Division

gambling), the impersonal bureaucracy serves to deflect individual and community dissatisfaction from individual actions.

However, among detectives and their organization we find little of the military aspect that is said to characterize both police-academy training (Harris, 1973) and uniformed patrol work. The marked attention to differences in rank and strict formality characteristic of patrolmen's interaction with officers is not apparent among detectives. Niederhoffer (1967, p. 83) points to such nonmilitary behavior as a detective's calling a superior officer by his first name while discussing an important case and a generally relaxed demeanor in daily routines.

The Mountainbeach detectives, while certainly less formal in demeanor than the uniformed patrol, were not on totally familiar terms with their superior officers. Some of the detectives called their sergeants by first names, but others referred to them by rank or used the formal title (e.g., Sergeant Jones). Officers above the rank of sergeant were addressed by rank or title, never by first name. Nevertheless, there did not appear to be any military aspects to the interaction between the detectives and officers higher in rank than sergeant. None of the men stood when a superior officer approached, and none of the detectives were ordered around by superiors in a way suggestive of a military command.

The relation of the detectives to their superiors and the overall organization might best be described in terms of bureaucratic semiformality. That is, the interaction between the detectives and their superordinates was neither military-formal nor friendly-informal, but instead was guided by the bureaucratic need for impersonal objectivity in interaction; at the same time, the formality of the bureaucracy was tempered by *Gemeinschaft* relations that had developed over the years. The Detective Division was not a "mock bureaucracy" (the term Niederhoffer used to characterize New York City detectives), for the official rules, departmental policies, and other bureaucratic guidelines were certainly employed and acknowledged, even though the Mountainbeach detectives did not see being good bureaucrats as synonomous with doing good work. A number of the organizational and bureaucratic policies were regarded as helpful in doing detective work. Detectives' complaints about patrol officers' failure to fill out crime reports pointed to the support of certain bureaucratic precepts, but there were many rules and regulations that were considered "chickenshit" or "mickey-mouse," and no one believed that a policy or regulation was essentially correct or should be followed merely because it was so ordered.

OTHER ORGANIZATIONAL COMPONENTS AS INFORMATIONAL RESOURCES

Most writers who have studied detectives, especially Nieder-hoffer (1967) and Skolnick (1966), have stressed the importance of informants and have neglected or minimized the utility of organized operations in terms of bureaucratic structures. Nie-derhoffer (1967, p. 85), for example, states that the detective "performs best when disregarding formal regulations and official procedures." However, as we will show throughout this study, even though informants were used, detectives also relied extensively on organizationally produced information.

In terms of the detectives' day-to-day work, the relevant organizational others include the Main Patrol, the Foot Patrol, the Main Jail, Criminal Records, Identification (ID), and Special Investigations. The various patrols are the main source of "basic information" for the detectives, and typically the patrol reports set the stage for an investigation. Usually, a citizen's call is taken by the communications center and relayed to a patrol unit, which is then dispatched to take a report. The report is then reviewed by the detective sergeants to determine whether or not an investigation is necessary. Sometimes the detectives receive complaints directly from citizens, but most of the cases the detectives work are first reported to them by patrol.

For cases involving physical evidence to be examined, such as fingerprints, vaginal smears, blood samples, and so on, the ID bureau provides technical analysis and recommendations. The ID bureau is also responsible for maintaining "rap sheets" (i.e., criminal records of individuals, including photographs, finger-prints, and criminal histories). If detectives need a photograph of a suspect, the names of his friends or relatives, or the address or place of his last employment, they contact the ID bureau. The "rap sheets" should not be confused with the records kept in Criminal Records, which generally consist of patrol and detective reports. If an old case is thought to have information that might be useful in a current investigation, Criminal Records is contacted instead of the ID bureau.

Occasionally, a suspect in jail has information that he is willing to give the detectives in the hope of receiving a lighter sentence; sometimes a deputy working in the jail overhears something or is given information that he believes to be useful. In these instances the jail can be considered an organizationally relevant source of information. By and large, though, the jail is not seen as informationally useful, and detectives spend little time using it as a source.

Finally, Special Investigations is sometimes useful, especially in a narcotics case involving burglarized or stolen property or when the detectives have information linking a narcotic user with some other crime. At the time of this study there was only minimal cooperation between Special Investigations and the Detective Bureau, but detectives in these units were taking steps toward greater cooperation. For example, if Special Investigations got a warrant to search a house for narcotics, they would invite a Burglary detective along to try to spot stolen property in the house; similarly, if Burglary detectives were able to get a warrant to search for stolen property, they would take along a narcotic investigator to look for drugs. This arrangement was in effect on a number of occasions, but for some reason it was not instituted on a regular basis. At least one major narcotic arrest occured when Burglary detectives searching an apartment for a stolen pump found it attached to a device used for manufacturing illegal drugs. Cooperation was usually in the form of information passed on after a search and arrest. Someone from Special Investigations would drop by the detective office and talk about an arrest he had made, mentioning that there were a lot of television sets or other typically burglarized items in the place where a narcotic arrest had been made. If the Burglary detectives could get a warrant they would then make a search on the basis of information from Special Investigations.

Thus, other units in the organization sometimes provided accounts, artifacts, documents, and reports that were seen as potentially useful information to be employed in "clearing a case" (solving a crime). From the detectives' point of view, these other units sometimes provided information or possible information, and even though they had to "make sense of" and "make informative" anything they were given, they treated it as factual.

For example, if a narcotic officer during a raid on a heroin user's home found several CB radios that had been reported stolen, such information was regarded as unproblematic. However, at other times the detectives would be given a vague account, such as: "There's a lot of stuff in this guy's place you might want to look at," or the ID bureau would give the detectives a photograph of a crime scene and say, "Here, see what you make of it." This vague type of situation provides a better ground for examining the process whereby information is developed, since there is not yet a definite sense that something is information.

The flow of information was affected by the spatial arrangements of the different units. Often receiving or giving information depended on the location of the units. During the research period the detectives moved from one building to another, and the move changed the flow of information. In the old offices, Special Investigations and Investigations were in two entirely different buildings separated by a parking lot. After the move they were in the same building but at opposite ends, separated by the patrol squad room, a locker room, and a bathroom. In both locations, all three details of Investigations were in the same building, but, as can be seen in figure 2–3, the new office had fewer physical barriers than the old one.

In the old building there was a definite separation of the three details. Major Crimes and Burglary shared a common room, but the room was divided by a traffic pattern from the front door to the stairs leading to the interview room. The Juvenile Detail was totally apart from Major Crimes and Burglary, in the back part of the building. There was little interaction among members of the different details except during lunch, when they gathered in the interview room to play cards. Most of the talk during these card games was general discussion about the department (e.g., pay, promotions, who was doing well and who was not). Only occasionally was a case discussed, and the daily card game rarely resulted in the exchange of information.

In the new building all the details were put into one large room with rows of desks. Basically, the rows were arranged into three lines, with the Major Crimes detectives in one, Burglary in another, and Juvenile in the last. The Burglary sergeant and the Burglary detective who worked forgery cases had their desks in line with the Juvenile Detail. In this arrangement there was

Figure 2-3 Spatial Arrangement of Investigative Division

OLD OFFICE

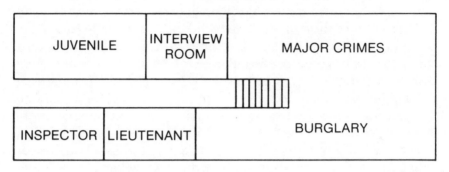

NEW OFFICE

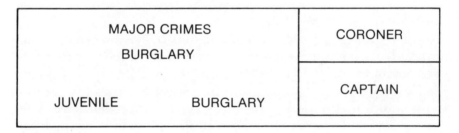

greater interaction among members of the details, and information was passed more freely. Until the move, the Juvenile sergeant had discouraged the detectives from discussing their cases with men in other details, claiming that each should concentrate on his own assignments. After the move it was more difficult to enforce this order, since there was less pronounced boundary maintenance.

THE STATUS OF DETECTIVES IN THE DEPARTMENT

As Niederhoffer (1967, pp. 81–85) has pointed out, the police detective enjoys high status in relation to uniformed patrol and even certain higher-ranking officers in other divisions. During this study the rank of detective was only one step above the rank of basic deputy (Deputy 1), but the step was a large one. Instead of having to wear a uniform and drive a black and white patrol car, the detectives could wear regular street clothes and drive in an unmarked (though obviously official) detective car. They were not limited to a single beat, and they were able to spend a good deal of time out of the office, away from direct supervision either by radio commands or by in-person orders. If something interesting happened (e.g., a robbery in progress), they could go to the scene of the action without asking special permission to leave their zone or their duties. On one occasion, a detective I was accompanying was interviewing a forgery suspect in his car when he heard over the police radio that a bank was being robbed. He told the suspect to get out of the car and wait until he returned, then took off to the bank robbery with his red emergency light flashing.

Newspaper, radio, and television reporters were eager to interview the detectives, and on numerous occasions the publicity-minded Burglary sergeant took television crews along on raids. Whenever an interesting case was solved or occurred, the media would send reporters to talk to the detectives assigned to investigate it. Only rarely did the patrol deputies receive the same kind of attention or celebrity status as the detective. The extra pay and step up the organizational ladder were often secondary to the special prestige that went with being a detective.

The social boundaries between investigations and patrol were maintained in a number of ways. If someone who is unknown to the officer or receptionist on duty enters a police department, he is greeted with, "May I help you?" or some similar phrase conveying both cool courtesy and a demand that the newcomer state his business. At the beginning of the research, this query-challenge was given to me every time I entered the building, and I soon learned that it was more a demand that I identify myself and explain my presence than an aspect of some program to make the police more responsive to citizens. The query-challenge also serves to tell some persons that they do not belong there. After a while, when I was accepted in my comings and goings, I began to notice that the query-challenge was given to others who came into the detective offices. One group to which that unwelcoming greeting was routinely addressed was uniform patrol. Since everyone in the sheriff's office used this same query-challenge with outsiders, in effect it told the patrol officers that they should not be in the detective office except on official business. Since the police as a group are cliquish to begin with (Manning, 1976, pp. 109–15), one might expect that any police officer, especially someone so obvious as a uniformed patrolman, would be accepted as belonging in any department. However, in the context of the departmental status hierarchy, the uniform patrolman was a long way from a detective.

When a deputy was moved into the Detective Division, his demeanor went through a noticeable transformation. In addition to the obvious changes in dress (from uniform to civilian clothes), there were more subtle changes related to the status of detective. New detectives still used the patrol demeanor, which called for a continual air of authority and a "take-charge" attitude. This demeanor gradually relaxed as the newcomer came under social pressure from other detectives. The authority was still important, but it was a casual authority based more on intelligence than on muscle. When an officer is in uniform, he is highly visible to the populace, and if anything happens that would normally call for police action, he is under heavy obligation to take charge. Therefore, he must at least appear capable of taking charge when in uniform, and this becomes a feature of his demeanor. However, when an officer is driving a detective car and dressed in a business suit, he is not immediately identifiable as a policeman, and no one expects him to take command of a situation.

For example, one day a detective was given a patrol car to drive because no detective car was available. On the way to talk to a burglary victim, he remarked to me that he disliked driving a "black and white" since people expected a patrolman to "do something." Just as he was explaining why he did not like driving a patrol car, another car made an illegal U-turn against a traffic signal and went roaring off with its tires squealing. A number of people saw the incident and looked expectantly at the patrol unit. The detective then said, "See what I mean? Some asshole pulls a stunt like that and all those people are wondering why I don't go after him."

The "Romantic Bureaucrat"

Bittner (1970, p. 61) has characterized the police role as that
of a "soldier-bureaucrat." The detective role, however, is significantly different. As was pointed out above, the severe "take-
charge" demeanor characteristic of both patrol and the fighting
soldier is rarely seen in the Detective Bureau. The detective
might rather be seen in terms of the romantic. In this context the
romantic   is   adventurous,   heroic,   individualistic,   and
independent—aspects of detective work glorified in fiction. The
celebrity status of the detective is tied to the romantic image,
and even though much of it is fictional, detectives, like everyone
else, frequently come to see themselves in terms of what others
believe they are.

At the same time that the romantic aspect of the role blooms,
the bureaucratic aspects remain the same and sometimes even
increase. The bureaucrat in the detective is the man who sees to
it that the paperwork is done and that policies are carried out;
the detective bureau in this study, far from being a mock
bureaucracy, was a very real one in its requirements of massive
paperwork and meeting regulated ways of doing investigations.
Every case investigated, and even some that were received and
not investigated, required a follow-up report of some sort. Some
of this paperwork was described in terms of "C.Y.A." (cover
your ass) and was carried out for the sole purpose of meeting
bureaucratic requirements. However, much of it was done with
the understanding that a good report might later prove to be
important in an investigation. One detective who had been
investigating a case in another city criticized that city's detective
bureau for its poor paperwork. He explained that each detective
took his own notes on scraps of paper, and when another
detective took over the investigation or some other agency
wanted information, they could not rely on departmental records but had to find the detective who investigated the case and
hope that he could remember pertinent details and was willing
to share them. The department, which was one of the largest in
the state, represented "old-fashioned" detective practice to the
Mountainbeach detectives. Even though similar operations existed in the New York City department at the time of Niederhoffer's study, they are seen as anachronisms.

The detective as a romantic bureaucrat is a contradiction. On the one hand the role emphasizes the detective as a free agent using his individual intelligence; on the other hand, the detective is the good bureaucrat, a cog in an impersonal machine. There is both respect and annoyance shown toward detectives who "screw up" by not doing good follow-up reports even though they make good investigations. Mild sanctions are taken against "headline grabbers," but the same detectives who apply the sanctions delight in seeing themselves on television or named in the papers. Those who explain everything in a successful investigation in terms of good bureaucratic organization or who totally embrace departmental policies and regulations are seen as unimaginative hacks or "ass-kissers," but all of the detectives acknowledge the need for good record keeping in the department. Thus the role, while apparently contradictory in many respects, gives the detective both the celebrity status and relative freedom of the romantic, and at the same time access to the organizational resources of the department.

The Status of Crimes and Detectives

The status of an individual detective is linked to the kinds of crimes he investigates. Detectives who typically work homicides are held in higher esteem, for example, than those who normally work cases involving runaway juveniles. On the whole, homicides are seen as more important than runaways, and the detective who works them is seen as more important. More generally, since the type of crime a detective works depends on the detail he is assigned to, a detective's status on this informal ranking is tied to his detail. Those in Major Crimes have the highest status, Burglary detectives the middle status, and Juvenile detectives are at the bottom.

I first noticed this hierarchy when I was talking to a former detective from another city. He explained that when he was working a special robbery detail he had developed an ulcer and was consequently moved "all the way" from Robbery to Juvenile. He had traversed the social distance seen to exist between the two details. Juvenile detectives were called "kiddie kops," and while their work did not involve any less skill, and indeed required a good deal of skill in that they had the widest variety of cases, they nevertheless were not regarded as highly as members of the other details. Sometimes the Juvenile detectives would get an important crime, such as an assault, a robbery, or a burglary, but a "big case" involving a juvenile was usually given to one of the other details. For example, in a case involving a 15-year-old bank robber, Major Crimes carried out the investigation and made the arrests, since bank robberies were considered "big cases." This suggests that even when it involved a juvenile, the Juvenile Detail was not considered entitled to handle a "big case." As a result, Juvenile detectives had few opportunities to obtain the status that went with the important crimes.

In examining the more general view of the social significance of various crimes, it was found that nondetectives shared the views of the detective bureau. A sample of 14 respondents, about half in law enforcement and half in other occupations, was given a list of 12 crimes and asked to rank them from 1 (most significant) to 12 (least significant). Crimes believed to be of equal importance were to be given the same rank. The scores were compiled by multiplying the number of choices for each rank by the rank number, with results as shown in table 1.

This social ranking of crime significance follows the hierarchy of the Detective Bureau: Crimes ranked from 1 to 6 are all investigated by the Major Crimes Detail. The eighth- and ninth-ranked crimes, annoying phone calls [653m PC] and disturbing the peace [415 PC], do not fit the pattern since both are received for investigation by the Major Crimes Detail. However, since only rarely did Major Crimes ever carry out an actual investigation on either of these crimes, they do not

TABLE 1.   Social Significance of Typical Crimes

RANK	CRIME	SCORE
1	Homicide	14
2	Sex crimes (e.g., rape, sexual assault)	43
3	Kidnapping	47
4	Felony assault	49
5	Robbery	85
5	Arson	85
6	Battery	109
7	Burglary	112
8	Theft	132
9	Juvenile	159
10	Annoying phone calls	186
11	Disturbing the peace	190

constitute a contradiction to the basic pattern. Annoying-phone-calls and disturbing-the-peace reports are merely received and inactivated or closed, and so do not represent the *work* done by Major Crimes.

Our sample is far too small to be significant, but it represents the only available data concerning crime significance in the community where the study was conducted. However, in a much larger study dealing with the seriousness of crimes as subjectively viewed by citizens, Rossi and associates (1974) found the same pattern, suggesting that the status of detectives as informally determined in the Detective Bureau reflects general social understandings of crime significance.

Detective Administrators

The administrative rationale above the rank of sergeant in the Detective Division was unclear. Detective sergeants functioned to allocate investigative work and organize the day-to-day office routine. Additionally, sergeants would lend a hand with certain cases and thus provided extra investigative help during periods of heavy work or on important cases.

On the basis of observations, not organizational job description, it did not appear that the lieutenants and captains who were in charge of the detectives did very much to affect the day-to-day operations of the Detective Bureau. This is not to say that they did nothing; rather, the manner in which a routine investigation was conducted did not depend on anything these officers did. During the observation period, the only thing the captain did that had much impact was to introduce staggered work-hours, so that the homicide detective, for example, came in at 10 A.M. instead of at 8 A.M. and left at 7 P.M. instead of at 5 P.M. Since investigations took place at all different times of the day, all this order did was to cut down on the amount of overtime the department had to pay.

Transfers were filtered through the captain, new departmental policies were announced through him, and the needs of the detectives were supposed to be taken up to the sheriff through him. However, since there were no observations made of what the captain did other than those actions that directly affected the daily routine of the investigators, I cannot say with any empirical confidence exactly what the captain did.

At the beginning of the study, before the move to the new office, there was no captain in charge of detectives; instead, a lieutenant occupied his functional position. After the move a lieutenant was placed in charge of Special Investigations and a captain in charge of the entire Detective Division, with no lieutenant in Investigations. This change did not appear to affect the detectives' daily operations in any way, and most of them believed that the changes were made for "political" reasons (i.e., to increase the sheriff's power and punish those who were out of favor).

One way to assess the actual functions of a position is to note what happens in the absence of the incumbent. When the captain went on vacation, nothing in the office routine seemed to change. However, when one of the sergeants left for two weeks and a detective was made acting sergeant, the morale of the other detectives in that detail improved and so did their efforts to solve cases. These observations, while admittedly from the detectives' point of view, serve to show that the higher-level administrators may have had power in determining general patterns and careers, but none of the policies they administered had much affect on the daily routines.

SUMMARY

In this chapter we have examined the Detective Division in the context of the organization of the sheriff's office. While the position of detectives in this study was only a step above the bottom rung, it was one of relative autonomy and high esteem. At the same time, the detectives were not totally free from bureaucratic demands and policies, nor did they wish to be, for the bureaucratic structure provided resources for solving crimes. In fact, the recognition given to individual detectives for solving cases was seen by the detectives to be due in part to the bureaucratically generated resources for making a successful investigation possible. In order to maintain the romantic image of the free-agent sleuth who "got his man" or "broke the case," the detective found it necessary to attend to paperwork, routine follow-ups, and other bureaucratic details. At the same time that the bureaucracy worked for and determined the actions of the detectives, the routine that grew up around the overall structure was only minutely affected by adjustments in the form of new policies and administrators above the level of sergeant. As a result, only the most momentous policy change could affect the routine.

3

The Organization of Information

When I began the research for this book, the detectives' paperwork seemed overwhelming. They seemed to be filling out reports of one sort or another for everything they did, and it was not until I was well into the research that I could tell one report from another. The amount of paperwork was a source of constant complaint from the detectives, but most of them nevertheless acknowledged that it was necessary, for all their reports were filed in the Records department, and they never knew when a report would be useful. Even the reports of cases in which no investigations were made were seen to be potentially useful information. Later in the research, when a disturbing-the-peace report proved to be helpful in making a decision in a homicide investigation, I was given a "See what I mean?" look. The detectives showed me how they had used the report to document the victim's potential for violence. Thus, even though none of the detectives seemed to be a slave to bureaucratic ritual, they all recognized the practical utility of certain rituals.

In their study of a morals detail, Skolnick and Woodworth (1967, p. 99) point out that information on legal infractions underlies the work of any social-control agency, for without awareness of infractions there can be no control. They go on to show how the police have organized themselves to maximize their awareness of lawbreaking, especially of instances not typically reported by citizens. Their methods of awareness extension include surveillance by traffic police, undercover narcotic and vice agents, and police patrol in general. Skolnick and Woodworth (1967, p. 100) describe the police organization that would result if police did not play this "proactive" role:

> Imagine, as an example, a social system where criminality could be accused only if a citizen *complained* that a law was being violated. In such a system we would have a grossly different conception of police than the one commonly held, at least in the United States. In such a system police would be men who sit in rooms and investigate only when accusing citizens are moved to complain by the occurrence of events regarded as violations of the law.

The characterization of men sitting around waiting for someone to complain essentially describes the detectives in this study. The detectives in the Skolnick and Woodworth (1967) study of a morals detail and in Skolnick's (1966) study of a vice squad, like those in Special Investigations in MCSO, would have little to do if they waited for someone to complain. Skolnick (1966, p. 35) also studied the burglary and robbery/homicide squads, "where there is typically a complainant," but most of his attention is directed to "proactive" information gathering.

In Reiss' (1971) study of the police, the main focus is on patrol duties. Unlike Skolnick, Reiss (1971, p. 11) found that most patrol mobilizations (87 percent) were dispatched from headquarters, which received the information initially from citizens who called to request police service. Thus, Reiss characterized the police organization as "reactive," pointing to the comparative rates of "on view" mobilizations and "citizen request" mobilizations in patrol.

In his study of robbery, Conklin (1972, p. 124) found, similarly, the following:

> Officers assigned to individual stationhouses learn of robberies from headquarters, since most are initially reported to the central headquarters switchboard. In 1964 and 1968, three-quarters of the robberies recorded by the police were initially reported to the switchboard, usually by the victim of the crime. Only one robbery in 20 was discovered by an officer sighting the offense in progress. One in 14 was reported to the police by

a citizen who approached an officer on the street, and about the same proportion was reported directly to officers in district stationhouses. Obviously the police are greatly dependent on the public for information about robberies, since more than nine-tenths are reported by private citizens.

After the patrol officer has investigated the complaint, in cases where the robber is not apprehended, he turns his report over to the detectives. Conklin (1972, p. 125) describes the process as follows:

> If the investigating officer (Patrol) does not make an arrest at the scene, the case is assigned to a district detective for investigation the following morning. He makes a follow-up investigation, contacting the victim or witness for information to help solve the case, but this is quite uncommon in robbery cases.

Thus, 90 percent of robbery cases are reported by citizens directly to the police, and the detectives who investigate rely on citizen reports for mobilizing an investigation. In this sense, then, the detectives who investigate such crimes are literally "men who sit in rooms and investigate only when accusing citizens are moved to complain by the occurrence of events regarded as violations of the law."

THE FLOW OF ACCOUNTS AND INFORMATION

The detectives of the MCSO Investigations unit were truly "citizen-response detectives," in that they were typically mobilized by an account supplied initially by a citizen and passed on to them by patrol. However, such accounts are interpreted and reformulated as they are processed through the organization, traveling through various points in the manner of a lump of clay that everyone molds as it goes along, "making it information."

For example, suppose that a citizen calls the MCSO and claims to have been burglarized. The account provided by the caller is recorded on tape and logged in Communications. On the basis of this information, the watch commander requests that a patrol car be sent to the crime scene to contact the reporting party. A departmental dispatcher then assigns a patrol officer to the address given by the caller. The patrolman "takes a report" of the burglary in an effort to provide the detectives with the following information: type of crime (e.g., Burglary, 459

PC), the victim's name and addresses, the names and addresses of witnesses or persons who may have information, a description of possible suspects, and a narrative description of the crime, including a list of items or amount of cash taken, the degree of harm or nature of acts committed upon the victim, method of committing the crime, and any physical evidence found at the scene.

On some occasions, after a call has been made to the department and a patrol unit assigned, documentation of the crime may not proceed in a chronological fashion from patrol to detective investigation. Sometimes patrol officers who are dispatched to major burglaries, or more typically to major crimes such as homicides, robberies, or bombings, call detectives and request their copresence during the initial investigation. But whether or not the detectives begin their work before a written report has been received from patrol, a formal patrol report is always filed and eventually reviewed by detectives.

In most cases the patrol report is transcribed by secretaries from patrol's handwritten or tape-recorded report. It then goes to the detectives, who pass it around among themselves. Burglary and Major Crimes detectives read all of the reports, or at least have access to all of them; however, as has been noted, the Juvenile sergeant in Mountainbeach for some time discouraged the men in his detail from reading any reports other than the ones he gave them, in the belief that this would keep the detectives from being distracted and thus enable them to do better work. Furthermore, the Juvenile detectives were also discouraged from talking with other detectives. The consequences of this arrangement were that the Major Crimes and Burglary detectives were able to draw on and make use of information in reports assigned to other details, whereas the Juvenile detectives were not.

In the old office, where the Juvenile Detail was located in a room separate from the other details, the sergeant was able to keep the detectives effectively ignorant of what the others were doing, and sometimes he wasted resources and time enforcing this policy. On one occasion, for example, three Juvenile detectives were each given different cases, all involving the same suspect. Two of these detectives arrived at the suspect's house simultaneously, and it was only then that they realized they were working cases involving the same person. The third detective arrived as the other two were leaving and found that he, too, had been given a case with the same suspect.

The forced lack of communication between Juvenile detectives and everyone else in the office not only led to redundant efforts but also hampered the development of information. As we have pointed out, for something to be seen as informative, it must be viewed in terms of some scheme or context. If, for example, a Juvenile detective received a report identifying a certain juvenile as a principal in a case, and that person was known to the Burglary detectives to have been involved in burglaries, the report would probably be seen as less informative by the Juvenile detective than it would have been if he had reason to believe that the juvenile was also a burglar.

In the other details, every detective knew the cases all the others were working, and information was frequently shared. In one case that the Burglary Detail had been working, which they believed to be phony, a family had made numerous complaints about a "prowler." When the Major Crimes Detail received a case involving the same family, a Burglary detective provided the interpretive scheme pointing to the phoniness of the complaints. The Major Crimes sergeant then told his men not to worry about the report since it could probably be interpreted as false.

Related to this interaction is the role of memory in detective investigations and the organization of information. A detective working a particular detail is expected to "know about" the types of persons, techniques, crimes, and criminal relationships typically involved in the kinds of cases he works. For example, one of the Major Crimes detectives was responsible for arson and bombs, and he knew a great deal about fuses, explosives, and other related matters that most of the other detectives did not know. Similarly, the theft detective knew a great deal about bicycles and bicycle parts, the fraud detective was extremely knowledgeable about false signatures, and all of the other detectives had specialized knowledge depending on the type of crime they usually investigated. The length of a detective's tenure in a position determined the amount of knowledge he had about a set of crimes, criminals, and criminal situations. Not all of this information is written down in reports, and what is written down is expected to be elaborated orally by the detective who worked the case. Memory serves to interpret reports in terms of "what really happened," link people to one another, and recall old cases and criminals. For example, one detective remembered a warrant issued a year and a half before in a grand theft case. He spotted a van which had been described as belonging to the suspect, called in to check if the warrant was still outstanding, and subsequently arrested the man on the warrant.

In developing information, memory is often used to make something out of the bits and pieces that crop up in a case. During the investigation of a gas-station robbery, a detective who used to work narcotic cases remembered that a former employee of the station was involved in drugs. The name of this former employee was taken as a possible break in the case, for the connection that was "made" between the drug case and the robbery provided an informative framework. The detective explained that even though the robbery suspect was a male, the former employee, a woman, might have helped to plan the robbery by pointing out the best time to get the most money, where the safe was located, and other details. All of this was "made as information" from the detective's recollection of the woman's one-time involvement in drugs when he saw her name listed as a former employee of the station. Without this recollection, it is doubtful that the name of the woman would have been treated as useful information.

The extent of a detective's specialization and his tenure in a single position constitute a contingency in the organization of information. Greater specialization implies more detailed knowledge of certain types of crimes, methods, and typical perpetrators. The amount of communication between detectives was also a contingency in the flow of knowledge that was offered as "information" or "something you might want to know about," including possible interpretations for the bits and pieces that surrounded a case and, most important, the establishment of a scheme of interpretation for characterizing whatever had been found in a case.

REPORT FORMS

The informal communication among detectives was not a planned pattern in the flow of information, but, as we will see,

Figure 3-1 OAI Form

1. CLASSIFICATION O AI

SHERIFF'S DEPARTMENT

2. CASE NUMBER O AI
CITATION NO.

3. ☐ CHECK IF JUVENILE

OFFENSE REPORT ☐ | ARREST REPORT ☐ ON VIEW ☐ WARRANT ☐ CITIZEN'S ☐ OTHER | INCIDENT REPORT ☐

4. DAY AND TIME OCCURRED OR ARRESTED O AI | 5. ADDRESS OR LOCATION DESCRIBE PREMISES OR VEHICLE O AI | 6. DAY AND TIME REPORTED. O AI

7. VICTIMS NAME (FIRM NAME IF BUSINESS) O AI | RACE | SEX | AGE/D.O.B. | OCCUPATION | RESIDENCE ADDRESS (BUSINESS ADDRESS IF FIRM) | RESIDENCE PHONE

8. PERSON REPORTING OFFENSE O AI | RACE | SEX | AGE/D.O.B. | RESIDENCE ADDRESS | RESIDENCE PHONE

9. PERSON WHO DISCOVERED CRIME O AI

10. PRINCIPALS O AI | CONT. MADE | HOW INVOLVED

11. VEHICLE INVOLVED ☐ O AI | SUSPECT VEHICLE ☐ | LICENSE NO. STATE | YEAR | MAKE | MODEL | COLOR | ID NUMBER | REG/OR LEGAL OWNER | RESIDENCE ADDRESS | RES. PHONE | STORED ☐ | IMPOUNDED ☐ | RELEASED ☐

CRIMES AGAINST PROPERTY OR THE PERSON

12. EXACT LOCATION OF PROPERTY *OR VICTIM* AT TIME OF OFFENSE O

13. POINT OF ENTRY *OR APPROACH* O

14. OCCUPANTS *OR VICTIM(S)* ACTIVITY AT TIME OF OFFENSE O

15. METHOD *OR INDUCEMENT* USED TO GAIN ENTRANCE O

16. INSTRUMENT USED (DESCRIBE) *OR WEAPON,* FORCE *OR MEANS USED* O

17. APPARENT MOTIVE PROPERTY TAKEN *OR ACT COMMITTED* O

18. TRADEMARK OF SUSPECT(S) ACTION *OR EXACT WORDS USED* O

19. TELETYPE SENT BY O AI ☐ DDL ☐ CII

20. EVIDENCE TAG NO'S. O AI

21. SUSPECTS AND/OR PERSONS ARRESTED: NAME, ADDRESS AND PHONE O AI	CONT. MADE	RACE	SEX	AGE/D.O.B.	HEIGHT	WEIGHT	HAIR	EYES	BOOKING NO'S.

22 O AI LIST CONTINUATIONS. (A) FURTHER DESCRIPTION OF SUSPECTS OR PERSONS INVOLVED (B) SUMMARIZE DETAILS OF OCCURRENCE OF ARREST (C) DESCRIBE PHYSICAL EVIDENCE, LOCATION FOUND, AND GIVE DISPOSITION (D) SUMMARIZE OTHER DETAILS RELATING TO THE CRIME (E) TIME AND LOCATION WHERE VICTIM/WITNESSES CAN BE CONTACTED BY DAY INVESTIGATORS, IF NO AVAILABLE PHONE NUMBERS (F) ITEMIZE AND DESCRIBE ANY EVIDENCE SEIZED, LISTING ALL SERIAL NUMBERS AND OTHER MARKS OF IDENTIFICATION. (G) IF JUVENILE, LIST NAME, ADDRESS, PHONE NUMBER AND RELATIONSHIP OF PARENT OR GUARDIAN, WHETHER NOTIFIED, AND IF SO, HOW AND BY WHOM.

(NARRATIVE SECTION)

the official reporting devices designed to organize information were dependent on this informal communication. The forms on which the reports were written were so designed that if the officer writing the report filled in the blanks with the pertinent accounts, the report would "automatically" have the necessary information. However, the actual use of the completed forms was dependent on a good deal of interpretive work.

OAI Form

The OAI form (figure 3–1) is used by patrol to report "offenses," "arrests," and "incidents" to detectives. "Offenses" refers to crimes; "incidents" to noncriminal matters, such as a lost child; and "arrests" to taking a person into custody. Reports reviewed by detectives are typically checked off as "offenses." The items on the form are grouped into a "background section," where the crime classification, names and addresses of victims and other principals in the case, and other typified details are recorded; and a "narrative section," in which the offense situation is summarized.

The OAI form is used by detective sergeants to determine whether or not to work a case, how to begin an investigation, and which detail is to do the work.

Follow-Up Form

When detectives investigate a case, usually by talking with crime victims, witnesses, and suspects, the follow-up form (figure 3–2) is used to report their activities. In format it is essentially the same as the OAI form, but the narrative section is longer and contains fewer specific check-off items. Generally, the form is used by detectives simply to describe what they have done in a case. The following example of item 12 is typical of theft and burglary follow-ups:

A. Unknown

B. See original report (patrol report on OAI form).

C. Victim (name) was unavailable for contact at (name of high school) in regard to the theft of radio and tools from his pick-up truck. Mr. S. (school administrator) was requested to advise victim to contact this department if further information is located.

Figure 3-2 Follow-Up Form

1. OFFENSE OR CLASSIFICATION	**SHERIFF'S DEPARTMENT**			2. CASE NUMBER
	FOLLOW UP REPORT			

3.
FOLLOW UP TO: ☐ OFFENSE REPORT ☐ ARREST REPORT ☐ INCIDENT REPORT ☐ OTHER _____

4. DATE AND TIME OF ORIGINAL REPORT	5. DATE AND TIME OF THIS REPORT	6. FINAL OFFENSE OR CLASSIFICATION

7. VICTIM/COMPLAINANT	ADDRESS	TELEPHONE NUMBER

8. VEHICLE INVOLVED LICENSE NO.	STATE	YEAR	MAKE	MODEL	COLOR	9. STORED IMPOUNDED	10. DISPOSITION OF VEHICLE (GARAGE, LEFT AT SCENE, ETC.)

11. WITNESS(ES) OR PRINCIPALS CONTACTED OR IN ADDITION TO ORIGINAL REPORT	RACE	SEX	AGE/D.O.B.	ADDRESS	PHONE	HOW INVOLVED	CONT. MADE

12. ITEM NO. (A) IF SUSPECT(S) LISTED, GIVE FULL NAME(S) AND DESCRIPTIONS INCLUDING D.O.B. IF AVAILABLE (B) DESCRIBE EVIDENCE AND/OR PROPERTY OBTAINED, SERIAL NUMBERS. (C) GIVE ANY NEW INFORMATION AS TO WHEN AND WHERE PRINCIPALS CAN BE CONTACTED.

21. RECORDS USE ONLY		
19. ATTACHMENTS TO REPORT: YES ☐ NO ☐	ENTERED	AREA NO.
	INDEXED	
13. REPORTING OFFICER	BODY NO.	14. DATE AND TIME REPORT WRITTEN	15. VALUE OF ADDED LOSS OR RECOVERY	20. TIME OFFICER SENT	EDP NO.
16. ASSISTING OFFICER	BODY NO	17. SUPERVISOR APPROVING/BODY NO.	18. TYPED BY / DATE	10-97	
				10-8	

FORM SH 224 (REV. 10-70)   **RECORDS/ORIGINAL**   EXCEPTIONAL DISTRIBUTION IS AUTHORIZED
TO: _____
BY _____ BODY NO. _____ DATE _____

Figure 3-3 CPC Form

1. OFFENSE OR CLASSIFICATION	**SHERIFF'S DEPARTMENT** — 2. CASE NUMBER

SHERIFF'S DEPARTMENT

CLEAR-UP, PROPERTY, COMPLAINT REPORT

□ SUPPLEMENTAL □ MULTIPLE

1. OFFENSE OR CLASSIFICATION
2. CASE NUMBER

3. TYPE OF REPORT: □ CLEARANCE □ PROPERTY □ COMPLAINT
4. FOLLOW-UP TO: □ OFFENSE □ ARREST REPORT □ INCIDENT □ OTHER ___

5. DATE AND TIME OF ORIGINAL REPORT
6. DATE AND TIME OF THIS REPORT
7. FINAL OFFENSE OR CLASSIFICATION
8. ARREST MADE □ YES □ NO

9. VICTIM/COMPLAINANT | ADDRESS | TELEPHONE NUMBER

10. VEHICLE INVOLVED LICENSE NO. | STATE | YEAR | MAKE | MODEL | COLOR | 11. STORED (IMPOUNDED) | 12. DISPOSITION OF VEHICLE (GARAGE, LEFT AT SCENE, ETC.)

13. PRINCIPALS | RACE | SEX | AGE/D.O.B. | ADDRESS | PHONE | HOW INVOLVED | CONT. MADE

14. COMPLAINT OBTAINED □ YES □ MISD. □ NO □ FELONY
15. D.A. NO.
16. COURT:
17. COURT CASE #
18. □ CITED TO APPEAR □ D.A. TO SEND NOTICE
19. □ WRRT. TO BE ISSUED □ SUBJ. IN CUSTODY □ OUT ON BAIL

20. IF OFFENSE CLEARED, INDICATE WITH "X" ALL ITEMS WHICH APPLY TO THIS REPORT
21. IF PROPERTY INVOLVED:

□ UNFOUNDED
□ ARRESTED AND PROSECUTED HERE.
□ ARRESTED BY OUTSIDE DEPARTMENT FOR SBSO.
□ ARRESTED FOR OUTSIDE DEPARTMENT?
□ ARRESTED AND REFERRED TO JUVENILE COURT.
□ ARRESTED AND PROSECUTED BY OUTSIDE DEPT.
□ ARRESTED BUT NOT PROSECUTED, EXPLAIN.
□ DISTURBANCE OR NUISANCE ABATED.
□ CLEARED, OTHERWISE - SPECIFY

□ INVESTIGATION CONTINUING.
□ INACTIVE, NO FURTHER LEADS
□ COMPLAINT WITHDRAWN BY COMPLAINANT.
□ COMPLAINT REFUSED BY D.A. ___ NAME
□ INSUFFICIENT EVIDENCE
□ CIVIL MATTER
□ WARNED (HANDLED, W/IN DEPT.)
□ REFERRED TO ANOTHER AGENCY
□ REFERRED TO PROBATION

□ RECOVERY - COMPLETE
□ RECOVERY - PARTIAL
□ RECOVERED BY PAWNSHOP
□ RECOVERED BY OTHER POLICE
□ RECOVERED BY OWNER
□ RECOVERED OTHERWISE, EXPLAIN
□ RECOVERED OUTSIDE S.B.
□ RECOVERED FOR OUTSIDE AGENCY ___

□ ADDITIONAL LOSS
□ CHANGE OF VALUE
□ RELEASE ORDER

22. RECOVERED BY (LAST NAME, FIRST, INITIAL) | RESIDENCE ADDRESS | CITY | RESIDENCE PHONE | BUSINESS PHONE

23. WHERE RECOVERED
24. DATE AND TIME OF RECOVERY
25. CONDITION WHEN RECOVERED

26. PLACE OF STORAGE | ADDRESS | CITY | PHONE NUMBER

27. OWNER NOTIFIED BY | BODY NO.
28. DATE AND TIME NOTIFIED
29. REPORTED TO CII □ YES □ NO
30. TELETYPE NUMBER
31. APB NUMBER

32. ITEM NO. (A) IF MORE THAN ONE REPORT INVOLVED, INDICATE REPORT NUMBERS, ETC. BELOW. (B) IF SUSPECT(S) LISTED, GIVE FULL NAME(S) AND DESCRIPTIONS INCLUDING D.O.B. IF AVAILABLE. (C) DESCRIBE EVIDENCE AND/OR PROPERTY OBTAINED, SERIAL NUMBERS.

MULTIPLE REPORT NOS. OR BOOKING NOS.	VICTIM OR DEFENDANT	DATE REPORTED	CRIME TYPE	PROPERTY RECOVERED (LIST AND GIVE PROPERTY TAG NO.)

(NARRATIVE SECTION)

THIS CASE INACTIVE PENDING FURTHER INVES-
TIGATIVE LEADS

CPC Form

The "Clear-Up, property, Complaint" form (figure 3–3) is one of the most interesting because it is the most specific. For example, it supplies 18 categories for the manner in which the case was resolved (item 20). The CPC form serves as a "cap" on cases that have been finished (not inactivated) and is generally the last report in the case file. Its categorization of events structures cases far beyond the complex and haphazard events that were observed to take place; however, because it is used more to catalogue than to inform, it is not thought to be as useful as reports on other forms that "explained what really happened" in the large narrative sections. (The CPC form has a relatively small narrative section.)

Specialized and Short Forms

The OAI, follow-up, and CPC forms are used for virtually any type of crime, but other forms are intended for only certain crimes. Thus the bicycle and surfboard form has blanks for bicycle and surfboard characteristics; the check and forgery form (figure 3–4) includes such items as what type of instrument (e.g., pen, pencil) had been used in forging the document and contains the outline of a check so that the detective can show how it had been filled out; the coroner's form (figure 3–5) has items relating to causes of death. A property form (figure 3–6) was developed during the course of the study, used, mainly by Burglary detectives, to log stolen and recovered property as well as evidence.

Another group of forms used by the MCSO included the field interrogation card (FI card), field report form, and pawn-shop cards. The FI card (figure 3–7) was used by patrol to record any interrogation in which the subject appeared to be "out of place" (cf. Sacks, 1972) and consists of items relating to personal biography and appearance. The field report, a shorter version of the OAI form, was used when patrol noticed something that they believed should be recorded but did not warrant the longer OAI report. One weekend's batch of field reports, for example, included the following items:

Figure 3-4 Check and Forgery Form

SHERIFF'S DEPARTMENT — CHECK AND FORGERY REPORT form

1. SPECIFIC OFFENSE

SHERIFF'S DEPARTMENT

CHECK AND FORGERY REPORT

2. CASE NUMBER   SUPPL.

3. DATE AND TIME OCCURRED   4. LOCATION OF OCCURRENCE   5. DATE AND TIME REPORTED

6.

NSF	RTM	SIG. IRREG.	ACT. CLOSED	UTL	FORGED	STOLEN	FICT. PRINT	RAISED	PERSONAL	PAYROLL	MONEY ORD.	CRED. CARD
☐	☐	☐	☐	☐	☐	☐	☐	☐	☐	☐	☐	☐

7. CAN ACCEPTOR I.D. S?   WILL V SIGN COMPL?   FORGERY AFFIDAVIT SIGNED   PORTION ALTERED   AUTHORIZED SIGNATURE   BANK LETTER WRITTEN

YES ☐ NO ☐   YES ☐ NO ☐   YES ☐ NO ☐   DATE _____

8. AMOUNT OF LOSS   9. TYPE OF PROPERTY AND/OR CASH OBTAINED   10. IDENTIFICATION USED TO PASS CHECK:

D.L.#   S.S.# _____ OTHER _____

11. WAS DOCUMENT OR ENDORSEMENT WRITTEN IN HIS PRESENCE?   12. SPECIFY WHAT PARTS   13. SIGNATURE OF ENDORSER   DESC. _____

YES ☐   NO ☐   EMPL. _____

14. VICTIMS NAME (FIRM NAME IF BUSINESS)   RACE   SEX   AGE/D.O.B.   RESIDENCE ADDRESS (BUSINESS ADDRESS IF FIRM)   RESIDENCE PHONE

OCCUPATION

15. PERSON REPORTING OFFENSE   RACE   SEX   AGE/D.O.B.   RESIDENCE ADDRESS   RESIDENCE PHONE

16. PERSON WHO ACCEPTED DOCUMENT

17. PRINCIPALS   CONT. MADE   HOW INVOLVED

18.

PEN WRITTEN ☐	19. BUSINESS OR PERSONALIZED. (NAME AND ADDRESS)	NO. _____
BALL PEN ☐		
PENCIL ☐		DATE _____
TYPEWRITTEN ☐	PAY TO THE ORDER OF _____ (NAME OF PAYEE)	$ _____
HAND PRINTED ☐		
PROTECTOGRAPHED ☐	_____ (WRITTEN AMOUNT)	DOLLARS
RUBBER STAMP ☐	(NAME OF BANK) (CITY AND BRANCH)	(NAME OF MAKER)

20. SUSPECTS AND/OR PERSONS ARRESTED: NAME, ADDRESS AND PHONE   CONT. MADE   RACE   SEX   AGE/D.O.B.   HEIGHT   WEIGHT   HAIR   EYES   BOOKING NO'S.

21. TRADEMARKS OF SUSPECTS (ACTS, CONVERSATION, ETC.)   22. VEHICLE INVOLVED ☐   LICENSE NO. STATE   YEAR   MAKE   MODEL   COLOR

23. DETAILS: DESCRIBE EVIDENCE: SUMMARIZE DETAILS NOT GIVEN ABOVE:

24. ANY PREVIOUS CASE NUMBERS OR OTHER AGENCIES ALSO WITH CHECKS

25. REPORTING OFFICER   BODY NO.   26. DATE AND TIME REPORT WRITTEN   27. CHECK COPIES ATTACHED: SBSO ☐ CII ☐   28. TIME OFFICER SENT   10-97   32. RECORDS USE ONLY   ENTERED   AREA NO.

29. ASSISTING OFFICER   BODY NO.   30. SUPERVISOR APPROVING/BODY NO.   31. TYPED BY: / DATE   10-8   INDEXED

EXCEPTIONAL DISTRIBUTION IS AUTHORIZED   EDP NO.

TO: _____

BY: _____ BODY NO. _____ DATE _____

FORM SH-325 (REV. 6/70)   **RECORDS/ORIGINAL**

Figure 3-5 Coroner's Form

1. CLASSIFICATION		**SHERIFF—CORONER**	2. CASE NUMBER	CORONER'S NUMBER
		CORONER'S REPORT		

3. DATE AND TIME PRONOUNCED DEAD	4. LOCATION OF OCCURRENCE	5. DATE AND TIME REPORTED DAY OF THE WEEK

| 6. DECEASED: LAST NAME | FIRST NAME | MIDDLE NAME | 7. AKA | 8. SOCIAL SECURITY NO. |

| 9. DATE OF BIRTH | 10. RACE | SEX | HEIGHT | WEIGHT | HAIR | EYES | 11. CITIZENSHIP | 12. PLACE OF BIRTH |

13. LAST USUAL RESIDENCE OF DECEASED: (CITY-COUNTY-STATE)   14. OCCUPATION

15. MORTUARY: 16. OUTSIDE AGENCY: 17. OFFICER:

18. PERSON REPORTING DEATH: (NAME, ADDRESS, CITY, COUNTY, STATE, PHONE-RESIDENCE & BUSINESS)

19. PERSON WHO DISCOVERED DECEASED: (NAME, ADDRESS, CITY, COUNTY, STATE, PHONE-RESIDENCE & BUSINESS)

20.	RELATIONSHIP	NAME	ADDRESS	TELEPHONE
NEXT OF KIN, POLICE INFORMANTS-WITNESSES MEDICAL PERSONNEL				

21.	PRIVATE PHYSICIAN:	ADDRESS:	TELEPHONE:
MEDICAL SUMMARY TREATMENTS-MEDICATION INJURIES -DIAGNOSIS	NATURE OF ILLNESS: (INCLUDE ANY DIAGNOSIS)		DATE OF LAST VISIT
	TREATMENT & MEDICATIONS: (INCLUDE ANY HOSPITALIZATION)		

22.	PLACE OF INJURY: (ADDRESS-DESCRIBE LOCATION)	DISTANCE FROM RESIDENCE:	DATE & TIME OF INJURY:	INJURY AT WORK: YES/NO
INJURY INFORMATION	TYPE OF PREMISES OR LOCATION: (HOME, FARM, FACTORY, FREEWAY, HIGHWAY, ETC.)	HOW DID INJURY OCCUR:		

23. NOTIFICATION OF DEATH: (NAME & RELATIONSHIP)

NOTIFIED ON: AT:

VIA: BY: AS VERIFIED BY: DATE/TIME:

24. PATHOLOGIST: DR.

,M.D. NOTIFIED: TIME:

25. **PARTICULARS SURROUNDING DEATH:** (A) LIST AND DESCRIBE ALL PROPERTY SEIZED, WHERE FOUND, DISPOSITION AND PROPERTY TAG NUMBER. (B) LIST ANY DOCUMENTS, I.E. WILLS, SUICIDE NOTES. (C) NARRATIVE SECTION, RELATE ALL PERTINENT FACTS OF INVESTIGATION. (D) IF VEHICLE ACCIDENT, LIST WHETHER DECEASED WAS DRIVER, PASSENGER OR PEDESTRIAN AND AGENCY AND OFFICER INVESTIGATING.

34.	RECORDS USE ONLY
ENTERED	AREA NO.

	32. ATTACHMENTS TO REPORT YES ☐ NO ☐		INDEXED

26. REPORTING OFFICER BODY NO.	27. DATE AND TIME REPORT WRITTEN	28. INITIAL CALL RECEIVED BY	33. TIME OFFICER SENT	EDP NO.
			10-97	
29. ASSISTING OFFICER BODY NO.	30. SUPERVISOR APPROVING/BODY NO.	31. TYPED BY: / DATE	10-8	

FORM SH141 (REV. 11-72)   **CORONER'S /ORIGINAL**   EXCEPTIONAL DISTRIBUTION IS AUTHORIZED
TO: _____

BY _____ BODY NO. _____ DATE _____

Figure 3-6 Property Form

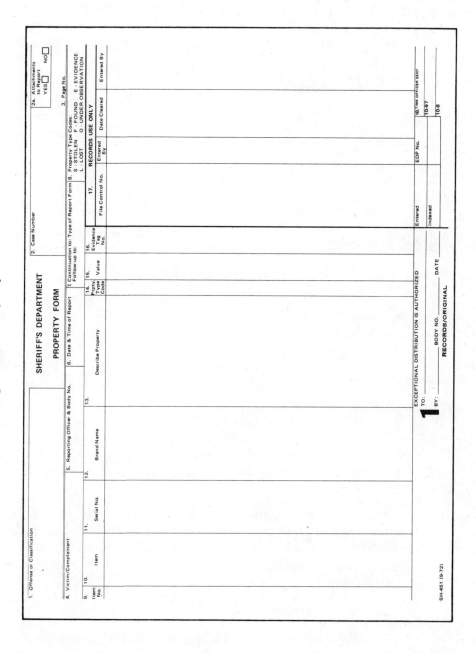

Figure 3-7   Field Interrogation Card

NICKNAME		OFFICER	VEH. OPR. LIC. NO.
NAME:			SEX
			PHONE
ADDRESS			
SCHOOL OR EMPLOYMENT (PLACE)			HOW LONG
		DATE	TIME
LOCATION			
PARENT OR LOCAL REFERENCE			

AGE	DATE OF BIRTH	HT.	WT.	BUILD	COMPLEXION
RACE	HAIR	EYES		MARKS OR SCARS	

DRESS

MAKE OF CAR	TYPE	YEAR	COLOR	LIC. NUMBER

FIELD INTERROGATION   SH-248

[Reverse side of field interrogation card includes blanks for 1) reason for interrogation; 2) disposition and 3) officers (who were involved in the field interrogation)].

1. Suspicious vehicle.
2. Alarm ringing.
3. Firecrackers or shots.
4. Outside agency assist (helping highway patrol, city police, or some law-enforcement agency in another county or state).
5. Public assistance.
6. Open door.
7. Voided citation (traffic ticket canceled).
8. Suspicious circumstances (anything that "didn't look right").

Finally, the pawnshop cards are filled out by pawnshop customers when they bring in something to sell, and include, besides the name, address, and other identification of the seller, a description of the items sold. They are used in attempts to locate stolen property.

THE USE OF REPORT FORMS

The following examples of observed cases demonstrate how what is developed as information flows through the organization and how certain things come to be treated as information. Case 50 illustrates the use of an OAI report, a follow-up report, and an FI card in addition to records from other agencies.

CASE 50

A girl reported that she had been raped at knifepoint while walking on the beach. The patrol report [OAI form] classified the offense as rape (261 PC) and kidnapping (217 PC). A Major Crimes detective contacted the victim and the witnesses listed in the patrol report and talked with them about the crime and the rapist. From these talks, he learned that the suspected rapist was a Negro male wearing red pants with a stripe down the side, and this description went into the follow-up report [follow-up form]. Going through the FI cards for the day of the crime, the detective found that a person had been "FI'd" who matched the description given by the victim and witnesses. Using the name from the FI card, he learned that the man had a criminal record as a juvenile. He was able to obtain a photograph from the State Youth Authority records. The photograph was identified by the victim and witnesses as the rapist.

CASE 101

Burglary detectives had made a raid on a suspected burglar's house (with a search warrant) and had found a great deal of suspected stolen property. All of these items were logged on the property form, categorized mainly as "O" (under observation), but some of the items were found to have been reported as stolen on other property reports or follow-up reports and were logged "R" (for recovered). The detectives were able to clear four burglaries at once by comparing records of items found with old burglary reports, but they expected to clear more by examining other reports of burglary and theft investigations in both the sheriff's office and the city police department.

The detectives believe that the information either is or is not on the forms; what is on the forms is information. However, by examining the actual uses made of the various reports, we can see that what is finally regarded and acted upon as information is not given but developed through interpretive work. For example, in case 50, when the detective found the FI card with a description of the suspect, he did not know at the time that the man was the suspect or that he had found a solid lead in the rape case. Only after the victim had identified the photograph of the person named on the FI card was the card seen as a lead and what it contained as informative. The definite sense of what was on the FI card was retrospective; before identification by the victim, it was seen as only a "possibility."

The forms are instrumental in creating a sense of order in information. Since the forms constitute standardized means of reporting crimes and incidents, they are also ordering devices themselves. They can be seen as reflections of the real world in that they contain places for reporting standardized, routine events. What is called for on the form is seen to exist in the real world. On the other hand, report forms serve to order the world in that accounts are directed and bounded by their format. If one uses a report form and wishes to complete it, a report must be constructed that follows the order suggested on the form.

The view that the reports reflect the real world is held by the detectives and anyone who believes that the detectives are doing their job honestly. The contrary view is held by groups which believe that there is a real world to be reported but that detectives and police generally lie, either for legal reasons or to "cover" themselves for disobeying bureaucratic procedures. Others perceive that the accounts in the report serve to order the reality and construct the world. The last view, of course, is the one embodied in this book. There is a reflexive interaction between the phenomena reported and the reporting accounts; each is a part of the other (cf. Garfinkel, 1967, pp. 7–9). Report forms constitute a way of reading the world of events encountered by the detectives and thus are themselves interpretive devices. At the same time, they provide a sense of order, for they follow the standardized format in which the reality of a case is arranged.

The utility of reports, however, is contingent on the informal flow of communication. As we pointed out earlier, memory plays an important role in the organization of information, for access to particular knowledge is often stored in somebody's head and not in a file. A detective may remember something that is not in the records and that may ultimately be useful. Also, in order to make use of something in the records it is necessary to be aware of it, and communicated recollection is an important source of such awareness. Thus, access to the possible information in the records depends to a large extent on informal communication among detectives.

Such communication is used by detectives to provide the "scenery" and "texture" generally absent from written reports. If a detective knows of circumstances relevant to an official report, he will provide an interpretive scheme for reading the report. For instance, a detective who had had prior contact with a suspect in a new case might point out that the suspect was a "scroat,"* and the items in the report would be read in terms of this view of the suspect's character. Alternatively, one detective might tell another that even though a report made the suspect look bad, the suspect was really a "good kid," essentially a victim of circumstances, a "patsy" or "fall guy" for another's misdeeds. Thus, depending on the interpretive scheme offered informally, the items in a report could be seen as informative or not. On a number of occasions I was told by detectives, "You really can't tell what happened by reading an old report unless someone who knows about it is around to fill you in on the details." As a Scotland Yard detective explained to me in an interview, "Reports consist of what the officer should have done." What "really happened" is often hidden and must be explained conversationally by someone who knows.

For example, let us say that a detective was investigating a case and needed to know something about an old case involving a current suspect. Suppose the case involved violence, and the suspect was involved in an assault case some years earlier. The detective is going to want to see the old report on the assault, but he is also going to ask the detective who wrote the report to explain or elaborate the details. The detective who wrote the old report might say something like, "Well, this guy you're looking at really wasn't at fault. He had been drinking when some loudmouth picked a fight with him. When the patrol officers showed up, they've got two guys in a fight, and only one of them has been drinking. So when they write their report, it looks like

---

*One of several terms used to characterize anyone who was not liked. Such terms as "punk," "puke," and "asshole" were used to convey the same idea, but at the time of the study, "scroat" was the favorite. Since most nonpolice did not know what it meant, the term could be used with little risk that someone would complain.

the guy who was drinking started it. By the time I start the follow-up report nobody wants to charge anyone with anything, and so I just write on the follow-up report to see the patrol report, and close the case. I'm not about to go into a lot of detail about it if the case isn't going anywhere." As can be seen, not only does a conversational report fill in details left out either because they did not meet the legal requirements for inclusion (e.g., the information was illegally obtained) or because the report writer was in a hurry and saw no reason to include them; more importantly, having someone available who "knows about" the reported incident can provide the context for the proper reading of the details. This suggests the contextual dependence and bond of such communications. Even though reports are written in a style that suggests objectivity, their exact sense is always dependent on having background details and a context.

INTERORGANIZATIONAL FLOW AND ORGANIZATION OF INFORMATION

The flow and organization of records and details between the MCSO and other organizations took two forms. First, there was a state-wide and nation-wide network of law-enforcement records and a tacit understanding that information and assistance would be provided by various other local law-enforcement agencies, in and out of the state, when requested for an investigation. This type of information consisted largely of copies of reports prepared for the other agencies.

The second type of communication between MCSO and other agencies had to do with information used in court by the defense, prosecutor, and judge, and by the probation officer and any other agency or person involved with a case outside the sheriff's office and other police agencies. Everything written down and handed over to the courts, including virtually every report in a case, had to be presented in a "legal style" which excluded opinions, hunches, and anything that had not been gathered in strict adherence to due process. For example, a hunch that led to the successful conclusion of a case was not presented, even though without it the case would never have been solved.

With the exception of "voluntary statement" forms, filled out by victims, witnesses, and suspects, everything in the reports is written by the patrol officer, detective, or some other member of the MCSO, in a manner that conforms to the rules of admissible evidence. In contrast, the reports used by Scotland Yard are quite short, consisting of a paragraph or so by the reporting officer and perhaps the detectives, with the bulk of the case file made up of witnesses' statements. Instead of having to record every interview, Scotland Yard detectives simply arrange the various statements, including the reporting officer's and the detective's, in a case-file for court.

The requirement that "reasonable" or "probable" cause must be shown for bringing a person before the D.A. also leads to confusion and ambiguity. LaFave (1965, p. 245) points out that "reasonable cause" is defined in Michigan (and several other states) simply as "cause to believe that a felony has been committed and reasonable cause to believe that such person has committed it." The definition is tautological and does not resolve the problem of what constitutes grounds for such a belief.

LaFave (1965, p. 249) illustrates probable cause in a number of questionable situations. For example:

> A patrolman came upon a man walking in a residential neighborhood late at night. The community in question was experiencing a particularly serious wave of nighttime offenses. Although the man could identify himself, he did not live in that neighborhood, and his explanation for being there was equivocal. The officer placed him under arrest.

Given this example without the information that there had been a high number of offenses in the area, one might conclude that no one is safe from arrest. LaFave suggests that it takes less evidence to meet the reasonable-cause requirement during a crime wave than when things are relatively peaceful—in other words, reasonable cause depends on the context of the situation. The sense of reasonable cause rests upon "what everyone knows" or a common understanding of ethnographic details that provide the context (Garfinkel, 1967; Leiter, 1971).

Similarly, in the course of this study the notion of "probable cause" (PC), especially in cases where the evidence was taken to be circumstantial, was embedded in assumptions about what "everyone knows." Case 105 illustrates this point:

CASE 105

A suspect was arrested on a warrant based on circumstantial [indirect] evidence. The detective who made the arrest
explained that a burglary victim had given him a list of
ex-employees, and from this list he had deduced a suspect.
The physical evidence indicated that the point of entry was a
window that had been broken; since the window was relatively small, so, too, would the suspect be. Second, the burglary
alarm switch had been turned off, and from this it was
deduced that someone familiar with the alarm system was the
burglar. Money was the only item taken; this also pointed to
an ex-employee, who knew where the money was stored.
Finally, the fingerprints that were taken were smudged but
indicated a whorl pattern on the left hand, and the suspect had
whorl patterns on his left hand.

It is doubtful that a district attorney would accept any one of
these inferences or deductions alone as probable cause, but
given the number of not-inconsistent deductions, plus the
suspect's refusal to take a polygraph examination and his
inability to account for his activities on the night of the burglary,
the D.A. concluded that there was "plenty of PC" to arrest the
suspect, although not enough for a complaint (a case that would
be accepted for prosecution by the D.A.). He therefore suggested
that the detective arrest the suspect and let him sit in jail over the
weekend, in the hope that the man would "cop out" (confess) to
the burglary and ask for a deal with the D.A. If the suspect did
not cop out, he would have to be released.*

This case suggests the contextual embeddedness of "reasonable cause" in two important ways. First, as we have noted, the
detective saw probable cause on the basis of a number of
unstated assumptions and the context provided in the account.
Second, the D.A. saw reason to believe that the suspect had
committed the crime, but he knew that by providing a different
context for the circumstances under which the arrest was made,
a good defense lawyer could offer other formulations. Not only
the context but the events themselves could be transformed.

In interviews with police at The Hague and detectives at

---

*This tactic, which stretches due process to its limits, was not the detective's
idea, but rather it was initiated by the D.A., a member of the BAR and an
attorney at law.

Scotland Yard, I found the same situation-bound, ad hoc use of "reasonable cause." The following exchange took place with a high-ranking Dutch police officer:

RCH: What criteria do you use for reasonable cause?

OFF: If we don't have a reasonable cause we don't arrest a man.

RCH: What constitutes reasonable cause?

OFF: I think it's impossible to give you a reasonable answer. It all depends upon the crime and what you know about it. And what has occurred to you. What is reasonable cause? It's something that bothers me, yes.

RCH: In other words, it's the same as in the United States?

OFF: Yes. To me it is reasonable, but it may be that the public prosecutor says it is not reasonable to him. It's a question of crossing your heart and not always of the law.

RCH: Are there differences between what the police consider to be reasonable cause and what the judges consider it to be?

OFF: Oh yes. They are different people.

From this interview it can be seen that the officer relied on "what is known about the situation" as an account of what "reasonable" comes to mean. The sense of "reasonable cause" for the Dutch as well, then, is embedded in the context of its use. While unstated, the explanation proferred by this officer relied on "what everybody knows to be reasonable." What the police and the magistrates see as reasonable may differ, but the sense of "reasonableness" was not described as independent of the circumstances of a given case.

In a Scotland Yard interview concerning the notion of reasonable cause, little was said that was relevant to the concerns here; however, each description of reasonable cause was either tautological or given in an example where the sense of "probable cause" was assumed:

RCH: There is another thing that I'm interested in. This is, you make an arrest—we call it probable cause, or reasonable cause, in America. There are essentially two ways an arrest can be made. (Well, there are a few more than that but two basic ways.) One is on a warrant signed by a magistrate, and the other is what they call probable cause [to believe] that the person has committed a crime and there is no time to get a warrant. You can arrest the person.

DET: It's the same here virtually. Our powers of arrest are laid
down by act of Parliament, and the power of arrest is usually
contained in the act which provides the penalty. . . . For
instance, the Metropolitan Police Act is a very old act of
Parliament, I think perhaps even 1839. Section 66 of the act
gives power for a police officer to stop, search, and detain
any person who he has reasonable grounds to think may be
carrying anything stolen or unlawfully obtained. Now, if he
makes up his mind there and then, if he thinks that person is
carrying stolen property, having seen the property, and the
person isn't able to give a good account of it, he can then
arrest.

Again, what constitutes reasonable cause for arrest is left unspe-
cified. "Having seen the property" still leaves in question the
nature of the property seen as well as what is considered as "a
good account of it." This is "reasonable" cause only in terms of
a number of assumptions and is in no way independent of the
situation in which it is used. Moreover, the assumptions of what
"everybody knows," of what constitutes "a good account," and
what looks like stolen property is never specified.

In the course of their work, police develop skills in "seeing"
reasons to make arrests (Sacks, 1972), but while these skills may
lead them to make initial searches that sometimes lead to arrests,
they may not be accepted by the courts as reasonable grounds
for a search or arrest. The Dutch police official noted this in his
explanation of reasonable cause, and it was a concern among the
detectives on Mountainbeach. Therefore, in making out their
reports for the D.A. and the courts, the detectives attempt to
formulate their accounts of what happened so that "anyone,"
not just other police officers, will agree that "reasonable cause"
was present. This practice does not involve deception so much
as omission of the subjective elements that may be the real
reasons a suspect first came to be noticed. Thus, in the development of information, detectives keep an eye out for what they
know the D.A. and courts will want to see.

INFORMATION NETWORKS IN SOCIETY

The detectives saw most of what was taken as information
not as made up or constructed, but as gathered, generally by

sifting through interviews with people somehow related to a crime. That is, from the detectives' point of view, the information was in the world waiting to be uncovered. There were certain people the detectives would typically see and places they would go outside of the department. By examining those who detectives believed normally had information about a crime or criminal, as well as the "nature" of the information they had, we can determine the picture of social order and social organization the detectives held.

Crime and Criminal Relationships

As was pointed out earlier, most of the crimes investigated by the Detective Division were reported initially by crime victims or other citizens. In most cases, therefore, it was assumed that the victim of a crime and witnesses, listed as "principals" in the report, had information. The crime situation itself gave rise to a number of relevant relationships for the detectives. For example, in a bar fight where someone is seriously hurt or even killed, normal patrons of the bar "become" possible witnesses, the bartender is assumed to have information, and anyone who knows the people involved in the fight is assumed to have possible information.

A number of items on the OAI form (page 54) guided the reporting officer to formulate the crime in terms of such relationships. For instance, items 7 through 10 point to relationships assumed to have typical relevance in crimes (e.g., person who reported crime). Thus, those persons with an assumed relationship to the crime, as outlined in the OAI form, are "automatically" brought into the investigation, and at the same time reify the assumption that they have information.

By checking out those listed on the crime report, the detective hopes to find a lead to the suspect. Case 62 illustrates some crime-situated relationships that were traced in the hope of locating information that would lead to a suspect:

CASE 62

A girl had been found in a near-fatal condition after what appeared to have been a rape. Upon questioning her, the detective found that she could remember nothing of the assault or her assailant. Since the victim was unable to

describe the attacker, the investigation centered on contacting
the people she had been with shortly before the attack. She
had attended a party before the assault, and the detectives
began interviewing *other guests at the party.* They were able
to identify *a boy who had taken the girl for a ride* shortly
before she was last seen unharmed. The boy claimed that she
had vomited in his car and that he therefore told her to get out
and returned to the party. He was identified as having been at
the party during the time of the assault and was not a prime
suspect.

In addition to crime-situated relationships, such as victim
and witness, there are also criminal relationships, or a set of
relationships among people who commit crimes. Since it is
believed that criminals have information about one another,
certain criminals are questioned. If a detective knows someone
who is typically involved in the criminal subculture he will
approach that person for information. Those who give information about other criminals are referred to as "informants" or
"snitches."

The detective-informant relationship is a tenuous one at best,
for to remain privy to information about other criminals, the
informant must have the trust and confidence of those who
commit crimes, which may involve committing crimes himself.
If the crimes committed by the informant come to be known to
the detectives and are of a relatively minor nature, they can be
used in an exchange of "favors." The detective may try to
convince the informant that the crime he committed is more
serious than the detective actually believes it to be, and that by
overlooking the crime he is doing the informant a favor and is
owed a favor (i.e., information) in return.

The "favor" may be given before or after the fact. The
detective may do a favor for a criminal and collect on it later. For
example, the theft detective was once instrumental in saving a
convicted juvenile from going to the Youth Authority. The youth
was grateful and on subsequent occasions gave the detective
information about thefts and thieves. On the other hand, after a
criminal has been arrested he may wish to make a deal with the
police or district attorney in the hope of getting a light sentence.
For instance, a convicted rapist awaiting sentencing in the jail
asked to talk to a Burglary detective about some property he

knew had been stolen. The detective promised only to let the informant "talk to the D.A." (supposedly to discuss a light sentence), and for this the rapist gave him information which resulted not only in the recovery of a large cache of stolen property but also in the discovery of an illegal narcotics factory. The information the rapist had supplied was assumed to have been passed on in the network of criminal relationships.

Primary and Secondary Relationships

Essentially, primary and secondary relationships refer to family, friends, and close associates (Cooley, 1902). Sometimes these relationships are criminal ones, as we discussed above, but relationships independent of criminal identities may also be information resources for the detectives.

In some crimes, family and friends are typically involved. For example, most homicides are committed by acquaintances of the victim, and a good place to begin looking for a suspect is among such others (Luckenbill, 1973). Similarly, assaults, beatings, rapes, batteries, as well as other crimes against the person, generally involve people who are known to the victim. To understand such relationships, then, is to understand whom to contact for information. The "closer" the relationship, presumably the more information those involved have about each other. Thus, a man's wife is assumed to have more information than a distant cousin or a casual associate. On receiving a report of a runaway (601 WIC), Juvenile detectives first interview the parents or guardians. The sense of the structure of these relationships provides investigators with a "map" of whom to contact, and the relationship stands as a "good reason" for such contacts. Case 33 illustrates the use of normal relations for information:

CASE 33

The victim had reported a burglary and had listed her ex-husband as the suspect. Taken were some beds, end tables, and other items the victim believed were of interest only to her husband. The detective contacted the victim at work. She said all she wanted was to get her things back. She was not interested in criminal prosecution.

Next the detective went to the address of the husband, and

a small boy who answered the door identified himself as the suspect's stepson. He explained that his mother had married the victim's ex-husband, the suspect. He said the suspect would not be at home until 5:30. The detective asked where he could contact the suspect during the day, but the boy did not know. The detective gave the boy a card and instructions for him to give it to his stepfather and have him call the number on the card. The next day the father called, admitted that he had taken the property, and said he had initiated civil action to keep it; so the detective closed the case, citing it to be a civil matter.

In this case information was sought through the relationship and the suspect was identified by the victim through the same relationship. A typical burglary usually involves such resalable items as television sets, stereo components, or cash (cf. Sudnow, 1965). In this case, since beds and end tables were taken, the victim, as well as the detective, saw the burglary as something other than typical.

A second feature pertaining to relationships is illustrated by the detective's momentary confusion as to the identity of the boy. When he said he was the suspect's stepson, the detective at first thought he meant that he was the victim's son, but after the new family structure and relevant kinship patterns had been explained, the detective understood the boy's relation to the suspect. However, it was not until the relationship had been fully explained that the detective could provide a scheme for understanding the information the boy had to offer.

Organizational Relationships

Relation to some organization is another source of information when attempting to establish a crime or identify or locate a suspect. Individuals are linked not only to the organization itself but also to others in the organization. Thus the organizational scheme provides detectives with the identities and location of people who are potentially linked to someone they are trying to find. In investigating the burglary of a business, for example, detectives usually ask for a list of employees and former employees. These organizational links are used as a map of possible suspects and witnesses and sometimes lead the detective to other contacts as well. For example, in a case involving the theft of some tools from a small factory, the employees were taken as possible suspects and witnesses. After listening to the owner's account of how the tools were believed to have been taken, the detective decided that the culprit was someone employed there. By examining the work schedule, he drew up a list of possible suspects.

In another case, a rape suspect had been traced to a security guard firm. Even though he was no longer employed there, the man had not picked up his final paycheck. When he came to get paid, the detectives were waiting for him. In this way organizations are used to locate people in time and space.

The various relationships that are seen to exist in society serve as guides to investigations. The detectives' analysis of relationships in society is very much like the analysis employed by sociologists. Not only are they aware of the positioning potentials of relationships, both formal and informal, but they are equally aware of the form a certain relationship would have. For example, they characterized a "manager-worker" relationship as functional and impersonal and were therefore relatively free about asking managers about information that might damage the worker if revealed. Since they saw the relationship as not involving sentimental ties, it was believed that the manager would not try to protect a worker suspect. On the other hand, when interviewing a relative of a suspect, they would ask where they could find the suspect to "talk with him" instead of saying they were going to arrest him. Such relationships were seen in terms of Gemeinschaft characteristics, which include loyalty to those who are part of such a relation.

CONCLUSION

Detective work can be seen in terms of various resources for developing information. The organizational resources of the MCSO included reports of various sorts to which detectives had access in their investigations. Effective use of these reports, however, was often contingent on an understanding of their context that could be provided only by someone who "knew about the case." Likewise, the existence of a report came to be known only if the detective himself had worked the case or if another detective told him that it might be of possible use in an investigation. Generally detectives did not rummage blindly through reams of reports in the hope of finding something that might be of use. Rather, they communicated with one another on an informal basis, and such communication appeared to be more important in formulating something as useful or possibly useful information than did simple access to the files.

Another contingency that affected the use of reports was the requirement that they be written in such a way that they could be used in court. The unopinionated tone of the reports, produced for the D.A's office, constituted one reason the detectives saw them as needing "explanation" by someone who "knew the case."

The extraorganizational arrangement of information was seen to exist in the myriad of social relationships that exist in society. Some of these relationships affected the way in which detectives typified crimes and the people who are generally related to a given type of crime. Thus, investigative contacts served to point to the sense relationships held by detectives. More generally, detectives pursued primary, secondary, and organizational relationships as sources of information, and the evidence they took to be informative was formulated in terms of their understanding of the relationship between the person who gave it and the others possibly involved in the case. Thus, while these relationships were seen as informational resources, the sense of the relationship elaborated and defined how informational evidences were to be treated.

4

Working a Case

*Every morning when I got to the office, the detectives would
be there going through the morning's batch of reports. They sat
around reading and commenting on them trying to decide which
ones should be worked and which ones shouldn't. If a case
involved someone who had been in habitual trouble, the detectives would comment on it, letting everyone know that so-and-so
was at it again. If the case involved particularly funny circumstances, it would be read aloud for everyone's amusement.
Serious and interesting cases would be noted, and everyone, even
the detectives who would not be involved in the investigation,
would read the report closely. Most of the cases were routine
ones involving burglaries, thefts, and disturbing the peace, and
no one was particularly interested in them, other than to give
them to a detective for assignment. Sometimes, especially if they
were busy writing follow-up reports, the sergeant would give one
of us researchers the batch of reports to go over and determine
which ones would be worked and which ones would not. The
selection process was so routine that we rarely made mistakes.*

Law-enforcement agencies of all types share the broad and
vague mandate to enforce the law and keep the peace (Bittner,
1967; Manning, 1971). With rare exceptions, detective work
involves enforcing the law; the peacekeeping functions are left
up to patrol. But showing how the law-enforcement mandate is
met involves far more than simply pointing to an investigation
initiated by law violation.

The formal rules regarding law enforcement vary from state to state, but typically the police are required by some statute to enforce all laws (LaFave, 1965). In addition, and as in all bureaucracies, there is also a set of informal rules and policies (cf. Turner, 1947) which to some extent mitigate the formal rules; thus, there are informal rules requiring that only certain laws will be enforced, based on a consensus that some laws, such as Sunday blue laws, are unpopular and that nonenforcement would cause no public outcry (LaFave, 1965, p. 127).

Examining police conduct in terms of the statutory requirements can explain very little, for exceptions to the rules are so pervasive that police actions almost appear to be arbitrary. On the other hand, if we follow a sociological approach, concentrating on formal bureaucratic rules and polices *and* informal norms within the police organization, we can begin to discern and understand patterns in police actions. Studies by Westley (1953), Piliavin and Briar (1964), Skolnick (1966), Reiss (1971), and Rubinstein (1973) all document the impact of informal understandings on police activity. Underlying all these studies is the Durkheimian notion that the norms are independent of the occasions and situations where they are applied. That is, the application of norms can be seen in many types of situations, and while the norms governing different situations and occasions vary, essentially the same norms prevail in the same kinds of situations. Other than pointing to a consensual definition of the situation, the normative theorists from either the symbolic-interaction or the structural-functionalism perspective pay little attention to the actor's role in analyzing the situation (cf. T. Wilson, 1970, pp. 59–70). That is, they ignore how actors develop a normative understanding of their own reality. In this book we will explore the ways in which actors develop a sense of "following the rules" and will see a "rule being followed."

In examining how detectives establish a case, we will first provide an overview of what constitutes "working a case." Since establishing a case provides us with the best data for understanding how detectives formulate reality, this chapter will treat that phase separately from the other aspects of detective work. In chapter 5 we will look at the investigations that make up the bulk of detective work once a case has been established. Both chapters, however, focus on the development of information.

WORKING A CASE: AN OVERVIEW

A detective investigation can be divided into five parts or steps. The first step is to *establish a case* of a reported incident as an instance of a specific crime or as otherwise warranting investigation. Then detectives begin work to *identify a suspect.* The third step is to *locate the suspect.* Then the detectives attempt to get a confession from the suspected culprit (*"cop the suspect"*), usually by presenting irrefutable evidence. This fourth step may end in an unexpected manner, for the detectives may learn that the suspect can show *them* irrefutable evidence of innocence, and they will have to start all over again in trying to identify a more likely culprit. Finally, the case is *disposed of* in one of a number of ways.

Investigations do not always follow this sequence. Often a crime is immediately disposed of after it has been established, thereby short-circuiting the sequence and going from first step to last. However, a typical investigation leading to the apprehension of a suspect follows the five-step sequence described, as is illustrated by the following case:

CASE 25

A young girl reported that a man had exposed himself to her. The detective contacted the girl and after talking with her decided that she was telling the truth and that the exposure was deliberate (*establishing a case*). Upon further questioning he found that the suspect had been driving a truck with a distinctive marking. By tracing the truck to a local company and contacting the manager of the company, the detective learned that a certain employee had reason to be at the location of the crime during the time the victim claimed it took place (*identifying a suspect*). The manager then asked the suspect to come down to the company office to talk with the detective (*locating the suspect*).

The suspect denied that he had exposed himself to any young girl. The only reason he could think of to explain why anyone would say he had done so was that the company uniform he wore had holes in the crotch of the pants. The company manager confirmed that he had been having difficulty with the laundry and that there were indeed holes in the pants of some employees' uniforms. Then the detective recontacted the victim, questioning her as to the possibility that there was a hole in the man's pants and no deliberate exposure, but she insisted that the man had masturbated in front of her. After further investigation and attempts to obtain either a confession from the suspect or a change in the victim's story, the detective decided to use a polygraph examination (*copping a suspect*). The suspect agreed to take the examination, but it turned out to be inconclusive. Eventually the case was turned over to the D.A.'s office, where charges were filed against the suspect. Later, however, the charges were dropped and the case was closed for lack of evidence (*disposition of a case*).

Each of the steps described here is a characterization used by detectives in talking about their work. Moreover, the sense of each step is embedded in its occasioned use (i.e., the sense was derived from the occasion, while characterizing the occasion). By outlining the sequence of an investigation I do not mean to imply that these steps are independent of the actor's accounts.

The End of the Work

Detectives generally see their job to be catching criminals, and therefore the goal of an investigation is just that. In their view, "monkeying around" with "nickel and dime" cases (trivial crimes with little chance of being solved) is not what they are paid to do; instead they conceive of their task as dealing with "righteous crime"* and "real criminals." Moreover, this is to be done within the constraints imposed upon them by organizational requirements, typified by the paperwork and the legal requirements of due process.

"Doing their job," then, is seen in terms of *clearing a case*. A case characterized as "cleared" was one that had been solved, as far as the detectives were concerned, with a suspect in custody or identified. For instance, in theft cases involving little loss, when a detective identified a suspect and located him in another state, it was unlikely that extradition proceedings would be initiated to bring the suspect back. From the detectives' point of

---

*The term "righteous" was used by detectives to refer to an "actual" crime, one worth investigating.

view, however, such cases were deemed to have been solved and were treated for all practical purposes as cleared.

Conviction, therefore, is not a necessary requirement for clearance, for as Manning (1971, p. 156) has pointed out, the detectives see themselves and not the courts as the most reliable judge of a suspect's innocence or guilt. For the detectives a cleared case is "solved as far as we're concerned." If a lawyer is able to get his client off "on a technicality," the detectives do not assume that the suspect was innocent and begin again to look for the culprit. This is especially true of sexual assaults, where the victim is often seen to be more on trial than the suspect: In one case where a sexual-assault suspect "got off" in court after having been positively identified by the victim, the detectives saw no cause to question their original belief that the suspect was guilty and to look for a new suspect. If, however, strong evidence is introduced at a trial showing that the suspect could not have possibly committed the crime, an investigation may begin anew. This prospect is not regarded as very likely, for by the time a detective nominates a suspect for the D.A.'s attention he has no doubt about the person's guilt.

Sometimes a case will arrive that has already been cleared by patrol, and all the detective will have to do is write a follow-up or clear-up report. For example, a rapist fell asleep in the victim's bed and was picked up by patrol when the victim summoned the sheriff's office. A Major Crimes detective was assigned to the case and prepared a follow-up report even though the case was already cleared.

Old cases are sometimes cleared when a suspect arrested for one crime confesses (cops out) to others (Skolnick, 1966). This is especially true of burglary cases. During the period of the study, numerous burglaries were cleared by suspects in custody for other burglaries. In some departments (but not in the MCSO) cases were cleared on method of operations (M.O.). If a suspect is caught whose M.O. has been used in other crimes, those crimes are considered cleared.

Finally, a case can be cleared without an arrest if the detective decides merely to warn the culprit to behave himself in the future. For example, in juvenile trespassing cases the detective might simply tell the kids not to do it again.

Cases may also be closed or inactivated. Logging a case as

"closed" indicates that the detective has finished with it. Sometimes cases are closed as soon as they are received, such as
various "415's" (disturbing the peace). These are not seen as
"real crimes" and are believed not to warrant investigation.
Cases seen to be "phony" are also closed as soon as they are so
characterized, either on initial receipt of the case or after an
investigation. Finally, if the detective decides that the case is a
civil matter (e.g., a divorce settlement), he tells the victim that
the issue does not involve a crime and closes the case.

The difference between an inactivated case and a closed case
is that the former is seen as potentially solved, while the latter is
seen either as not solvable or not in need of a solution.
Generally, a case that is inactivated is so classified after some
investigation. The investigation "ran out of leads" or there were
seen to be no leads to begin with. Typically the last line in an
inactivated case reads "CASE INACTIVE DUE TO LACK OF
INVESTIGATIVE LEADS." Often the investigation preceding
inactivation is perfunctory. By reading the initial report, the
detective determines whether the case has any leads. If it does
not, he proceeds on the assumption that time should not be
spent on it, and the case will be inactivated, sometimes after no
more investigation than a phone call to the victim.

A Note on "Stats"

Other studies of the police, especially Skolnick's (1966), have
found the concern for "stats" (i.e., statistics on "clearance
rates") to be a driving force in police work. While this is true to
some extent, especially among some members of the Burglary
detail, it did not appear to be a general concern of the MCSO
detectives. The ratio of crimes cleared to those reported and
treated as actual crimes was viewed with general cynicism. The
detectives pointed out that how "stats" were defined and manip-
ulated by different departments was far more important than the
actual number of arrests made for reported crimes. If "stats" had
been a major concern, all of the reported "415's" could have
been investigated and cleared with relative ease. However, these
cases were closed as soon as they came to the detectives'
attention, since disturbing the peace was seen as a relatively
harmless act generally not involving "real criminals." I accompanied a Burglary detective for his initial few months with the

detail, and it was not until he cleared his first "real burglary" that he expressed any satisfaction with his work. He had cleared some other burglaries involving little loss and suspects who were juveniles and only warned, but when he identified and arrested a suspect in a burglary/arson case who he believed was "really a criminal," he said he felt that at last his work was showing results. The "stats" from the other cases had little significance to him or his sergeant; praise for a job well done came only with the successful clearance of the burglary/arson case.

Another indication that "stats" play only a tangential role in some detective details was found when I offered to compute the clearance rates of two Juvenile detectives. One detective who worked theft cases did not know what a clearance rate was and, after I had computed the rate for the cases to which he had been assigned, asked me what it meant. While he was pleased to learn that his clearance rate was well above the national average, because this indicated that by some measure he was doing a good job, it was not of great interest to him. Moreover, this detective received little recognition for his work. Other detectives with lower clearance rates were held in higher esteem and were higher on the promotion list.

This is not to suggest that the sheriff and others in the MCSO did not know or care about clearance rates, for the rates were one indicator of how well the department was doing. Rather, the focus in any single case was not on "stats" so much as it was on identifying a "real criminal" or a "real crime." The more serious the crime, the more concern there was for solving it, and while the numbers in the "stats" were based in part on lesser crimes, the office procedures and priorities were organized in such a way that the more serious crimes would be investigated while lesser ones with the same stat-generating potential were not.

Investigative Orientation

Given that detectives conceive of their "real work" as catching criminals, organizationally realized in the form of a "cleared case," we can begin to examine investigations geared to generate information to this end. We must keep in mind, however, that detectives are not oriented in terms of clearance rates so much as in terms of "good rips" (arrests). Developing the sense of a lead

or some other form of information, then, is viewed in relation to
the overall mandate of enforcing the law by catching criminals,
and not in terms of producing clearance rates "to make the
department look good."

ESTABLISHING A CASE

As we have pointed out, cases received by detectives are
initially taken by patrol. When the case reaches the detectives
the sergeants must decide what crime it exemplifies and whether
or not to spend investigative time on it. The patrol report's
definition of the case in terms of the State Penal Code serves as
shorthand for pointing to "real criminals." And whenever a case
is reported in terms of a penal-code classification, the detectives
read the particulars of the report to determine whether in fact it
is a "righteous crime" or something else. For example, attempted murder (217 PC) is seen to be a "righteous crime" involving
"real criminals," or at least people who are potentially dangerous and should be dealt with. However, what constitutes an
actual case of attempted murder is not, as is theorized in the
legal code, a set of circumstances independent of an account of
attempted murder, or for that matter any other form of crime.
The legal requirements for a person to be charged with a crime
are that elements of the crime must be shown to exist and the
person must be shown to have committed it. In establishing a
case, the detective is not so much looking for elements of the
crime as he is formulating the reported events into typified
wholes. For example, a crime was reported as an attempted
murder, but when the Major Crimes sergeant read the report, he
said, "This is nothing but a glorified domestic." By this he
meant that the case should have been reported as a domestic
disturbance and logged as disturbing the peace, 415 PC, the
usual penal code used to characterize domestic quarrels. Characterization of the incident as an attempted murder did not, he
believed, reflect "what really happened." Instead of a "real
attempt" by a woman to kill her husband, it was *really* just a
family fight.

The problem for the detective sergeant, as well as for the
detective who makes an investigation, is to discern "what really

happened." For our analysis, however, the problem is how the sense of what really happened is developed. That is, what methods are employed so that the sense of something "really" happening is made available to the social actor? In the attempted-murder report that was reformulated as "really" just a family squabble, the sense of the incident is not in the actions taken by the husband and wife but rather is provided in the account that it was "just a family squabble." Supposing two alternative schemes of interpretation, from an infinite variety of possible schemes, it can be seen that the formulation was accomplished in terms of the documentary method of interpretation (Garfinkel, 1967). Attempted murder can be accounted for in terms of "woman pursuing husband with knife saying she is going to kill him." That is, the account of the woman chasing her husband with a knife may be given a specific sense by pointing to the underlying theme of "attempted murder." In turn, the interpretive scheme of "attempted murder" is documented and elaborated by the account of the woman with the knife. On the other hand, the specific sense of the account is changed, yet made equally available, by the formulation "domestic quarrel." That is, the sense of "what really happened" in the latter formulation is provided by the elaboration of the account of "woman pursuing husband with knife" as a "domestic quarrel."

When a reported crime reaches the detective bureau, it is treated as a case that is to be worked (i.e., investigated) or not worked. For a crime to be worked it has to be seen as: (1) a "righteous" crime (an actual instance of a type of crime); (2) a "significant" crime (a crime, in the context of the detail, that is important); and (3) a "workable" case (something that can be investigated).

Phony Cases

The sense that a crime is a "real" one is important for the detectives since they feel that it is a waste of time to initiate an investigation of a complaint that turns out to be false or something other than what it is reported to be. For example, a good deal of investigative time was spent on the following case even though it was suspected to be phony from the beginning:

CASE 86

One of the Major Crimes detectives was reading a report and said it sounded phony. "Looked like a man and his wife were in a fight. She reported him to the sheriff's office on a 242 [battery] and then went out and got laid. Then she decided it was rape." The patrol report listed the incident as a "possible" rape, thereby alerting the reader of the report that something seemed wrong. There had been a time conflict in the "victim's" account of what had happened, and since she had reported her husband for battery and disturbing the peace, there was a record of the time she had come to the sheriff's office.

The suspect was known to the victim, who supplied his telephone number, and he was contacted by telephone. The suspect's mother answered the phone and insisted on being present during interrogation, although the suspect was not a juvenile. The detective agreed to let the mother sit in on the interview, but since she kept interrupting, she was soon asked to leave.

The detective explained to the suspect that if the "victim" had consented to intercourse, no charge of rape would be made and the matter would be dropped, but the suspect refused even to admit having had intercourse with her. The detective then explained the physical evidence. When presented with this evidence, the suspect admitted having had intercourse but expressed the fear that he would get in trouble with his mother if she knew. The detective promised not to reveal the information if he was told what really happened. The suspect explained that he had met the girl and accompanied her to his house after she got into a fight with her husband. She had asked for a back rub, removed her blouse, and lay down on the bed, where she and the suspect had intercourse.

When this account was presented to the woman who had reported the "rape," she explained that when her husband found that she had had intercourse with another man, she was afraid to admit to him that it had been with her consent. It was when her husband took her to confront the suspect that they were stopped by the Highway Patrol for speeding; at that time the report of rape came to the attention of the sheriff's office.

(The highway patrol had turned the report over to the sheriff's office.)

Besides the time conflict in the report, the sense that it was phony was also established, to the detective's satisfaction, by what he took the "suspect" to be. He made such statements as, "You shoulda seen this guy. He's no rapist. He was more worried about his mother finding out he got laid than he was about a rape charge." Such particulars were part of a "nonrape" formulation of "what really happened," and along with the contradiction in the girl's story, the girl's record (a moderate delinquent one), and certain particulars of the account of the situation that preceded the report of rape, a context was established so that each element of the report derived the specific sense of "pointing to" a nonrape, while at the same time the context of "nonrape" or "phony rape" provided the specific sense of each element.

Other than filing a false report, no other crime was involved in case 86; however, the report of a phony crime sometimes masks another crime. For example, the following case was initially reported as an armed robbery and kidnapping; however, the "victim" who reported the crime was subsequently convicted of embezzlement:

CASE 51

The "victim" reported that as she was taking the day's receipts from the store where she worked to the bank, a man had robbed her of the cash. She said he was hiding behind the seat of her car when she got in and had forced her to drive to a deserted location, where she let him out. The robber had not taken the checks or the bags containing receipts but only the cash. There were some packages behind the seat of the car, but the officer taking the report noticed that none of them was rumpled or crushed. Since the car was the type with a truck bed behind it, there was no way the alleged robber could have climbed behind the seat without disturbing the packages. During the initial contact, the officer suggested that it would be unlikely for the events to have happened in the way she claimed without disturbing the packages. The next day, when the detectives went to talk with the girl further about the robbery, she said she had retained a lawyer and had been told not to talk to the police without his being there. She said that when she reported the crime, one of the patrol sergeants had suggested that she had embezzled the money, and since she was now a suspect, she shouldn't be required to talk to the police. The detective told her that he was going to talk to her only about the robbery and kidnapping, but she still refused to speak with him. From that point on, the investigation focused on a case of embezzlement, and eventually the girl admitted the crime.

Because of the characterization of this event as a "righteous crime," it was investigated. The investigators first formulated accounts that pointed to a false report of a robbery-kidnapping; subsequently they made reports pointing to an embezzlement. Unlike the case of reported rape that was considered phony and dropped after that characterization, this case was worked, but in terms of a different formulation.

Unusual Cases

In Another kind of case that was established to be something other than a "righteous" crime, the report was not seen as phony, but, as one detective said, "There was something screwy about it." A case can be seen as unusual, not fitting the characterization of a "normal crime" (cf. Sudnow, 1965), or it may involve an unusual M.O. in a "normal crime," and still be considered a righteous crime. For example, if a burglar breaks a hole in the wall of a house, this would be considered an unusual way to commit a residential burglary, but it would still be seen as a "righteous burglary." However, if a victim had been burglarized of photo albums that had great personal value but nothing else had been taken, the case would be seen as neither "righteous" nor "phony" but "weird." Generally, if the detectives characterized a case or a victim as "screwy" and the loss was not great, the harm minimal, and the visibility low (few people knew about it), they would not waste time on an investigation. Moreover, if the victim was reluctant to have the police pursue an investigation and arrest the suspects, an unusual case would not be investigated. Case 106 is an illustration of a case in which the detectives saw the circumstances and victim as "weird" and did not investigate:

CASE 106
(PATROL REPORT)

Narrative

B. Between 2130 and 2230 hours, suspects one and two attempted to sexually molest victim C.M. in the rear hallway area of the Pinball Parlor.

D. At 1730 hours, victim C.M. contacted Deputy V. at the Foot Patrol headquarters and related the following: C.M. stated she had been sexually molested by two W/M [white male] employees of L's Bookstore last night (2-27-73) between 2130 and 2230 hours, in the rear hallway of the Pinball Parlor. Victim C.M. stated that because of previous incidents she had been involved in with police in the Westville and Mountain-beach area, she had no confidence in "law and order." She wanted to handle the matter by talking to the suspects and "setting them straight" w/o police intervention.

C.M. related the following incidents took place between 2130 hours and 2230 hours, 2-27-73, inside the Pinball Parlor. C.M. stated she was playing the pin machines, then went to the rear of the Pinball Parlor to use the restroom. It was noted that the rear door to the Pinball Parlor is kept locked and adjoins a hallway that also leads to L's Bookstore. Both businesses use the same restroom, located in this hallway. Upon walking into the hallway and closing the door behind her, C.M. was grabbed by the two suspects and pulled to the floor. Suspect two pinned her arms down with his knees and, holding her head between his knees, used his hands to grasp and pin victim C.M.'s arms. Suspect one pulled victim C.M.'s pants down to her knees and was noted to be laughing constantly. Victim C.M. stated she screamed during this time. Suspect one then began kissing victim C.M. on the lower abdomen area and inserted his tongue in her vagina. Victim C.M. said she was on her monthly period and was wearing a sanitary napkin, the type that clung to her underwear, and stated that suspect one was not aware of this until he put his tongue inside her vagina, whereupon he said, "Oh shit . . . she's on the fucking rag!" Victim C.M. stated that suspect one also pushed her sweater up and was kissing her breast, and she told the suspect, "I'm going to call the fucking pigs if you don't get off me." Suspect two told suspect one to let her go.

Victim C.M. stated she was released and ran into the restroom, locking the door behind her, where she remained for approximately ten minutes to regain her composure. Victim C.M. then left the restroom and was pushed through the doorway into the Pinball Parlor by suspect one. Victim C.M. wandered around the 900 block of North Street for a while, then went home at approximately 2330 hours, 2-27-73, and told her roommate, V.E., about the incident.

Victim C.M. stated that during the scuffle with suspects she lost approximately eight dollars in quarters, probably picked up by the suspects, noting she had just received payment in quarters from the Pinball Parlor. Victim C.M. also stated that a female employee of L's Bookstore opened the door leading from the bookstore into the hallway during the offense, looked in briefly, then closed the door. Victim C.M. was unable to describe the suspects, stating it was dark inside the hallway, hindering vision. She stated she knew they were employees of L's Bookstore, having seen them there before.

The "weirdness" or "screwyness" of the case is in the characterization of the victim, the suspects, and the set of circumstances in the assault. It was clear that the patrol officer who made the initial investigation and wrote the report believed the girl knew the identities of her assailants but would not tell the police precisely who they were. The fact that she wanted the police to talk with the attackers and yet could not identify them, even though she said she had seen them before, led the officer to see her as a liar, and not a very bright one. If the case were pursued beyond the point desired by the victim, which was merely to "warn" the suspects, it was clear that the police would get no cooperation from the girl, and the D.A. was unlikely to accept the case for prosecution. On the other hand, the detectives felt it would be foolish merely to "warn" the two attackers on a serious felony charge. The incongruity between a "warning," a disposition generally reserved for misdemeanors or petty felonies, and a "rape" further brought out the unusual character of the case.

The circumstances of the case as described by the patrol report also gave the case its sense of atypicality. The detectives thought it was funny, and many remarked that the suspects "already got what was coming to them." The girl's comment during the assault—"I'm going to call the fucking pigs"—was taken to be funny in the context of the assault, for it revealed the girl's sentiments toward the police while at the same time naming them as her saviours. These circumstances, taken as a whole, led the police to see the assailants more as bumblers than as "serious criminals." As a result of the victim's assumed attitude toward the police and the assault and the circumstances of the assault, the crime was formulated as something other than a "righteous" crime, yet something other than a false report or phony case. Ultimately, the case disposition could be justified by the victim's unwillingness to cooperate in identifying the suspects, but it appears that the case, and all cases formulated as "weird," fail to receive investigative attention because of their strangeness and not purely for legal reasons.

Showing "Elements" of a Crime

In just about any case the detective can "show" that a certain set of circumstances has the elements of a crime more serious than he actually sees the case to be. For instance, the report of the "attempted murder" was written so that all the necessary elements of an attempted murder were available to the reader; however, the reformulation of the case as a domestic fight was taken to provide "what really happened."

Similarly, a detective will often "show" a suspect what a crime can be "made" to be if he wants to "be technical" about it, yet all along the detective does not believe that the case is "really" an instance of the more serious crime. For example, the following case could be "shown" to include all the necessary elements of an armed robbery, but the investigator said it "really was only some kids screwing around":

CASE 89

Shortly after ten, Bert and I went over to a junior high school to talk to some boys about an incident involving an assault and a stretched 211 [armed robbery]. What had happened was that a gang of boys had jumped a kid, taken a can of spray paint away from him, and sprayed him with it. A knife was supposedly involved in the incident, and since property had been forcefully taken, this was an "armed robbery."

Bert had no intention of laying a 211 on these kids for the

incident, but he said he might use it to scare some of them. During the interview the boys said they had caught a kid defacing a wall with a can of spray paint and had taken the can of spray away from him and sprayed him and his bicycle. By their account, they had struck a blow for law and order by dissuading a vandal from further mischief. Bert decided they weren't really bad, and instead of referring them to probation, warned them and had them make restitution to the boy for the shirt that had been ruined by the spray paint. One of the boys would not admit what had happened and was told that "technically" he could be charged with armed robbery. After hearing that, the boy began to cry and explained what had happened.

Here again it can be seen that "what really happened" was not conceived in terms of legal criteria. Rather, the sense of what occurred was provided in terms of an understanding assumed to underly the particulars of the case presented in the account. A classification of "kidnapping," "assault with a deadly weapon," "battery," "armed robbery," or "attempted murder could have been used to characterize the case. The California Penal Code (1971) defines a 211 as follows:

> Robbery is the felonious taking of personal property in the possession of another, from his person or immediate presence, and against his will, accomplished by means of force or fear.

The common understanding of robbery, however, conjures up images of muggers, bank robbers, liquor-store holdups, and so on. The specific sense of robbery is not provided in "a bunch of kids grabbing a spray can from another kid," and any detective who included such charges in his report would be regarded as foolish. Just as the officer who reported as an "attempted murder" what the detectives took to be a "domestic quarrel" was thought to be trying to make a federal case out of a family fight, the proper reporting procedures are not solely based on a literal reading of the penal code.

Established and Unestablished Crimes

In talking about the kinds of cases the detectives received and worked, a deputy D.A. referred to "established crimes" and "unestablished crimes." By an "established crime" he meant the "routine, everyday kind of crimes like burglary, theft, and check forgery." Similarly, Sudnow (1965) refers to "normal crimes" received and processed in a D.A.'s office as "those occurrences whose typical features, e.g., the ways they usually occur and the characteristics of persons who commit them (as well as the typical victims and typical scenes), are known and attended to by the P.D." He goes on to point out:

> For any of a series of offense types the P.D. can provide some form of proverbial characterization. For example, *burglary* is seen as involving regular violators, no weapons, low-priced items, little property damage, lower-class establishments, large-ly Negro defendants, independent operators, and a nonprofes-sional orientation to the crime (Sudnow, 1965, pp. 314–15).

As opposed to "established" or "normal" crimes, a class of crimes is seen to be unestablished if there are no routine guidelines. As an example, the deputy D.A. spoke of laws being used to initiate prosecution in consumer-fraud cases. The recent "consumer revolution" has been seen by district attorneys, as well as some police departments, as a way of gaining public support by initiating investigations and complaints against consumer fraud, but the routine for handling such cases has yet to be established. Any section of the penal code that is not typically used to characterize a crime constitutes an "unestab-lished crime."

In the detective bureau, when a case was formulated to be an instance of an "unestablished crime," it was treated as a special instance of a more "normal" crime, a unique case in and of itself, or an instance of some noncriminal activity. For example, the following case involved using penal code 244 PC (assault with caustic chemicals):

CASE 56

A man reported that while he was driving through an orchard, he came to a point in the road that was blocked by a tree-spraying machine. When he asked the man operating the machine to turn off the spray so that it wouldn't get on his truck, an argument ensued, and the suspect turned on the tree-spray machine and shot the victim in the face with the spray.

This case was treated as a unique instance of 245 PC (assault with a deadly weapon), and after the detective had worked the case and filed a complaint, the D.A. decided to classify it as a 242 PC (battery). Both 245 PC and 242 PC are "established crimes," and even though the detective logged the case as a 244 PC (assault with caustic chemicals) it came to be treated very much like a 242 PC.

Another course sometimes followed in cases of "unestablished crimes" was to close them, advising the victim to take civil action. Section 602 PC (trespassing), is a fairly "normal" crime, but 602(a) PC is a seldom-used unestablished crime. Section 602(a) PC reads: "Cutting down, destroying, or injuring any kind of wood or timber standing or growing upon the lands of another." Case 40 was reported by patrol, logged as 602(a), and so formulated by the detective:

CASE 40

A woman reported that a neighbor had cut down a tree on her property along with some shrubs. There was some dispute over whose property the tree was on, but the victim hired a surveyor and, according to the surveyor, the tree was on the victim's property. The neighbor admitted to the reporting officer that she had cut down the tree, but insisted that the tree was on her property. The D.A. advised that the case be handled as a civil matter, and the detective closed the case.

Given the particulars seen to exist in this case, as well as the wording of the relevant penal section, it would have been possible to bring criminal action against the suspect. However, because the case was formulated as an unestablished case and there was no normal routine for handling such cases, "referring it to civil" or "making it a civil" was a way of disposing of it. This, then, was an established way of understanding how a case was to be thought of and routinely treated, and was one option for dealing with an unestablished crime.

It was not only unestablished crimes that were normalized by referring them to a noncriminal, civil status. Burglaries were considered normal crimes, but sometimes what was reported as a burglary or theft was made out to be a civil case and dropped. We have already reported a case in which the complainant said that her ex-husband had broken into her house and taken some furniture (case 33). The case was reported by patrol as a burglary and assigned to be worked as a burglary. However, when the detective found that the victim's ex-husband had initiated civil action to get title to the property he had taken, he reformulated the case as "divorcee property-dispute" rather than a "burglary" or "regular burglary," even though all the elements of a burglary could be shown to exist. Were it the case that crimes are established by literal application of the law or that criminal circumstances exist independent of the work done in an account, it would not be possible to reclassify a case in this manner. In fact, any law is taken to include more than what is written in the penal code, and the sense of what law should be "used" is embedded in and underlies any reported crime.

Competent Rule Use

"Normal crimes" are seen to be "significant," "big," or "important," or "insignificant," "little," or "unimportant." A continuum from most to least significant was more or less understood by the detectives. There was an understanding that the big cases should be worked and the little ones ignored. However, in the context of the cases a detective or detail typically received for possible investigative action, what was considered a "big case" for one detective was a "little case" for another. For instance, the Major Crimes Detail received all reports of battery. As compared with the other crimes the detail investigated, batteries were "little" and therefore were rarely investigated. On the other hand, if the Juvenile Detail received a battery case, it was treated as fairly important in the context of the usual crimes they recieved, such as petty theft or malicious mischief.

From the standpoint of an informal rule, as opposed to the formal rule that all violations of the law must be investigated, one would expect that whatever was seen as a big case would be worked and that small cases would be set aside. In a normative framework, there was a set of rules for working cases, which can be called the *important case rule,* used as a resource in investigations. However, the sense of the rule was not readily available to an outside observer ignorant of common understandings among the detectives.

To begin with, as has already been discussed, certain crimes reported by patrol and logged as "significant crimes" with penal-code identifications are formulated to be something other than what a literal reading of the penal code might suggest, or are reformulated in terms of another code. Illustrative of this is the case reported as "attempted murder" which was reformulated to be a domestic quarrel, and the attempted rape that was seen as "screwy." Neither case was worked, nor were other cases seen to be like them. For the detectives, the sense of following the important case rule was preserved, for these were taken to be not "important cases," and therefore no investigation was necessary.

On the other hand, if only "important cases" are worked, an outside observer would not expect to see "little cases" investigated. For example, the theft detective in the Juvenile Detail was normally not given reported thefts of inexpensive bicycles to investigate. If a report of the theft of a $5 bicycle was received, it would typically be inactivated, and no investigative time would be spent with it. However, the theft detective said that he would rather work a case involving a $5 bicycle *where he had leads* than a case involving a $500 bicycle with no leads. He explained that bicycle thieves often work in rings and occasionally steal cheap bicycles. If leads are available to apprehend the thief of a $5 bicycle, it is believed that the time is better spent there than in chasing an unknown suspect in a case involving property of greater value. However, in working a case involving property of little value, the important case rule is preserved in that apprehending the thief may have far-reaching consequences.

Related to this is the detectives' *workable case rule.* Where leads or possible leads were seen to exist, cases that would not be pursued otherwise would be investigated. The existence of a lead is developed in the course of an investigation, and what turns out to be a lead is often not known at the outset. Therefore, whether leads "really" existed or not was always problematic at the beginning of an investigation.

However, crimes and reported particulars of a crime were typified in terms of normally having leads or not. Robberies, rapes, and assaults were typified as having leads, since the victim served as a witness. Most burglaries and thefts, on the other hand, were reported as not having leads. Moreover, detectives working burglary and theft inactivated more cases because of lack of investigative leads than did Major Crimes detectives. (How the various details worked cases and took them to be "workable" will be elaborated in later chapters, when each detail is examined separately.)

Another rule employed by detectives is the *prosecutable case rule*. During the observation period, detectives rarely justified not spending much time with a case on the ground that it was "unprosecutable," but this reason stands as an account in the form of a rule-governed activity. Case 63 was worked only for information relating to another crime that the detective was investigating, and the former crime itself, explained as "unprosecutable," was employed as a resource for making contact in the hope of receiving information on the latter:

CASE 63

Bill was working a 242 PC [battery], which is unusual since they're usually not worked. The victim and her boyfriend complained that the guy's ex-girlfriend had come into the bar where he played piano and hit the new girlfriend. Since they raised a stink about it and Bill didn't have much else to do, it was going to be worked. He said it didn't look prosecutable, and all he wanted to do was to talk to the suspect. He said that the suspect was single, had four kids, and was on welfare, and that it was unlikely that anything would happen to her in court even if the D.A. pushed it. Also, the battery looked more like mutual combat, since the boyfriend got into the act on behalf of his new girlfriend; so it wasn't a good 242. *The thing that interested Bill in the case was that the boyfriend had on racing gloves and matched the description of a 220 PC* [attempted rape] *suspect.*

The unprosecutable aspect of the case was explained in terms of the suspect's financial and domestic situation. The detective believed that a judge would be unlikely to do more than place the woman on probation. Moreover, since the case could be shown to be equivocal in terms of how the battery occurred, it was not worth the time to do the work necessary for filing a complaint.

Another reason for working a case that fell outside the important or workable case rules can also be seen from case 63. If the victim of a crime complained that nothing was being done about his or her case, a detective would be dispatched to PR (public relations) the case. This sometimes involved contacting the victim and pretending to be looking for the suspect; at other times a PR merely involved explaining to the victim that there was little that could be done to help him or her. Usually the victim would accept the situation as the detective explained it, but sometimes the detectives would be accused of laziness and disinterest. This was especially true in cases involving finger-prints. Victims believed that if the detectives found latent fingerprints at the crime scene they could identify the criminal, even though fingerprints are rarely useful in identifying a suspect. Victims would expect "someone in the lab" to examine the prints and pull an identical set from the departmental records, as is always done on television.* Thus, when a victim learns from a patrol officer or the detective that fingerprints have been found, he assumes that the suspect can be quickly identi-fied and cannot understand that no "solid leads" exist in the case. It is understandable that the victims become upset when they are told that the investigation has been inactivated, and it is also understandable why the detectives put on a "make-believe" investigation in these situations.

Detective Discretion

From our discussion of how detectives go about establishing a case, it can be seen how "discretion" operated in the Detective Bureau. The "rules" served as explanations of why a case was worked or not. Even though these informal norms were used by detectives in their own analyses of a situation, it is important to understand that the "rules" were embedded in the explanations and formulations used in establishing a case. The sense of "following the rules" was established by formulating a case as "one that is to be investigated." That is, since the investigations were carried out according to an understanding of a set of rules, which required that only certain crimes be given investigative

---

*The fingerprint myth cannot be blamed wholly on the mass media. During a tour of the FBI building in Washington, D.C., in 1975, I was led to believe that the minutest physical trace could be used to catch criminals. In one display, latent heel prints on a bank counter (which had been cut out and mounted for tour groups) were presented to show how a bank robber was identified. Upon questioning the tour guide, we learned that the bank robber had been caught a few blocks from the bank with the stolen money. The robber's heel marks were compared to those on the bank counter for additional evidence, but the prints were not instrumental in the case, and they certainly would have been of little use if the robber had not been in custody and identified.

attention, the fact that a case was being investigated was used to document the "fact" that the case was of a certain sort.

In locating the significant features of discretion, we must understand the work done in establishing a case as an instance of a certain type of crime, for it was in establishing the case that the actual decision was made. If a case was characterized as of a type that would be worked in accordance with a rule (any rule), then at least some investigative efforts would be made. By understanding how reported elements of a case came to be seen as characteristic of one type of crime or another, we come to understand how discretion operates. That is, instead of looking for the rules that are "automatically" followed in making decisions, we must look to see how a sense of rule-use is developed.

CONCLUSION

Establishing a case involves more than merely identifying elements that show it to be one sort of crime or another. Instead, an account is formulated in terms of an underlying scheme of interpretation embedded in certain assumptions about the nature of crime and criminals. Each element points to and receives its specific sense from this underlying pattern, inherent aspects of the event. The penal code is taken as a set of accounts to provide the sense of rule violation, pointing to still another set of assumptions about any given event. It is through such practices that the sense of establishing a crime is accomplished and the events of the crime are made available.

5

Making an Investigation

We had just left the bike shop where the burglary was reported to have taken place. Andy said he wished the patrol officer who initially contacted the victim had kept his mouth shut about finding fingerprints at the crime scene. If the victim hadn't known about the fingerprints, Andy said, he wouldn't have had to explain why they probably wouldn't help the detectives to catch the burglar. To me it seemed that it would be easier to say something like, "We're working on these prints," rather than go into a long discourse about needing all ten fingerprints to use the coding system and the rest of the speech Andy gave the victim. After being with the Burglary Detail for a couple of months, I also felt that the victims were being unreasonable in expecting the detectives to catch burglars on the basis of only a couple of fingerprints and a description of what had been stolen. Victims still tend to believe that if you send the prints to the FBI, they'll send you the name, photograph, and address of the burglar.

IDENTIFYING A SUSPECT

Once a crime has been established as one to be worked, the investigation centers around learning the identity of the culprit. For the detective, the identity search usually begins with the attempt to find the name of a suspect and, given a name, other information leading to his or her capture.

In the course of an investigation, the identity of a possible suspect can be "found" at a number of points. Other informa-

100

tion will also be developed along the way. Initially, certain types of crimes are characterized by the detectives as intrinsically "giving" more or less information about a possible suspect. As we have pointed out, in crimes against persons, such as assaults, more information is generally available about the suspect than in crimes against property, such as burglaries. In some cases of all types, a suspect is known and listed in the patrol report. In these cases the problem for the detective is to determine whether the named suspect is in fact guilty. Taking the name he has been given, the detective tries to find out whether the person has a criminal record, where he lives, where he works, and so on. More often, however, there is no name available at the outset, and the detective must begin by "finding information" that will lead him to a suspect.

Interviewing Victims and Witnesses

Most investigations begin by contacting the victim and witnesses. The detective asks if they have any idea who might have committed the crime; usually they have only a vague idea, such as "probably some kids in the neighborhood," or none at all. If there is an eyewitness, he or she will be asked to describe the suspect, and the detective hopes he can recognize or find a name for the person described. For example, see the following transcript of an interview with the victim of an attempted rape. The victim had been picked up hitchhiking, and when she realized that the suspect was taking her somewhere other than to her destination and was demanding that she submit sexually, she grabbed the car's gearshift and jammed the gears. This action was enough to frighten the would-be rapist, and he took the victim to her destination, apologizing for his attempt to molest her. The interview segment begins after the detective has asked the victim to try to identify the suspect:

CASE 54

VIC: I won't say yes to it if I'm not sure of it.
DET: Okay.
VIC: I'll say no to it if I have the least doubt.
DET: Okay, here are the pictures I'm going to be showing you. I want you to look at them real carefully.
VIC: Uh huh.

DET: Okay, because we've had an investigation under way
and we're interested in these people. And, ah, I don't want
you to necessarily to think that you're going to be held
responsible.

VIC: For doing what?

DET: For identifying this set of pictures.

VIC: Oh, okay.

DET: Now I want you to take your time and look at them
carefully.

In this case the detective had a set of photographs of
suspected rapists who fit the general description of the suspect
(i.e., black male, six feet tall, approximately 18–22 years old) and
he was able to give something to the victim to start with. In other
cases the detective has nothing but the victim's description to go
on, and he tries to get her to go into detail about the suspect's
physical characteristics (height, complexion, moles, scars, tat-
toos) and method of operation (e.g., knife or gun, what was
taken, night or day). By asking the victim and other witnesses to
supply these particles of possible information, the detective can
narrow down the universe of probable suspects and begin to
formulate a picture of the suspected culprit.

If, based on the information developed from interviewing
victims and others surrounding a case, the detective can come
up with a name, the other details can be filled in to make an
unsatisfactory account useful. An M.O. may suggest a particular
known criminal, for example. However, if no name is known,
the detectives can still have an unknown culprit identified as
"one person" or "this kind of person." This means that even
though they don't know exactly who the culprit is, they know he
is the same person who has committed a series of other crimes or
is a certain kind of person (e.g., a junky, a juvenile). For
example, Scotland Yard detectives said in an interview that they
can distinguish between the professional house burglar and the
amateur by the way the bureau drawers have been left. If all the
drawers are found open, the detectives assume that they are
dealing with a professional, since professionals open the drawers from the bottom one up so that they don't have to take the
time to close each drawer after searching it. Amateurs tend to
begin with the top drawer, having to close it to get to the
contents of the next one down. If several burglaries in an area

typically visited by amateur burglars were seen to have professional characteristics, the burglar in all these cases would be "identified" as the same person.

In the following cases, the suspects came to be "known" from witnesses' accounts of their method of operation:

CASE 52

A number of reports of obscene phone calls had been received where the suspect would begin by asking, "Is your pussy hairy?" The caller was identified as a single person on the basis of the wording of his initial inquiry. One of the victims was able to schedule a call with the suspect, and the detectives were able to locate the source of the calls and eventually catch the caller. Twelve 653m PC cases [annoying phone calls] were cleared with the suspect's capture.

CASES 69 AND 71

The sheriff's office and city police department had received complaints of a number of robberies in which two robbers wore dark blue watch caps, bandanas covering their faces, and used knives. They came to be known as the "Bandana Bandits," and because they appeared to be spending their take in the robberies at the rate of $50 per day (the amount taken in a robbery divided by the number of days between robberies), they were believed to be heroin users each with a $25-a-day habit. Stake-outs were set up in and around the types of stores the bandits were robbing, generally small grocery and liquor stores, and eventually one of the robbers was caught when he attempted to hold up a grocery store.

While the specific identity of these culprits was the subject of much conjecture, it was provisionally determined from the victims' accounts that these two reported series of crimes involved the same person or people.*

In cases where no suspect was seen, detectives will try to elicit details about a vehicle or anything else that might be a lead in identifying a suspect. Thus, a detective might ask the victim if he saw anything or anyone that "looked out of place." If

---

*Such famous cases as "Jack the Ripper" and "Zodiac" involved suspects who were similarly identified as unique individuals, but neither Jack the Ripper nor Zodiac has been specifically identified, except in speculation, as a person whose "real name" was known.

someone or something is seen in the neighborhood that does not belong there, it is taken as suspect.

Another line of questioning when there are no witnesses is to ask whether the victim knows of anyone who could have committed the crime. The following case involved the theft of an electric grinder with no witnesses:

CASE 83

DET: Where was it [the grinder] located?
VIC: Out in the shop area.
DET: On the inside of the building itself?
VIC: Yes.
DET: O.K., was it taken sometime during . . .
VIC: Between Thursday, had to be between Thursday after-noon or y'know Thursday evening before we cleaned up and Monday morning.
DET: Do you feel it was taken sometime during the day?
VIC: No, because it was being used. So I really had, it's like I told, ah, what's his name that was here, ah . . .
DET: The deputy?
VIC: Yeah, O.K. I told him the only way we could figure out how the guy who did it was during clean-up time between 5:15 and 5:30 while everybody was going around sweeping, cleaning off their benches, rolling up their cords, somebody snuk outside and put it underneath some paper in the trash bin and then came back over the weekend and picked it up.

The detective then went on to question the victim about employ-ees who might have taken the grinder. The victim's assumptions about the circumstances of the theft and the work routine supported the employee-theft hypothesis.

In this case the victim's formulation provided the lead. In other cases, much of the speculation based on victim's accounts is formulated by the detective. In a case involving the theft of property from a truck parked outside the victim's house, the victim said she had seen a small white camper in front of the house at 4:00 A.M. Because of the hour, this was taken to be the thief's truck. With this information the detective, who had originally gone to PR the case, decided that the theft could have been the work of some thieves he knew in the neighborhood. The victim had not suggested any possible suspects, nor had she given any description of the culprit. Formulating the burglar to be one of a cohort of known thieves, the detective proceeded to drive past their residences looking for a truck matching the description given by the victim. The theft was never solved, but it is nevertheless an example of a case in which a suspect was sought with little information given by the victim.

Although witnesses are used extensively as resources, they are generally considered to be unreliable. Detectives believe that most witnesses' stories are only approximations of the facts. The victim of a sex crime described her assailant almost perfectly and identified him from a photograph ten years old, but she somehow forgot that he had a beard. When the suspect was picked up and was found to have a beard, the detectives called the victim and asked her if the man who attacked her was bearded, and she insisted he was not. When they showed her a recent photograph of the suspect, she remembered the beard. In a bank robbery the teller said she was certain that the robber was wearing a hat, but the bank's camera took a photograph of the incident and he was hatless. Witnesses to a burglary/stabbing described the culprit as wearing a brown sweater with a diamond pattern, but when the detectives found him near the crime scene, he had on a solid purple sweater. Such instances indicate the frequent unreliability of witnesses' reports of what transpired in a crime. Even though some witnesses may be precisely accurate, detectives never know for certain whether they are or not. What is generally a vague description of people and events becomes even more vague because the detective is uncertain of the extent to which the description reflects what might be seen in calmer circumstances by a better observer.

Some witnesses attempt to protect a friend by giving false information or no information at all. Detectives assume that loyalties may exist between friends and relatives or between certain classes. For instance, it is believed that criminals will not inform on one another unless some pressure is brought to bear on them, and that blacks, Chicanos, and other minorities have intragroup loyalties that are in opposition to the police.

Where loyalties are seen to present a problem in the type of information gleaned in an investigation, detectives employ a number of stratagems. First, they attempt to get information through questioning without revealing the purpose of their interview. For example, in a case referred to earlier involving attempted murder, robbery, and sexual assault, the detective tried to learn the identities of the guests at a party the victim had attended before she was attacked by questioning a potential witness without telling her how he had gotten her name or the specific purpose of questioning her. He told her he was involved in a routine investigation and wondered if she could tell him about anyone she knew who was at the party. In this instance the witness guessed correctly where the detective had gotten her name and what crime he was investigating, but it serves to illustrate one strategy for getting around loyalties.

Detectives often try to pry information from recalcitrant witnesses by appealing to their sense of civic duty (which is generally of little use) or by explaining what might happen to them if they withhold information. If witnesses steadfastly deny that they have information, it is often difficult to impress upon them that they are criminally liable for withholding information. The following transcript of an interview illustrates the tactic of showing the witness that it is in his own best interests to tell what he knows about a crime and help the detective "to get this whole thing cleared up." The person being questioned knows who stole some bicycles and bicycle parts, but he doesn't want to tell the detective. A friend of his has been arrested for possession of stolen bicycle parts, and the detective, in referring to "getting the stuff," is talking about the goods the arrested boy received. This is a subtle statement of blame directed to the witness for not having spoken up sooner and saving his friend:

CASE 79

DET: Is there somewhere we could go to talk?

WIT: Sure. I'd really just like to stay out of this, y'know.

DET: Yeah, we're trying to work it that way. . . . You see, here's the thing. The whole thing would've been completely over by now if, in fact, it was only a few days after the theft occurred, y'know, that the whole thing came about, y'know, that he was getting the stuff from somewhere. I can't go on hearsay. (The detective is saying that if the witness had come forward earlier, his friend would not be in trouble.)

WIT: Yeah, that's true.

DET: And, ah, from what I hear, I understand you saw the bike. As a matter of fact you probably know who did it.

WIT: Ahhhh.

DET: Now, what I need is, I'd like you to tell me what happened at the time, where they were, who was there, the whole thing. I know most of it, but I need it from you.

WIT: Yeah.

DET: O.K.

WIT: Ahhhmmmm, oh, ah Jesus. I hope that [name] don't, y'know, I know 'em and I know [name] too, y'know they're not going to think too much of me if I go and tell you. Say something 'bout . . .

DET: Well it's, here's the thing. Ah, now that you've been, y'know, apprised of the situation you can be charged with withholding information.

WIT: Yeah, I know.

DET: See, here's the thing, Ken, you're not involved in any crime at all, fortunately.

WIT: No, no, I know that.

DET: But you would be if you withheld information.

The detective then said that the witness' friend, who had been arrested for possession of stolen property, "really isn't a bad kid" but had gotten mixed up with the person who stole the bicycle, an expensive ten-speed racing model. The detective said that he was in contact with the defense lawyer and would talk to him if the witness cooperated.

DET: So that's what I'm trying to do this time. You can possibly help Arnold, it's not going to hurt him, you know that. It can do nothing but help him. I need to know the whole thing, everything.

WIT: Well, I went over one day . . . (witness begins to relate what he knew about case).

Besides explaining to the witness what could happen to him if he did not tell the truth, the detective also appealed to his loyalty. The boy who had been arrested, Arnold, was a closer friend of the witness than the suspects were. At the same time, the detective explained that if the witness helped the detective to "clear the thing up" and got his friend to tell the defense lawyer from whom he had received the stolen bicycle and parts, there would be no involvement of the witness as far as the suspects were concerned. In this way the detective provided the witness with a means of protecting himself from a criminal charge, aiding his friend, and still keeping his cooperation from public knowledge. Thus, the detective set forth a situation in which the witness could talk and at the same time not see himself as violating a loyalty.

Some witnesses are hesitant to give information to detectives because they have been intimidated by the suspect's friends and relatives, either covertly or overtly through implied or direct threats. The following transcript is from a burglary/arson case in which friends and relatives of the suspect were pressuring the victim to drop the charges.

CASE 35

DET: I understand you're a little bit concerned about what might happen after this guy's arrested and, ah, once he gets out again.

VIC: Well, what do you do if you go down if, if they give you the warrant for his arrest and you go down and arrest him and he goes to jail and to the court, right?

DET: Uh huh.

VIC: Now somebody, I'm sure that somebody will, ah, bail him out the very second that he is there because he's got friends. I just know if he, ah, I don't know, I just don't want him to come knocking on my door late at night and mad or something because he thinks that, I don't know. What if I decided I didn't want to press charges, would you still be able to put him in jail? It has nothing to do whatever with me pressing charges.

DET: You don't have to sign anything or do anything and the statement you made was voluntary and I mean you didn't have to do it.

VIC: Uh huh.

DET: But I assume you did it in case you wanted to, see, and even given that, that isn't what's putting him in jail, you know, 'cause the information there is not, ah, that critical, but it's helpful.

VIC: Yeah.

Here the detective assures the victim that she will not have to sign anything in order for the suspect to be convicted, but he does remind her that she put the case in motion by making a voluntary statement. This remark is a subtle reminder that she has committed herself to a course of action and implies that she should carry through with it. At the same time, though, the detective reassures her and takes her off the hook by pointing out that the information she gave was not critical for the successful conclusion of the case.

In the following segment the detective is working to keep the victim from retreating from her position. To do this, the detective attempts to provide an interpretive scheme so that the victim can "see" the "actual character" of the suspect by pointing out the young man's previous criminal record. After this characterization, he promises the victim police protection, which she will obviously need if the man is as dangerous as the detective says.

Case 35 (continued)

DET: But, ah, it's always a problem with something like this, you know, he can probably put two and two together and figure where we got his name.

VIC: Well, I already told him that. When I went down there that Monday, one of the reasons that I went down there was to tell him so that he wouldn't be surprised, cause I didn't know what could happen after I gave you these names at school that day. Now I didn't know what the procedures . . . I thought you might just go to all their houses and visit with them, you'know, so I just didn't want it to happen out of the blue. So I happened to mention it to him that I gave a lot of my friends' names and that he was one of them. I told him Monday. So he acted a little bit . . . you see, when I talked to him I've been trying to think of that day, and he really seemed, ah, surprised that it had happened and really happy to see me and I just, ah, it's either a really big cover up or, ah . . .

DET: Oh, he had quite an extensive record, you know. No doubt he knows how to con people, y'know, and knows how to present the type of image that he wants presented.

VIC: Uh huh.

DET: The type of reaction he wants, so . . .

MOT: (Victim's mother) Yeah, look how nice Jim comes over, y'know.

VIC: Yeah, but when he first saw me, he didn't act nervous. He just said, "Oh hi, Sally."

DET: Yeah, one thing I can do, ah, if you say he'll probably bail out, if not right away, ah, at least sooner or later, say to him that if anything happens up here either to you or to the property, that he is going to be the first person we come looking for and hopefully that'll get the point across to him that we can't charge or anything, but it would be extremely foolish on his part to do anything.

The victim then asks if there is any way she can disinvolve herself, and the detective assures her that it is possible, since her testimony is unnecessary in the case because of other evidence. He tells the victim that the suspect was "really" identified on the basis of his fingerprints, to give her further assurance that she is not responsible for identifying him. However, he does not want the victim to refuse to support his case and so goes on to tell her that the suspect should pay for his misdeeds. The victim's mother helps by reminding her of the fire the burglar started in her room.

CASE 35 (CONTINUED)

VIC: What if I just told him that, ah, that I didn't necessarily press charges, that I didn't have anything to do with it, just so that he wouldn't get mad at me?

DET: You can tell him or I can tell him that his name was given to us along with several others and it's a long list and that . . .

VIC: And you're not going to show him the statement, O.K.?

MOT: You just remember you didn't put him in jail, he put himself there, dear.

DET: Yeah, see, we just . . . see, once his fingerprints turn up at the crime scene, the way they have, ah, you get back to the district attorney and there's no problem at all getting a complaint and subsequently getting a warrant for the guy. The only thing we had to have to begin with was his name to get his fingerprints to make the comparison.

VIC: Uh huh.

DET: So that much you've done, but, ah, I think you owe it to yourself to know, to try and find out who's responsible.

VIC: Oh, I know, I, I, I don't know, I don't really feel guilty about it, I just don't want him to think . . .

DET: Well, if he isn't caught he might decide later on to come back and, ah, nail you again, who knows?

VIC: I know that.

MOT: Well, there's that about that fire too.
DET: Yeah.
MOT: Talk to him about it, I'd really like to know.
DET: Yeah, I intend to ask him that if he'll agree to talk about it.

Before the detective left to talk with the victim, he had been told by the sergeant that she was thinking of backing out, and there was some concern that she would not want the case to go to trial. Additionally, the suspect had convinced the victim by his demeanor that he was innocent of the burglary and fire. The victim's mother, however, wanted the culprit prosecuted and aided the detectives by reassuring the victim that he deserved punishment. Finally, the victim wanted to be assured that the suspect could be convicted without her help and that the fingerprints and bloodstains found at the point of entry could be used to establish his identity without her testimony. Even though she was instrumental in the detective's identification of the suspect, he was quite willing to let her believe that he could proceed without her, so that she would be able to disassociate herself from whatever fate came to the suspect.

This case also illustrates how relationships between the victim and others are used in identifying a suspect. The suspect was an acquaintance of the victim. When the case began, the detectives asked the victim if she knew anyone who might have committed the crime, and she gave them a list of her acquaintances. Similarly, in burglaries involving the theft of certain kinds of items not typically taken in such crimes (e.g., beds and tables), an ex-husband or ex-wife is often sought as the culprit. In homicides the victim is generally known by and sometimes related to the suspect, and detectives often establish the identity of the murderer by examining the victim's relationships.

Uncovering and Covering Identities

Given the problematic nature of witnesses' accounts, detectives take a "wait and see" stance toward much of what they say. If a witness describes a suspect as having certain characteristics and the detectives have a suspect in mind, the witness will be shown a photograph of the person (if one is available) along with photographs of others who the detectives do not believe were involved. If the witness identifies someone from a photograph, the detectives will judge the witness' descriptive account in terms of the photograph and the information that usually accompanies a police photograph (e.g., height, weight). At this point, the detectives believe that they can find what the suspect "really" looks like. Until then they regard the witness' account as a vague description that serves to narrow some of the grosser classifications (sex, race, and so on).

Depending on the type of crime, the suspect may or may not take pains to disguise himself. In crimes in which the victim comes face to face with the culprit, often he will mask himself. But a mask, while it hides the identity of the culprit, alerts the victim and witnesses that something "out of place" is going on. Interactionally, Goffman (1969, pp. 12–17) refers to this type of concealment as a "control move" where there is an "intentional effort of an informant (anyone who gives or gives off information) to produce expressions that he thinks will improve his situation if they are gleaned by the observer." In crimes involving face-to-face interaction between the criminal and the victim, control moves are necessary either to delay or prevent giving information to the victim that can be passed on to the police. One of the more ingenious disguises was used by a robber who would attach a simple red ball to his nose just before committing the crime. All the witnesses could remember was the red ball; they were at a loss to recall the robber's height, clothing, or eye color. In chapter 8, where we discuss Major Crimes investigations, we will examine the nuances of masking, but here it is enough to point out that some kind of control move is often employed by criminals who confront their victims.

In some face-to-face crimes, such as check forgeries and confidence games, the victim does not know that a crime is being committed at the time he is being victimized, and there is no need for masking. However, other types of control moves are employed. In confidence games, elaborate misrepresentations are concocted by the confidence men so that the mark (the victim) believes that he has stumbled across an immensely profitable, if slightly illegal, situation. For example, in the confidence game known as the "wire," the mark is led to believe that the confidence man has a friend in the telegraph office who can tell him which horse has won a race before the information is transmitted to the betting room. There is just enough time to place a bet on the winning horse before the betting window closes. What the mark doesn't know is that the "betting room" is staged, and all the "bettors" are confederates of the confidence man. After letting the mark win a few small bets they set him up for a large bet, which he loses. If the mark suspects he has been cheated, he cannot turn to the police, for to do so is to admit that he has engaged in illegal activities. Therefore, the confidence men, who usually can explain that they, too, had heavy losses, have no need to mask their physical identities even though their entire form of criminality is based on masking their social identities. In a similar vein, check forgers, at the time they are committing a crime, have no need to mask themselves, for during the crime they appear to be engaging in a perfectly legal transaction, and an obvious mask would only alert the victim that something illegal was taking place.

Bank robbers, check forgers, and other criminals who must come face to face with a victim rarely use their correct names. Obviously, a lone check forger would not want to provide his name and address, but teams of robbers have to make a conscious effort to refrain from calling one another by their real names. Detectives try to keep lists of known aliases, but usually they have to work at getting a name when suspects make an attempt to cover their tracks. If a suspect in custody gives a false name, it can be checked against a criminal record file, including fingerprints and photographs; however, if a suspect gives a false name in a jurisdiction where he or she is unknown, his fingerprints and photograph are rarely compared with all the fingerprints and photographs on file. It is likely, then, that many people use false names successfully.

Physical Evidence

As was pointed out earlier, physical evidence is rarely used to identify a suspect independent of witnesses' testimony. More typically, a suspect has been identified through some other means, and the physical evidence is used to persuade him to admit the crime and "get the whole thing over with." Detectives generally need to have a suspect, or at least a few possible suspects, before they can use latent fingerprints to identify a culprit.

However, there are cases and situations in which the physical evidence is all that is available for identifying a suspect. Physical evidence is sometimes used to "associate" a specific individual with a specific crime (Osterburg, 1967, p. 4). Fingerprints, shoeprints, tireprints, tool striations, bullet cartridges, and the like are seen to constitute various forms of "associative evidence."

In the main branch of the MCSO, only the most unusual circumstances call for a "blind run" on fingerprints. That is, given some latent prints, it would be rare for a fingerprint examiner to begin rummaging through the huge number of prints on file; in a large city like New York or Los Angeles, it would be even rarer. However, in one of the sheriff substations that was responsible for a relatively small population, such "blind runs" succeeded in identifying suspects in a total of 45 cases during the course of this study. Most of the criminals in the area were known, and by narrowing the field to a few who engaged in the kind of crime being investigated, it was a simple matter to make "blind runs" with some success.

In mass society, with mass production and uniformity, easily identifiable associative evidence is difficult to find; in smaller groups with unique craftmanship, it is relatively simple to find. For example, stereo sets, bicycles, television sets, and so on, have serial numbers which make them uniquely distinguishable, but most people do not record these numbers. Most valuable jewelry has unique characteristics since it is not mass-produced, and unless the stones are reset or recut, it is easily identifiable.

The similarity of most goods produced in mass society makes it difficult to associate an individual with a unique item of stolen property. One television set looks very much like all others of the same make and model. If a burglar took such a set he could put it in his living room for anyone to see, and there would be little likelihood of proving that his television set was a specific set stolen in a given burglary. On the other hand, if a person is suspected of burglary, any television set he has, as well as other items typically taken in burglaries, is suspected as stolen. For example, in the following case three brothers were identified as suspects in a series of burglaries. When detectives went to recover the suspected stolen property, instead of taking for observation just those things that were listed as burglarized in a specific case, they took every item that was typically stolen in burglaries:

CASE 101

In the first raid on the burglars' house a whole roomful of property had been recovered, and this time the detectives took a truck to make a second arrest of the suspects, who were now out on bail. There was so much listed on the search warrant that it allowed the detectives to take just about anything. Since the burglars had stolen so much, it was impossible to differentiate between what was legally theirs and what was not. Most of the things the detectives took were items seen to be typically taken by burglars or mentioned in connection with a specific burglary—radios, traffic signs, and automotive accessories. The specific burglary in this case involved a sportswear shop, so certain kinds of ski jackets and equipment were sought. Everything picked up was logged to identify where it was found since, depending on what room the property was found in, one or another of the brothers would be charged. The log was also used to compile a receipt for the owner of the house (the parents of the suspects) so that anything found not to have been stolen could be returned.

During the search some items were found that were listed on the search warrant, but, as we pointed out, one mass-produced item usually cannot be distinguished from thousands of others. Some of the things that were found could have been obtained only through theft, such as street signs. The other items "recovered" by the detectives were taken for "observation," to see whether or not they were stolen. Going through their records of unsolved burglaries, they would look for items of the same description as those recovered, then they would ask the victims of these robberies to come in to look at the property to see if it was what they had lost. The sheriff's detectives would generally call the city police detectives and invite them to look over recovered loot for the same purpose.

Another form of physical evidence is items of clothing and the like found at the crime scene which can be used to trace the criminal. Footprints, tireprints, bullets, and cartridges are used to begin the identification process; however, depending on the formulation of the situation, such things may or may not be seen as useful. For example, in a homicide investigation a bloody shoeprint was evident on the rug. The footprint was huge, and the suspect in custody was quite large himself, but on further investigation it was learned that the print had been made by the ambulance driver who had picked up the victims after they had been shot. In another homicide a shoeprint was used to link the suspect with a specific organization. The print was traced to a shoe issued by the Air Force. A number of shell cartridges found in the area were also traced to a lot sold to a nearby Air Force base; thus, the suspect was identified through physical evidence as possibly being in the Air Force.

Physical evidence also can be used to establish M.O.'s and "types" of criminals. If a house is torn up and the only thing taken is money, the crime is thought to be the work of a "hype," on the ground that "hypes" are desperate for money to buy heroin and rarely steal things that will take time to sell. At the opposite extreme, if a house is entered with a minimum amount of damage and only valuable things which cannot be readily sold are taken, the crime is believed to be the work of a professional who has the necessary connections to sell such items. "Normal burglaries" are generally identified as those in which such items as television sets and stereos are taken, and a specific burglar is identified by the method used to make entry.

One burglar employed an interesting control move in this respect. Several schools had been vandalized, and the police were searching for a group of delinquents. But when the "vandal" was identified, it was found that he had been stealing business machines from the schools and covering his intentions by vandalizing the school offices. Such creativity is rare; by and large detectives believe that "reading the evidence for what it is," or letting it "speak for itself" (Stuckey, 1968, p. 176), gives them a better chance of identifying the culprit. Physical evidence, however, is made available for practical use only through the interpretive schemes employed by the detectives. Without their interpretive work physical evidence would not only remain mute, it would cease to exist.

Summary

The work of identifying a suspect further illustrates the accomplished character of information. In their investigations, detectives characterize certain crimes as having the same M.O., which is taken to point to the same person as guilty of committing the crimes. That is, M.O.'s come to serve as interpretive devices. The fact that the accounts detectives receive in their interviews are given a "wait and see" status further points to a retrospective realization that an account can be taken as informative. Finally, the recognition and use of physical evidence are dependent on the detective's interpretive work, and such evidence exists only through the interpretive practices that make it available as informative.

LOCATING A SUSPECT

The sequence of an investigation, beginning with the establishment of a case, reaches its climax when the detectives have positively identified a suspect. The remainder of the investigation is typically anticlimactic. Locating a suspect whose name is known is generally not a difficult matter. However, sometimes a suspect's name is unknown but he is known to be a certain person through his M.O. In such cases the location of such a suspect may precede his identification and is taken to identify him as the suspect. For instance, in a burglary/stabbing case the suspect fled the scene of the crime, and sheriff patrol and detectives flooded the area searching for him. A man found crouching in a hole nearby was arrested, and his location and posture were taken as the identifying characteristics, thereby reversing the sequence of identity-location.

In other cases involving a known but unnamed suspect, the suspect's M.O. is used to locate and then identify him. A stratagem frequently employed for finding such suspects is the stake-out, where detectives sit and watch a building or an area where the culprit is expected to attack. When the suspect comes along, he is caught in the act. During the research period I participated in such stake-outs in two cases. These cases exemplify different types of location-identification stratagems and problems involved in locating a suspect:

STAKE-OUT 1

A number of liquor and grocery stores had been robbed in the city and county. In order to catch the robbers, detectives organized stake-outs in and around several liquor and grocery stores. The problem was to set up the stake-outs in locations where the detectives could see the relevant parts of each store without being seen and tipping off the suspect. Some of the stores had lofts with two-way mirrors, and these locations presented no problems for unseen surveillance. Most, however, did not. One location used was the walk-in refrigerator, where the detectives could observe the store without being seen. Another location was in a car or truck situated so that the stake-out team would not be noticed. Generally, this meant that the vehicle was parked across the street or in some other place away from the store.

Our stake-out point was directly in front of a liquor store in the back of a van provided by the store. The van was normally parked in the stake-out location so that its location was not seen as unusual, and a blanket was placed behind the driver's compartment so that the detectives were not silhouetted by the light shining through the front window. We sat in the van watching the store until it closed, but the suspect never arrived.

STAKE-OUT 2

A "burglar" had entered several women's apartments and observed the women as they slept. In one case he had taken some money from a dresser, and in a few other instances he had awakened the victim by fondling her. However, he had not assaulted any of the women. In addition, he had been seen breaking into a car and was run off by an apartment manager. From witness reports it was believed that he attempted break-ins and, if seen, ran and hid in the bushes, then returned and made further break-ins.

The stake-out plan was to have the detectives walk or drive around several areas where the man was known to have struck. Each member of the stake-out team had a walkie-talkie, so that if one of them saw the suspect he could contact the others spread out over a wide area. The walkie-talkies presented a problem in that any communication loud enough to be heard by members of the stake-out team might also alert the suspect to the status of those on stake-out. Also, since the stake-out took place from about 1 A.M. until 5 A.M., anyone seen between those hours was noticeable, further alerting the suspect to the fact that he was being sought. Apparently the stake-out teams *were* noticed by more than one would-be criminal, for not only did the suspect, when he was later caught, tell the detectives he had seen them on stake-out, but during the stake-out period there were no burglaries in the entire area, which normally had the highest burglary rate in the county.

STAKE-OUT 3

We were still looking for the "burglar" who had been bothering women. He still hadn't assaulted anyone, but he was fondling the women and leaving when they woke up. This time, instead of a "walking" stake-out in the streets, only cars, rooftops, and apartment houses were used for the stake-out. We sat up all night in a vacant apartment watching a parking lot the suspect had been seen crossing. Every movement in the lot from 1 A.M. to 5 A.M. was monitored, and everything that happened in the lot was subject to suspicion. No one fitting the suspect's description walked through the lot, and although I heard a lot of talk on the walkie-talkie about people who looked like the suspect, no one was arrested.

Stake-outs where a sizable area has to be covered with a limited number of men have limited success. During the search for the robber, a store where no stake-outs had been used was hit. A policeman had been on stake-out at the time in a van on the other side of a wide boulevard from the store. The van would not start, and even though the robbers escaped on foot, the man on stake-out was unable to catch them.

On the other hand, the stake-out team can be too close and therefore visible. During the stake-out no one wears a uniform or a conspicious outfit. Normally, except for undercover vice or narcotic detectives, detectives "look like cops." That is, they appear to have recent haircuts, no facial hair other than neatly trimmed moustaches, pressed clothes, and shined shoes. Most of the people they arrest have longer hair, facial hair that is untrimmed, unpressed clothes, and never-shined shoes.

Another problem in concealing a stake-out team is that often other people know of the stake-out. During the stake-out for the "burglar," arrangements had to be made for the detectives to occupy apartments. Only the apartment managers knew about the stake-outs in vacant apartments, but even they could not be trusted to keep silent. Other tenants in the apartment complex might tell the manager they saw someone going into or looking out of a vacant apartment, and the manager would be obliged to tell them about its use as a stake-out post. Where stake-outs were posted in occupied apartments, notice had to be given to the tenants well in advance so that preparations could be made. The fact that no burglaries took place in the area during the stake-out nights suggests that there was general knowledge of the police activities.

It is important to note how the efforts of the detectives reflect and point to social arrangements (i.e., the patterned organization of social life). The intention to carry out a stake-out can be kept secret from all but those who participate unless special arrangements have to be made for occupying private space. Where no arrangements are made to occupy private space, such as empty apartments, those who occupy such spaces are suspect, since under normal conditions to occupy empty apartments at night is "out of place." If the stake-out is to be conducted in public places, especially at night when everybody else is at home in bed, the detectives either must keep out of sight or must appear in a normal nighttime role (e.g., as a late-evening partygoer); otherwise their presence is cause for alarm (Goffman, 1971, pp. 238–47). Those who occupy such spaces as automobiles, rooftops, and public streets during the late night hours are seen to be bent on crime or on preventing it. Location in such spaces during certain hours informs the observer that something is out of place. For the criminal, it serves as information that a stake-out is underway; for the detective, it serves as information that a crime is in progress. Thus, because of the patterns of social arrangements in regard to space and time, being out of place is an alarm to the events afoot.

What's in a Name?

If, during the identification sequence of an investigation, the detectives learn a suspect's name, locating him is a matter of linking the name to one of several places. With the exception of unattached transients, whose location is seen to be general, a name generally ties an individual to a specific location. The name is assumed to go with certain other names, such as friends and family, and this assumption is employed as a resource in determining where a person is likely to be found. Given a name, information about the person is available from schools, businesses, clubs, criminal records, the Department of Motor Vehicles, and the telephone company, as well as other organizations that keep lists of names and information about them. The following examples illustrate how a name can be used to locate individuals both spatially and socially:

Case 67

A sexual offender was identified by the victim from a mug shot that had been taken when the man was arrested for drunk driving. The man no longer lived at the address listed in the police files, but the detective simply looked up his name in the phone book to find his address. The detective then went to the address and arrested the suspect.

Case 94

The name of a woman accused of child stealing was provided by her ex-husband. He also described the car she was driving, including the license plate number, and the address where he had been sending her money for the children. The detectives could not find her at this location so they waited until the car was seen near that address, and at that time found her and the children.

Case 54

A man identified as a rapist was traced to a factory. The detectives had his name and simply inquired as to the man's shift and arrested him at work.

Case 65

In a political bribery case detectives learned that the man they wanted was in a restaurant, but they did not know which one. To locate him, they called a number of restaurants and had the suspect paged, then arrested him outside the restaurant where he answered the phone.

Case 54A

In an attempted rape case the victim mentioned that her assailant had said his first name was something like "Tyrone." While at the city police department, the detective learned that

a man with a similar name had just been arrested for robbery
and was in the county jail.

CASE 50

In a rape case the culprit was known to have a grandmother
in Northtown. When the suspect was identified, the detectives
found his parents' address, and the parents told them about
the grandmother's residence, where the suspect had been
staying. From the grandmother the detectives learned that the
suspect had taken a job as a security guard. The manager of the
security-guard firm told them that the suspect would be by the
next day to pick up his paycheck, and the detectives arrested
him when he came to get it.

Socially, a name links an individual with relatives, an
occupation, a social class, and other aspects which are assumed
to "go with" relatives, occupations, and social class. In the
bribery case (65), for instance, the detectives phoned only the
better restaurants, since the social status of the suspect was seen
to be relatively high. Given a suspect's name, everything else
that goes with the name narrows the location of the person the
detectives are seeking.

The work of the ID bureau involves making available information about a name, and sometimes providing a name for
available information. For example, a booking jacket is made out
for anyone booked in the Mountainbeach County Jail, including
fingerprints, photograph, and such other information as:

Name	Eye color
Address	Hair color
City	Build
Date arrested	Scars
Charge	Tattoos
Disposition	Fingerprint classification
Birth date	Occupation
Place of birth	Relatives
Height	Remarks
Weight	Social Security number
Age	FBI number
Nationality	CII number (California Information
Complexion	and Identification)

It is noteworthy that everything on the booking jacket serves to identify a person as a unique individual. Even though the interest of the police in the individuals is not a tender one, their practices serve to establish identities for people who may otherwise be alienated. For an understanding of how identities are established in society at large, police activities in locating specific persons constitute a valuable resource. In terms of "knowing" people, albeit generally in uncomplimentary terms, the police stand as "intimates" to those with few ties to others.

We have noted that in order to circumvent police knowledge of their names and all that goes with them, people with criminal records, as well as some others, often use aliases when committing a crime. By carrying a set of forged identity papers, generally a driver's license or a selective service card, or no identity papers at all, the criminal can short-circuit the information that can be derived from an actual name. If a criminal on parole is stopped and questioned concerning some minor crime, he may be able to prevent his return to prison by the simple expedient of using a false name, and burglars dealing with pawnshops use false names so that they cannot be traced through pawn tickets. In one case Juvenile detectives found their youthful suspect in the county jail after she had lied not only about her name but also about her age in order to prevent her parents from learning of her activities. In drunk courts defendants sometimes give false names in order to avoid a jail sentence (Wiseman, 1970). Since drunks are sent to jail only when their visits to the court become frequent, such a defendant may use a whole series of names so that he can be told under each new name, "If I see you here again, you're going to do time."

However, since false names are known to be used by suspects, police incorporate "uncovering moves" (Goffman, 1969, pp. 17–18). Most forged documents can be verified, and by explaining to the defendant prints will be checked out against the name he gave, the police can usually get a defendant to reveal his name. Through the Division of Motor Vehicles detectives can uncover forged drivers' licenses, and other relevant checks can verify other documents. However, it is unlikely that all the prints in the ID bureau would be checked; even if they were, a person would have to have a previous arrest or be a civil servant for his prints to be on record. By acting as though it is of little importance whether or not he reveals his name, and pointing to the inconvenience that would be caused by withholding the name, detectives can generally persuade a suspect to tell who he is.

The Arrest

Once the suspect has been located, all the detectives have to do is pick him up. This constitutes the denouement of the case, and the arrest is often anticlimatic. On occasion there is cause for anxiety, especially with hefty or violent suspects, and the detectives take precautions to make the arrest in a situation they control. They prefer to have the suspect alone, away from possible allies. The suspect is thus relieved of any temptation to demonstrate to his friends that he has the guts to fight the cops (cf. Goffman, 1967, pp. 149–270); in addition, there are no external others to create incidents (cf. Goffman, 1961, pp. 45–48). During the observation period only two incidents occurred during an arrest, and in both situations it was others not being sought who caused the trouble.

Summary

Once a suspect has been identified, locating him is seen to be a relatively simple matter. This is because a name ties an individual to a place in society, and detectives work on the assumption that somewhere in the order of social arrangements will be their suspect's name. Merely by plugging the name into organizational, interpersonal, and subcultural networks, detectives can usually locate the body that goes with the name. Their activities and assumptions in these location operations point to their assumptions about the social order, and these assumptions in turn tell us about the order they construct and how they go about constructing it. Thus, we can see not only how investigators catch crooks in society but, more importantly, the sense of society as seen by social actors.

COPPING OUT A SUSPECT

Once a suspect has been arrested, the detectives generally try to get him to "cop out" (admit guilt). Ideally in the criminal-justice system, the police are only supposed to bring suspects before the court, where determinations of innocence or guilt are made by a judge or jury. However, the police are interested in screening out the innocent, not only to spare these citizens the expense and indignity of being booked and having to face court proceedings, but also to save themselves the work of preparing a case for the D.A. and spending a lot of time in court with no conviction to show for their efforts. It is routine procedure to interview suspects either before or after they have been arrested. The suspect is warned of his right to have a lawyer present before any such questioning and of his right to remain silent. If the suspect tells the detectives he does not want to talk to them, they cannot, and do not, pursue the interrogation. This rule is followed with special care when they believe they have a good case, for they are reluctant to risk the possibility that the case will be thrown out of court because of their failure to follow legal procedures. In a case where a deputy was stabbed, the Major Crimes detectives had strong evidence against the suspect. They made a point to tell the deputies who worked in the jail not to let anyone try to get a confession from the suspect lest the case be thrown out of court.

An interrogation aimed at getting a suspect to cop out will often open with a request for the suspect to give his side of the story. Sometimes the suspect's story will exonerate him; at other times there will be elements of the story which the detective believes from other evidence to be false. Aspects that do not correspond with the detective's information will be challenged, and if the story changes, it will often contradict some other part of the story that was consistent before the change was made. Generally, the detectives have already interpreted something about a case as informative before interviewing a suspect, and this is used as a resource both to check out the suspect's story and to impress upon him that there is little reason to hold back, since they already know what happened. Case 54 illustrates some of the detective's moves in an interrogation:

Case 54

DET: O.K., Larry, like I said, you've been arrested on a felony warrant, two charges, attempted rape and kidnapping. Do you understand what the charges mean? Attempted rape? Kidnapping?

SUS: Ah, kidnapping means you take someone where they
don't wanna go, right?

DET: Yeah. Or you prevent someone from leaving when they
wanna leave. O.K.? . . . O.K. It's a case that happened about
two and a half months ago. It dates back to the thirtieth of
September, approximately 12:30, one o'clock in the morning. Now, we're aware of what happened, Larry. If we
didn't, we wouldn't be here. I'm not a person who goes out
to harass people or anything else. As you know, I never dealt
with you before. I happen to know who you are, I have a
good memory, I remember you when you were in jail in
1967 or 1968 on similar charges. That's where I know you
from. O.K.?

SUS: Uh huh.

DET: O.K. I, that's where it is right there. I investigated the
case, and, I wanna be frank with you, I got you made on it.
You know if I didn't I wouldn't have $10,000 bail. I
wouldn't have the charges I got. It took me two months to do
it. I been working my back off. I just don't want you to think
that I'm here trying to snow you, 'cause I'm not. I also know
that there've been other capers you're involved in out here in
the county.

In this instance the suspect remained steadfast in his denial
of involvement, claiming, "I don't know a damned thing about
it." However, the tactic employed by the detective is a standard
one used in interrogations (cf. Kidd, 1940, pp. 77–104). The
detective tells the suspect that he has a great deal of evidence
against him without telling him what the evidence is.

In terms of linguistic interaction, the suspect "fills in" what
he assumes the detective already knows, whether or not the
detective actually has information. The details the detective
supplies to the suspect are taken as pointing to the total crime
(Garfinkel, 1967, pp. 39–40). This suggests an interpretive
practice of "skipping." With only sketchy information, a detective is able to communicate the sense that he has everything he
needs to implicate the suspect in the crime. In order to make
sense of these bits and pieces as standing for or pointing to
"everything else," the suspect must not only "fill in" what
constitutes "everything else" but must also "skip" or "pass by"
the points that have been left out of the detective's account.

Detectives are cautioned against bluffing when they have no

information at all. If the detective presents a detail of the crime that he guesses is accurate but in fact is not, the suspect may take this error as evidence that the detective is bluffing. However, if the detective presents only those details he knows from physical evidence or statements from witnesses he believes to be reliable, the suspect cannot interpret them as pointing to a bluff.

Another general rule of interrogation is that the suspect should be questioned in an interrogation room, with only one person present. As a result of this practice, I was not invited to be present at interrogations, although I sometimes listened to the detectives' tapes or asked them how they got information. However, I was able to be present in the field when a detective pumped a suspect or witness, and most of these confrontations took the form of Case 54 (pp. 125–26). That is, the detective would confront the suspect with known details of a case, and the suspect would either deny involvement or confess, filling in the details of the crime along with the other people involved, if any.

In cases where the suspect did not cop out, the detectives would often work with the defense lawyer to get a confession. This usually involved persuading the D.A. to accept from the defendant a guilty plea to a lesser charge in exchange for a lesser sentence. By presenting evidence to the defense attorney that his client was guilty, the detectives were sometimes able to enlist his cooperation. Blumberg (1967, p. 92) found that the defense attorney was likely to be the first person to suggest a guilty plea to a defendant and the most influential in getting the defendant to plead guilty. Moreover, the D.A. was also interested in getting a guilty plea, and although D.A.'s often worked out deals with defense attorneys to get guilty pleas that the detectives did not care for, the detectives were generally satisfied to get the cop out and close the case. As a result of arrangements with the defense attorney and the D.A., a detective who did not get a cop out in the interrogation room had a good chance of getting one later. In turn, this led to less pressure for the detectives to employ "third degree" methods on suspects; during the entire research period no such methods were observed.

SUMMARY AND CONCLUSIONS

Detective work, like any other job, involves a day-in, day-out routine that in one way or another is seen to accomplish some end. For the detective, this routine includes activities formulated and typified as "making contacts," "reading reports," "establishing crimes," "catching up on paperwork," "identifying suspects," "looking for suspects," "making rips" (arrests), "booking suspects," "talking to the D.A.," "getting cop outs," "going to court," and other such mundane tasks. In a single day a detective may have to catch up on paperwork for one case while trying to contact a witness for another case. Any single case can be seen retrospectively as following a given sequence from the time it is established until it is disposed of, but unless a detective is working a big case, devoting all his time to a single crime and suspect, a typical day consists of a mosaic of little tasks.

For the most part, but with notable exceptions, detective strategies have an institutionalized (typical and routinized) character (cf. Berger and Luckman, 1966). By going through such routines as looking for an M.O., contacting victims and witnesses, examining physical evidence, going through the pawn ticket file or the F.I. file, and digging up old cases, detectives maintain an everyday schedule that sometimes results in a cleared case. On occasions when a suspect is identified, located, arrested, booked, and eventually convicted, the strategies reveal themselves retrospectively. A neat sequence of events is explained in an account by the detective to "show" how the case was solved. When, however, the routines of detective work fail to yield a suspect, the strategies somehow are obscured retrospectively and come to be seen as "going through a routine investigation," and the case is inactivated "due to lack of investigative leads." Thus the sense of "using a strategy" or "doing detective work" is accomplished retrospectively, and it is only after the case is over that the sense of how the strategy worked is made available.

Another consideration in examining how the detectives' work gets done is the ongoing accomplishment of the sense of what they are doing. For a case to be investigated (or not investigated, for that matter), a reported set of evidences has to be seen to be one thing or another. If a case is reported as an attempted murder but is reformulated as "just a domestic disturbance," the case will not be investigated. Information in an investigation is developed through interpretive practices, and the sense of a case is accomplished by the same practices.

The typicality of any crime or criminal is not inherent in an objective set of conditions that take on certain forms but, rather, is a product of interpretive practices providing a sense of typicality that is taken to be independent of the actor's doing.

These practices are revealed when the accounts of crimes and casework are examined. A "man with a knife taking money" is seen to point to a robbery, while a report of some boys taking a spray can away from another boy is seen as "a bunch of kids screwing around." The sense of a "righteous crime" is an ongoing accomplishment. To be defined as such, the particulars of any reported events must be seen in terms of an underlying pattern pointing to a "righteous crime," for, as we have suggested throughout this study, at various points in the course of an investigation, a crime can be sensed as being something other than what it was seen to be at another point. It is insufficient to say that "new information" was found which revealed the "true conditions." The importance of the data lies not in how detectives as social actors go about uncovering clues, leads, and information but, rather, in how the stable sense of these activities is accomplished. All the routines of detective work stand as accounts and formulations from the actor's point of view. In turn, these accounts serve as data for documenting interpretive practices.

6

The Juvenile Detail

Harry had been looking for a woman from Tennessee who was charged with stealing her children from her ex-husband, to whom the court had given custody. He knew what her car looked like and where she was staying, but whenever he went there, the woman, the children, and the car were nowhere to be seen. When the car was finally spotted near her house, Sergeant Holsh and I went along with Harry to make the arrest.

Sergeant Holsh and I waited at the end of the driveway while Harry went in to pick up the woman and the children. After a short time we heard someone shouting and finally realized it was Harry calling for help. We ran down the driveway and to the side of the house, where Harry was holding off the woman's boyfriend while she and the children were trying to escape over the fence. A couple of the kids were already over the fence when we arrived, and Harry had his gun out, something I don't remember ever having seen before. Then the woman and the children began to cry, and the boyfriend was handcuffed. He was arrested for interfering with an officer, the children were taken into protective custody, and their mother was taken to jail.

Harry and the sergeant tried to calm them, but all they could tell the woman was that they had been given an arrest warrant issued by the State of Tennessee to return her and her children to that state.

THE ORGANIZATION AND WORK OF THE JUVENILE DETAIL

The MCSO Juvenile Detail consisted of a sergeant, two detectives, and a deputy. The deputy, a woman who was later promoted to detective, spent most of her time in a PR program the sheriff's office had set up with the schools. Since the school program did not involve investigations, almost all of my research time in the Juvenile Detail was spent with the two detectives who investigated crimes by juveniles and "status offenses." "Status offenses" refer to those violations for which only juveniles can be arrested, such as runaway, incorrigibility, and truancy. About 10 percent of the cases assigned to the Juvenile detectives were runaway investigations, but I gathered relatively few data on these cases because the detective I accompanied most frequently was assigned fewer runaway cases, and because very few of the cases that were assigned resulted in an actual investigation. By the time the case was assigned to a detective, the juvenile in most instances had returned home voluntarily or had been located at a friend's or relative's house. The "investigation" in these cases consisted of merely calling the parents and learning of the juvenile's whereabouts. The case would be logged as "cleared," and the detectives would be happy. To supplement the investigative data gathered on the few runaway cases where I accompanied a detective, I interviewed the detectives about past cases and reviewed follow-up reports on investigations that I was unable to observe.

In the division of labor of the detail, one of the Juvenile detectives, identified as the "theft detective," was given most of the bicycle and surfboard thefts to investigate because it was believed that juveniles were generally involved in such crimes. The other detective was more likely to receive cases involving runaways (about 20 percent of his case load). Even though the vast majority of his assigned cases were other than runaways, he spent most of his actual investigative efforts on runaway cases. This was true even though many of the cases required merely a phone call to "solve."

Priorities

According to the Juvenile sergeant, the investigative priorities of his detail ranged from runaway cases (the most important) to petty crimes without leads (the least important). He said that runaways were always investigated before anything else, then cases with leads such as an M.O., a possible suspect, or a license number, and finally cases where victims complained most insistently that nothing was being done to catch a culprit. He said that cases with no leads (except for runaways) were filed, and if no leads developed within three weeks, they were inactivated. At the same time, however, the sergeant said he believed that all cases, whether they had leads or not, should be investigated at least to the extent of making contact with the victim. This ideal, he explained, was impossible to attain since it was more important that the detectives use their time on cases with some chance of solution and on runaway cases.

It appeared that the sergeant tried to realize his ideal in practice. The detectives believed that they were being given every case that came in, whether it had leads or not, and that most of them did not; my observations confirm their belief. Thus, instead of filing cases that had no leads, as he claimed, the sergeant would assign almost every case the Juvenile Detail pulled (took out of the incoming batch of patrol reports for possible investigation).* For example, the following case was assigned to be investigated:

CASE 78

A man reported that there was a sticky substance in his mailbox. The theft detective was assigned to investigate the case although there were no apparent suspects or leads. The detective contacted the victim, who was surprised to find that his complaint was being investigated. After talking to the victim, the detective examined the mailbox, but there appeared to be no evidence there. The case was then inactivated.

During the investigation I asked the detective why he had been assigned to the case, and he said he didn't know, except that a number of mailboxes in the area had been destroyed or damaged, and the sergeant may have felt that it was good public

---

*The patrol report had a separate copy of every report entitled "Juvenile Division." The Burglary and Major Crimes Details used the "Detective Investigators" copy of the patrol report. This sometimes led to problems (as we will see later), since if one of the other details pulled a case to investigate using the "Detective Investigators" copy, the Juvenile Detail might pull the same case using the "Juvenile Division" copy.

relations to send a detective to make an investigation. However, unless the number of assaulted mailboxes was seen to constitute an M.O., the case did not appear to be assigned on the basis of the sergeant's stated criterion.

The cases pulled by the Juvenile Detail sometimes overlapped with those pulled by Major Crimes. The first time I accompanied a Major Crimes detective on a case we ran into a Juvenile detective who had been assigned to the same case. The report from patrol had been classified as a 245 PC ADW (assault with a deadly weapon) and, unless juveniles were reported to be involved, it was unclear why a Juvenile detective had been assigned to the case. Generally, when there was some question as to who should properly investigate a case, the Juvenile sergeant or a detective would ask the Major Crimes sergeant if Major Crimes was going to take the case. In cases involving Juveniles in assault or battery, the Major Crimes sergeant would usually give it to Juvenile on request.

In order to get an overall picture of the kinds of cases worked by the two Juvenile detectives, I summarized their work logs for a 10- or 12-week period, listing the type of crime. The compilations (logs 1 and 2) suggest not only the nature of the cases received, but also the volume of cases each detective handled.

The theft detective's log (1) reflects his specialty in theft investigation, but fully 37 percent of the cases he received to

Log 1   (12/30/72–3/20/73)

CRIME	NUMBER OF CASES	%
Theft	72	63.0
Malicious mischief	22	19.0
Mailbox tampering	8	7.0
Runaway	5	4.4
Burglary	1	0.9
Possession of stolen property	1	0.9
Loitering around schoolyard	1	0.9
Mental case	1	0.9
Assault (felony)	1	0.9
Child stealing	1	0.9
Forgery	1	0.9
	114	*99.7%

*Less than 100% due to rounding.

Log 2   (12/29/72–3/9/73)

CRIME	NUMBER OF CASES	%
Malicious mischief	18	30.6
Runaway	12	20.4
Theft	9	15.3
Mailbox tampering	4	6.8
Wife/child beating	3	5.1
Burglary	3	5.1
Possession of stolen property	3	5.1
Assault (felony)	2	3.4
Battery	2	3.4
Oral copulation	1	1.7
Child molestation	1	1.7
Prowler	1	1.7
	59	*100.3%

*More than 100% due to rounding.

work were not related to theft. The diversity of cases received by Juvenile is even more evident in log 2. While investigation of the three modal crimes (theft, malicious mischief, and runaway) constituted 66 percent of the work load, a large portion of the work still involved other types of crime.

The logs do not necessarily reflect actual work. As has been pointed out before, many of the runaway cases simply involve calling the juvenile's parents and learning that the child has returned home. Similarly, many of the other cases, especially theft and malicious mischief, receive minimal investigative attention—merely contacting the victim and writing a follow-up report that inactivates the case. For instance, in one malicious-mischief case someone had shot a BB pellet through a plate-glass window. There was a large plowed field near the building where the window had been damaged, and since the field was used by any number of people, especially young boys, who typically have BB guns, there was little to go on in the case.

With a runaway juvenile who has not been located, on the other hand, the detective has the names of the runaway and his relatives and friends, as well as other information that may suggest his possible location. Because there is a group of people who can be and are contacted (and can therefore be regarded as leads in the case), the detective generally spends a fair amount of time on such runaways.

Similarly, any case involving "possession of stolen property" has a suspect, since someone must be identified as possessing the property for the case to be reported as other than a theft or burglary. In a possession-of-stolen-property case the detective can work backward from the suspect to the person who committed the theft or burglary in the first place. The following excerpt from my field notes involved the leads that had been built up in a possession-of-stolen-property (496 PC) case investigated by the theft detective:

> Bert first contacted the owner of one bicycle shop, who told us that he believed one of the kids who worked at another bike shop knew something about the theft of the bicycles and the sale of the parts taken off the bicycles. Apparently this bike-shop owner had done some investigation on his own, and Bert felt that he was getting in the way by contacting too many people.
>
> A man at the second bike shop told us the person we were looking for was in school but would be in later that afternoon. We came back after lunch to interview the kid, and even though he said he didn't want to get involved, Bert finally got him to talk. Bert had learned of the leads in the case initially through the arrest of a boy who had been caught with the bicycle parts, who was a friend of the boy who now became the informant. The problem for Bert was to learn who had stolen the bicycles in the first place, and the informant, in order to take the pressure off his arrested friend, identified the thieves. Thus, beginning with the arrest of the kid on a possession-of-stolen-property charge, the investigation wove its way back to the thieves.

If every case had the kinds of leads inherent in 496 PC's, no detective would be able to handle two new cases a day, or even one. However, cases in which a single contact, either in person or by phone, is generally sufficient to "learn" that there are no leads, make it relatively easy to handle several cases a day. What irritates the detectives is to be working a case with good leads and nevertheless be given the usual number of new cases with no leads to be worked. It is difficult for the detectives to follow and develop leads, witnesses, and suspects, and at the same time have to make contact on cases that they see as petty. If what is taken to be a "typical petty theft" develops into a full-fledged case while the detective is still working on another case with good leads, the detective's situation becomes even more difficult. Instead of having one workable case, he now has two, along with his daily quota of "contact and inactivate" cases. Since a detective would rather have one good case with leads to develop than any number of cases without leads, the cases he receives while working a "hot" case get very little attention. Thus the likelihood that any one case will "have" leads is linked to the other cases the detective has when he receives it. One of the Juvenile detectives said that any case received could be solved if there were enough time to work it, and that every case could be found to have some leads. Therefore, when we speak of cases "with leads" and "without leads," we are talking about cases which are typified as having or not having leads. That is, cases are viewed in terms of a typified corpus of details which point to or suggest the existence of "leads" or "no leads."

The pace of the work in the Juvenile Detail is fairly constant and steady (for example, an average of three to five theft cases can be expected every day). There are always cases to be investigated even if the "investigation" involves no more than contacting a victim or going to a crime scene.

"Big" and "Little" Cases

To the Juvenile Detail, a "big" case is any battery or assault case or any case involving a suspect who has previously committed several crimes. Even though first priority in the allocation of investigative resources is given to runaway cases, there was no status reward for tracking down some youngster who had left home. Most 601's were located soon after a report had been filed that they were missing. Some would come home on their own, others would be found with relatives or friends, and some turned up in juvenile hall. On several occasions the runaway was seen to have good reason to run away from home, but the detective could offer such juveniles little more than, "We're just doing our job" and would deposit the youth at juvenile hall. One boy who had a history of placements in juvenile hall asked not to be returned to his home because his mother was "dealing" heroin, and he would only get in trouble again. When his mother was later arrested for selling heroin, he was picked up along with her and placed back in juvenile hall, even though he was not involved in the crime.

While 601 WIC cases are seen to be of little significance, not only by the detectives who are assigned to work them but also by the public at large, runaway cases are consequential in another way. If "something happens" to a runaway, the law-enforcement agency which received the report of the case will be criticized long and loud for not having done anything. Two years before the research project, a number of young people were murdered in Mountainbeach County. Ever since that time, any person under the age of 18 who was from another county was picked up on a 601 WIC charge and taken to juvenile hall. Generally this involved hitchhikers, but it also meant that other youths from all over the state and nation, many of whom had their parents' permission to make the journeys, were picked up in Mountainbeach. The relevant section of the Welfare and Institutions Code (601) states:

> 601. Any person under the age of 18 years who persistently or habitually refuses to obey the reasonable and proper orders or directions of his parents, guardian, custodian or school authorities, or who is beyond the control of such person, or any person who is a habitual truant from school within the meaning of any law of this State, or who from any cause is in danger of leading an idle, dissolute, lewd, or immoral life, is within the jurisdiction of the juvenile court which may adjudge such person to be a ward of the court. (Amended Ch. 1748, Stats. 1971. Effective Mar. 4, 1972).

The "out of county" criterion is nowhere to be found in this section. However, the reference to "beyond the control" can be interpreted in a spatial sense, to mean the physical distance separating the juvenile from his parents. Of course, other senses could also be made of the law. An interpretation could be so strict as to put the juvenile on the end of a leash, or it could be so liberal as to let the juvenile go anywhere he pleased. This is not because the section is poorly written but rather because when any law is applied to a specific situation, its meaning is specified by and specifies the occasion on which it is used. As Wieder (1970, p. 134) points out:

> Ethnomethodologists have found that, when one directly examines the activity of employing criteria for using names or titles (a certain law), one finds that the particular sense of the criteria is specific to the cases in which the criteria are employed.

Rather than having a stable meaning across a set of cases that are classified by their use, criteria are matched against cases by elaborating the sense of the criteria or the case to encompass the particular occurrences the name user faces. Explicating what members mean by their terms by stating criteria for using those terms would then be an inappropriate method, since criteria vary in their meaning over the occasions in which they are used.

While the "out of county" criterion provided a convenient account for a youth's being "out of control," it may have seemed absurd even to those who used it. Mountainbeach County is 100 miles long from the north to the south border and extends about 50 miles to the east from the coast. It is 70 miles from Mountainbeach City to North City, which is in the same county, but only 30 miles to South City, which is in another county. Thus, a juvenile from North City would not be picked up, but a juvenile from South City, who was much closer to home than the first youth, would be.

Even though the 601 WIC cases were not generally taken to be "big" cases and the application of the law appeared to be arbitrary in many of them, they were consequential.* Shortly after the research period ended, the bodies of a number of young boys were found in Texas. They were victims of a homosexual-homicide "ring," and the Dallas police were vehemently criticized for not having "seen the pattern," since several of the youths were from the same neighborhood. In defense, the police chief claimed that there had been 5,000 reports of runaways, and the 20 or so who were murdered constituted a small fraction of the whole. Such events are used by the Juvenile sergeant to document the importance of giving runaway cases top priority. If these cases are investigated, homicides and other horrors are less likely to occur. If they do occur, the sheriff's office can at least point to the vigorous efforts they made to find the runaways involved.

---

*I am using the term "consequential" in the sense developed by Erving Goffman (1967, p. 159). He refers to consequentiality as the "capacity of a payoff to flow beyond the bounds of the occasion in which it is delivered and to influence objectively the later life of the bettor." In this context the "payoff" is the trouble that would be caused by the discovery of murdered youths, and the "occasion" refers to the occasions on which the law is applied as well as to the occasions where youths are killed. The emphasis is on the fact that these occasions have consequences far beyond the boundaries of the occasion.

For the detectives, however, a "big" case or a "good" case is one involving high-status crimes such as battery or felony assault, or one whose solution permits the detectives to clear a number of smaller crimes, such as thefts or malicious mischief. Battery and assault cases are usually pulled by the Major Crimes detail and are considered "small" in the context of the rapes, robberies, and homicides that detail customarily handles. In the context of the petty thefts and malicious mischief more often handled by Juvenile, however, a battery or assault case is something "big." For example, the following case was a "big one" worked by the Juvenile theft detective:

CASE 74

Bert received a report of a theft/battery logged as a 484/242 PC. After initial investigation, he found that less than $200 had been taken so he reclassified the case as a 488 PC (petty theft) and battery. The situation was formulated as a shoplifter taking some liquor from a liquor store. When the owner intervened, the thief slugged him. Later, when the suspect was found to be a someone with a previous felony record, and because the victim had to have three stitches taken over his eye where he had been hit, the case was again reclassified as 667 PC (crime by felon) and 245a PC (assault resulting in "great bodily harm"). Finally, Bert decided that, given the circumstances of the case, it appeared that the suspect *had intended to take the liquor and not pay for* it; therefore, instead of petty theft, the case was now a burglary.* Thus, the final complaint that went to the D.A. included three felonies classified as 667/245a/459 PC. What began as petty theft and battery turned out to be "crime by a felon," felony assault, and burglary.

The case was a big one not only because it involved three felonies, but also because of the investigation, which involved a web of circumstantial evidence. The detective explained the investigation as follows:

Bert said that the whole case was circumstantial in that he had no solid eyewitness. When the suspect hit the victim, the

*Shoplifting was treated as a burglary (a felony) if it could be shown that the thief had entered with the intention of stealing. Normally, shoplifting was treated as petty theft (a misdemeanor).

victim's glasses were knocked off, and therefore he could not make a positive identification.

Upon interviewing various principals in the case, Bert found conflicting stories. The store owner said that when he stopped the suspect, the youth's jacket was taken off in the scuffle. The suspect told his parents that someone who had given him a ride had stolen his jacket and broken the cast on his wrist. His parents said he told them this story between 9:00 and 9:30 P.M.

The suspect went to the emergency room of a hospital at 9:15 P.M. and told them he had broken his cast by tripping on a curb. He was given a shot of demerol and left before they could reset the cast. At 11:15 P.M. that same evening, he went to another hospital and requested a shot of demerol for his broken wrist, still in the broken cast. He told the nurse he had fallen out of a truck. However, the attending physician recognized the suspect as a drug user and reset the cast but gave him no demerol.

Because of the contradictions in his story, it could be shown in court that the suspect was lying about something, and since it was believed he broke the cast when he slugged the store owner, his different stories were used to support that interpretation. Also, the hospital staff who assisted in resetting the cast said they did not believe the suspect could have broken the cast in the manner he described. Further, the suspect's parole officer said he was a chronic liar.

The physician who attended the victim said he did not believe that a blow from a bare fist could have caused the damage, but a cast could have. Finally, a witness to the scuffle said that there was something in the suspect's hand which could have been the cast.

To complicate the case further, a second "suspect" copped out to the crime. However, since he was a friend of the first suspect and a juvenile, so that little would happen to him if he was convicted, it was believed that this second suspect was doing the first boy a favor. His story did not coincide with what the victim had described. He said that the victim grabbed him from behind, wrapping his arms around him, and the victim said he grabbed the suspect by the collar of his jacket. The second suspect said that his jacket was pulled off, ripping his shirt, but the victim said the suspect did not have a shirt on, that his shirt was rolled up in his jacket pocket. Since the detectives had the shirt, they examined it, finding no rips in it. On this evidence, which showed the second suspect to be lying, and on the circumstantial evidence they had on the first suspect, they were able to get a complaint from the D.A.

By working through circumstantial evidence and discrediting the second "suspect," the detective was able to demonstrate skill as an investigator (cf. Skolnick, 1966, pp. 161–62). Further, he did so not in a simple case or a small case but in a triple felony. The prime suspect did not cop out, there were a number of witnesses' statements to piece together, and there was a phony admission to be discredited. All these details, compared with the petty thefts, malicious mischief, and runaways with which the Juvenile Detail is generally concerned, constitute the sense of a "big, complex case" that was "solved." In turn, this kind of work is taken as an indication of a good investigation and a good investigator.

The "worth" of a case, however, is typically retrospective. What began as a run-of-the-mill petty theft with battery "turned out" to be a big case, just as a traffic stop by a patrolman may "turn out" to be the arrest of a murder suspect. Retrospectively, the case described above came to be seen as a big case "all along," just as cases that "turn out" to have no leads even after a thorough investigation are seen retrospectively as having been "dead ends" all along. Each step in the investigation, which at the time is vaguely hopeful, is seen "after all" to have been a waste of time. Thus any single point in an investigation is understood in its "proper" light only after the case is finished.

Another kind of big case for the Juvenile Detail involves a thief who cops out or is found to be involved in numerous crimes. Thus, a bicycle-theft report may turn out to be a big case even though it is treated at the outset as "another 488" if the thief is found to have stolen many bikes. Likewise, a malicious-mischief report can lead to the apprehension of a group of vandals who have been destroying school property. (In one such case, which somehow was given to a Burglary detective, the vandals were caught. The local television station sent out a news crew to interview the detective, who was given departmental as well as community recognition for his work.) Obviously, big cases involving multiple clearances are so defined only after much more work is done than on the typical cases the detail receives.

Troublesome Cases

A "troublesome" case may be one that is seen to "have" leads but in which, for one reason or another, a witness cannot be contacted or will not cooperate, or various kinds of evidence cannot be obtained, or the detectives encounter other difficulties in identifying or locating a suspect. On the other hand, some cases are problematical because of the circumstances involved. One crime that is always considered to be a "bad" case is child stealing. During the research period two such cases were worked back to back, and trouble occurred in both. Child-stealing cases are typified as involving a separated or divorced couple: One parent illegally takes custody of the children, and the detectives have to take the children away from him or her. The trouble that occurs is caused by one or both parents, the children, or all of them. Here the detectives are seen as representatives of an unfair, impersonal order separating mother or father from the child. Cries of "Why are you taking my baby away?" and "I want my mommy!" punctuate the scene.

These tasks do not fit the detectives' image of "detective work," and many of them express great distaste for working these cases. The sense of this kind of case is provided in the following report:

CASE 99

A man from Florida came in with a court order from that state giving him custody of a child who was living with his father in Mountainbeach. The Florida man explained that he had married the child's mother and that she had obtained custody of the child, which had previously been given to the father. Also, there was a felony warrant for the arrest of the father for refusing to give up the child. Harry and Bert worked the case together and quickly located where the father and child were living. When they went to the address they found that the father was at work and the child was being cared for by a neighbor. A patrol unit was called to back up the two detectives since they felt the father might become extremely upset.

Harry called the father at work and explained that they had to turn the child over to the juvenile protection agency until he could be released to his mother. The father returned home immediately and was placed under arrest on the felony warrant from Florida. The neighbors, especially the woman who was looking after the boy, became upset and began sobbing. The father, choking back tears, was handcuffed (standard procedure in a felony arrest) and showed the detectives where his son's clothes and toys were. He asked to talk to his son once more before they took him away, situating himself so that the boy could not see the handcuffs. At this point I had to leave because I began to cry, too, and didn't want to embarrass the detectives, who were having a difficult enough time themselves.

The father claimed he had not been informed that the mother had received custody of the child, pointing out that she had not been given custody in the first place because she had been arrested for using heroin. He added that the mother would only use the child so that she could get more money from welfare, which she would spend on drugs. The neighbors said that the father had taken excellent care of the child and otherwise voiced their support for his plea to retain custody.

Because they had a felony warrant for the father's arrest along with a court order from Florida giving custody of the child to the mother, the detectives felt there was nothing they could do; were they to let the father and son go, there would be departmental sanctions against them. They did explain to the father some steps he could take to fight the court order and also extradition to Florida, suggested a lawyer they knew, and tried to offer condolences. The father said he knew they were only doing their job and in no way held them responsible for what was happening to him. This made them feel even worse. After the father had been taken to jail and the son placed in the custody of social services, one of the detectives said, "Now you see why I hate these cases."

The detective assumed that the researcher understood the sense of a "troublesome" or "distasteful" case. He assumed that the events that occurred during the arrest were there for "anyone" to see. However, during the arrest itself a number of assumptions about the events taking place were necessary for seeing why he hated "these cases." At the time of the arrest I had seen the court order and felony warrant as the work of some red-neck judge, probably corrupt and paid off by the mother, making a grievous blunder in taking the child away from a hard-working, loving father and giving him to a junkie mother. By formulating the situation as one in which a great injustice was being done, with the detectives as unwilling parties to such injustice, I could "see" why they hated these cases.

An alternative reading of the details, however, would transform not only the sense of the event but also the work that was done. Instead of being seen as a distasteful part of their job, the detectives' work in the case could be seen as saving a child from a disastrous future. In fact, this reformulation came about, and the whole incident was reseen as having been not so bad all along as it had first appeared. The next day, when they checked the father's story, the detectives found that he had been lying to them. He had a record of heroin use, he had applied for welfare, "using" the child as an account for need, and he had received notification of the court order to return custody of the child to the mother. Retrospectively, the father was seen to have been lying to them all along, his ignoring the court order pointed to lack of respect for the law, and he was a junkie himself, so they felt that even if they had not delivered the child to a good situation, neither had they taken him from one. In this case, and other cases in general, the detectives would much rather arrest a "scroat," "a con man," or a "real criminal" than what they see as "some poor slob who got caught up" in criminal circumstances.

Dealing with Juveniles

A good and bad aspect of working cases involving juveniles is the juvenile-justice system. The detectives are given a good deal of leeway in deciding how to handle a case, and many cases are cleared with only a warning. On the other hand, police are often frustrated by the lenient treatment juveniles generally receive at the hands of the courts. A 15-year-old bank robber, who was quite sophisticated in criminal behavior, received a short sentence to what the detectives regarded as a "resort" for boys.

Juvenile detectives often used the "warning" as a way of clearing cases. One detective told a suspect that if the boy "came clean," he would not be sent to the authorities and would merely be required to pay for any damage he had done or to return items he had stolen. In such cases the detective would explain that he was not going to warn the suspect of his rights since he was not going to place him under arrest; however, if the suspect lied, he would immediately warn the boy of his rights and place him under arrest. It was not clear to me whether the detective believed warning of "rights" to be a commitment point that forced him to make an arrest; whether he felt the juvenile was a "good kid" until he began lying, at which point he would find him to be "bad" and warn him of his rights; or whether all this was simply a stratagem he employed to keep the juvenile ignorant of his right to keep silent. (The last alternative was probably incorrect, since most of the juveniles knew of their right to remain silent and to have a lawyer present during questioning by police.) In all probability, it was a way of reassuring the juvenile that if he copped out and "came clean" there would be nothing to fear, since all he would get was a short lecture.

On a minor charge the lecture was usually a simple piece of advice, as illustrated in the following transcript:

CASE 104

DET: Now also, ah, legally, there is a law about trespass which is in the penal code, it is an offense. Before you go to one of these places, what were you guys doing? Collecting bottles or something like that?
JUV: Yeah, old bottles.
DET: You are? Yeah, as a matter of fact one of my ex-sergeants I used to work for, he's a bottle collector himself, I can understand that. . . . The thing to do when you go up to one of these places is to go up to the house and explain what you're doing and get permission to do it. O.K.?
JUV: (Nod)
DET: And that's the main thing.

With a more serious problem where the detectives do not want to take a juvenile to the juvenile hall, they will warn him by calling his parents. In an incident at a junior high school two detective units went to back up a patrol unit that had responded to a scuffle involving about 50 kids and was having trouble. When the detectives arrived, the patrol unit left them to handle the situation. Most of the juveniles had left, and all the detectives wanted was to get the others to leave as well. A small group was persistent in its refusal to leave. Finally, the detectives placed one girl in the back of their car and called her father at work to come and get her. This action was taken to convince the other youngsters that if they didn't leave the area they would get into trouble as well. When the father arrived they explained why he had been called:

DET: Mr. Ford?

FTR: (Nod)

DET: I'm Detective Knight of the sheriff's department. Sorry to meet you under these circumstances. Wonder if you could come over here and talk to me a minute. Ah, this afternoon at approximately 3:15 we had a fight occur in this vicinity. We rolled units into the area. There were 50 to 60 juveniles gathered here who wouldn't break up. . . . There was a small group who were harassing the officers. We asked them on several occasions to leave the area. This they failed to comply with. Your daughter, Alice, was standing out here. She, ah, was talking back, to put it in a blunt term, "hassling" the officers around here. I asked her to move on several occasions. She said I didn't have any authority to tell her to, that I couldn't tell her what to do. I asked her name several times. She refused to give me her name. I said "What about your folks, what are they going to say about this?" And she said, "I don't have any parents." I said, "Well, where's your home?" "I don't have a home. You can't do this to me. My father's going to take care of you." We had to fight tooth and nail to get any information out of her at all. She would not leave the area. We asked, ah, I asked her specifically on four separate occasions to leave the area, because of the danger involved and everything else. She refused to leave. Generally, she just tried to create a disturbance for the officers, and so it finally got to the point where she failed to obey our commands, and she was interfering with an officer in the performance of his duty and contributing to what we call a public disturbance, a 415. So I just finally just took her name and placed her in the car and decided to call you, rather than lock her up; so I'm going to release her in your custody. I thought you'd better hear about it.

FTR: Well, I'll take care of that.

The most serious warnings occur in cases where the detective is trying to decide whether or not to refer a youth to probation. An example is the case in which a boy was told that if he told the truth he would only be made to make restitution, but if he lied he would be referred to probation. Of course, if the warning does not seem to have any effect in terms of impressing the juvenile with the seriousness of the case, the detective can always turn the youth over to the probation department.

In juvenile cases the detectives have a sanction that is generally unavailable to other details: They can tell the juvenile's parents about the trouble the youth is in and leave it to them to take the necessary measures for dealing with their son or daughter. With adults who are involved in the same kinds of crimes, there is no expectation that the parents are willing or able to take control of their offspring. Because of the availability of the parents to take disciplinary action, it is not always necessary to use the juvenile-justice system, which to the detectives can turn a "good kid" into a delinquent. At the same time, the detectives can develop the sense of "doing their job," which they conceive as enforcing the law and "bringing to justice" those who break it.

Juvenile Offenses and Information

In the work of developing information about suspects and suspect location, the Juvenile Detail differs in some unique respects from the other detective details in MCSO. Juvenile-status offenses that are lumped into 601 WIC (e.g., runaway, truant, incorrigible) are reported with the offender's identity. If parents or the schools call and report such an offense, they do not report an "unknown perpetrator," as is the case in most other crimes. Thus, rather than having first to learn the culprit's identity, detectives investigating juvenile-status offenses have only to locate him or her.

A second informational resource uniquely available in juvenile cases is the school. In addition to the fact that the school is a location where investigators would normally go in search of an identified juvenile suspect, it is also a center of formal and informal information networks. The student body makes up what the detectives assume to be a "juvenile world clique" where information of delinquent activity abounds, but from which they are excluded because of their police and adult status. Nevertheless, it can be used to trace relationships (usually friendship patterns) through which information travels. Even though the detectives may not always be told what they hope to learn, they at least can find youths who have the information they seek. (Sometimes knowledge of the relationship is enough information in and of itself.) Additionally, the school is seen to have informational resources in the persons of administrators, counselors, and teachers. School records can be used to find students' addresses, relatives, and friends. Of course, access to school records is dependent on the cooperation the detectives get from the schools, but in my observation the schools appeared to be willing to cooperate with the police. This cooperation, moreover, was based on informal understandings the detectives cultivated with the schools. On a number of occasions the detectives helped to solve problems in the schools without invoking formal sanctions and bringing school problems to public attention. Although the schools were never observed to refuse requests for information on occasions when the detectives had no legal access to the records, the detectives were well aware of their right to do so. Therefore, in their interaction with school authorities and teachers, detectives went out of their way to make sure that they maintained good informal relationships.

Aside from the character of information in juvenile-status offenses and the unique informational resource the schools provided, most juvenile investigations were much like criminal investigations in the other details. The variety of cases received by Juvenile detectives gave them the opportunity to sample a broad spectrum of offenses and to assume informational keystones (starting points), as we will see in our discussion of the Burglary and Major Crimes Details.

CONCLUSION

The Juvenile Detail has a wide variety of cases to investigate, which make up a microcosm of the business brought to the Detective Bureau. In some respects, their assignment is the least rewarding in the bureau, since they deal with what are considered "petty crimes" and "petty criminals." If a "big" case involving a juvenile occurs, often detectives in other details are given the work and the status honor that goes with it. The detectives receive little social esteem for hauling in a runaway or catching a mother who has taken her children against a court order. The variety of the cases they have to work does not allow them to develop expertise in any one, except perhaps theft and runaways; instead, the juvenile detective has to become a jack-of-all-trades.

On the other hand, the Juvenile Detail was the most valuable for studying information because of the variety of information development that went with the many kinds of cases these detectives were given to work. They had to consider each type of case in terms of different information resources, and this led them to discuss their problems in working the case. In turn, these discussions served as data in finding how information is developed, adding significantly to the study.

7

The Burglary Detail

After having tried unsuccessfully to contact the 95-year-old victim at home, we finally found him sitting in his driveway in a car. He told us to talk to the woman who was taking care of him. She had listed several items taken in the original burglary report by patrol, and the list had increased by the time we talked to her. Andy asked her if she knew any possible suspects, and she said she did not, which was typical of burglary victims. She explained that the old man was friendly to everyone who talked with him and would show them around the house, so she thought it might be someone the old man had befriended. She didn't think the old man could remember anyone. When Andy explained the case to the sergeant, he was told to handle it "routinely," which meant to inactivate it unless other leads came up.

ROUTINES IN THE BURGLARY DETAIL

The research in the Burglary Detail began when a Juvenile detective I was accompanying was transferred to Burglary. I believed that since the Burglary Detail would be new to both of us, there were things I could learn that would be problematical-ly visible to the detective. That is, if I had begun my observations with a detective who had been in the detail a long time, a number of the procedures would be routine and unproblematic, and therefore not made visible to me. I also liked the detective who was being transferred, and it would be easy to continue to work with him. For the major period of my research in the Burglary Detail, I was with this detective.

Of all the details, Burglary underwent the most extensive a change in personnel during the research period. Three members of the detail—the sergeant, the check and forgery detective, who also acted as the complaints officer (i.e., he took complaints to the D.A.'s office), and one other Burglary detective—were there during the entire period, and four other detectives were transferred in or out. In addition, the department began a TDY program in which a patrolman would spend two weeks with the detail working as a Burglary detective. Thus, the detail at any given time comprised one sergeant, the check and forgery detective, three Burglary detectives, and one TDY detective. Near the end of the research an additional Burglary detective was added permanently.

The Burglary Detail received a constant flow of cases. Reports of about four cases per day came in from patrol. On some days there would be none and on others as many as ten. Most of the check and forgery cases were reported directly to the detective concerned, mainly by banks.

With the exception of not having runaway cases to work, the priorities in the Burglary Detail were much like those in Juvenile Detail. Cases involving substantial financial or property loss, those with good leads, and those where the victim complained that nothing was being done about his case would receive at least some investigative attention. Cases seen to have leads, however, were rare in Burglary, and a number of the bigger cases were cleared with information from an informant or witness.

Burglaries are difficult crimes to solve, and were it not for informants and multiple clearances on cop outs and M.O. even fewer would be "solved." In part this situation is due to the nature of the events characterized as burglaries. Section 459 of the Penal Code of California (1971) reads:

459. (Burglary defined) Every person who enters any house, room, apartment, tenement, shop, warehouse, store, mill, barn, stable, outhouse or other building, tent, vessel, railroad car, trailer coach as defined by the Vehicle Code, vehicle as defined by said code when the doors of such vehicle are locked, aircraft as defined by the Harbors and Navigation Code, mine or any

underground portion thereof, with intent to commit grand or
petit larceny or any felony is guilty of burglary (p. 111).

Thus, burglaries are characterized as "going inside," and this
feature makes the burglar invisible to witnesses unless they see
the entry. Moreover, burglaries generally occur when no regular
occupant is at the premises (Scarr, 1972), so the victim does not
see the culprit either.

A characteristic of private space is that passage through the
space is controlled by the space holder. Another feature is the
right to carry on private activities within the space, free from
view through a window or some other viewing device. These
same features that provide for privacy will shield housebreakers,
and any person entering and burglarizing such space is not
likely to be seen or caught. Stinchcombe (1963) proposes that a
good part of the arrested population are those without access to
private space, such as homeless men or runaways, for while
inside the sanctuary of a house, hotel room, trailer, or any other
place deemed to be private, people are generally left alone.
Ironically, burglars, who do their work in such places, are left
alone as well.

The one Burglary detective who works forgery deals with a
crime that involves different types of social arrangements. When
a check or credit-card forgery occurs, the culprit and the victim
typically have face-to-face contact. A person writing a check
leaves a signature and possibly a face to be recalled and
identified. Also, the exact time and method of the crime can be
determined. The hour and day of a burglary, by contrast, are
often established by vague estimates based on when the victim
last saw the missing property and when he realized he had been
burglarized. Thus check cases typically are characterized as
having leads, and therefore something to work. When the
detective receives a case he will spend more time investigating it
than he will a typical burglary, and fewer check cases are
inactivated at the outset than are burglaries.

Big and Little Cases

Since most of the cases received by the Juvenile Detail are
misdemeanors (e.g., petty theft, malicious mischief), a burglary
case received there is considered to be a big case since it is a
felony. However, other than some of the check and forgery

cases, almost all of the cases received by the Burglary Detail are burglaries. On occasion burglary will be combined with another charge, such as arson or malicious mischief, but for the most part it is reported simply as an instant of 459 PC, burglary. Thus the differentiation between big and little cases is not characteristically based on types of crimes but on types of burglaries, and sometimes burglars.

Of the 42 burglary investigations on which I accompanied a Burglary detective, only three were cleared. One of these was considered big, and that was only because an arson was involved and the suspect characterized as a "real criminal" (i.e., an adult who was believed to continue committing crimes). The other two that were cleared involved juveniles, and nothing more than a warning was used. Later, through other investigations, an additional seven cases were cleared by other detectives who got cop outs from burglars in custody.

Retrospectively, several of the "little" burglaries came to be seen as having been part of a series of burglaries by a "big" burglar. One such case involved two burglaries, in each of which only one item was taken. Each burglary occurred in a house that was offered for sale by the same realtor, and it was suspected that someone who worked for the realtor was the burglar. After talking to one suspect, the Burglary detective decided there was no further reason for his pursuing the suspect and inactivated both cases. In a subsequent investigation of a burglary/fraud case, the same suspect was identified as the culprit and admitted in interrogation that he had committed several other crimes as well.

In other cases, especially burglaries of businesses where a great deal of property is taken, the case is seen from the outset as "potentially big." In the burglary of a sporting goods store, for example, an informant who was tangentially involved gave the names of suspects who were subsequently arrested. Using a search warrant, the detectives not only recovered property stolen from the sporting goods store but also recovered property (and saw other property that they did not confiscate) that was not on the warrant but appeared to be stolen (see case 101 below). Items typically taken in burglaries "appear to have been stolen" in the context of other items known to be stolen. The detectives went through their records of old cases looking for descriptions of property matching the property they had recovered or seen, and then obtained a search warrant for this new property as well. In the second raid, on which I accompanied them, the detectives invited the local television station to send a crew to film their activities. The following television report of the raid was aired, making this a truly "big" case.

CASE 101

ANN: Property from burglars operating in the Mountainbeach and Northside area was seized this afternoon by sheriff detectives, and three brothers were rearrested on suspicion of burglary. This brings to a total of some ten arrests and $8,000 worth of stolen property recovered this week following a month-long investigation by the Sheriff's Department. The three brothers, Mac, Harry, and Pete Smith, all between the ages of 18 and 21, were arrested on burglary-related charges and released on bail. After obtaining a search warrant, detectives went to the Smith residence where they made today's seizure and rearrested the brothers on additional burglary-related charges. Sergeant Gomez of the sheriff's Burglary Detail talked to QUSV's Horace Nell about today's seizures.

SGT: Well, the arrest was based on a search warrant and the information we had previously developed concerning the involvement by the two suspects that we presently have in custody. (The third was not in jail at the time.)

TVI: Are these thefts related to any other thefts that have been going on in the past month or two?

SGT: Yes, they are. We have definitely established on the basis of the inventory of property that we sus . . . that we have determined some involvement by the individuals in connection with numerous burglary offenses, both residential and vehicular.

TVI: What, what sort of property that you just mentioned is involved here and what value is placed on it?

SGT: Well the largest volume of property consists basically of stereo equipment, electronic. There have been some items of jewelry that was recovered, one in particular which is valued in excess of $1,000. We also found numerous automotive accessories and parts that have been established as being stolen from various business firms in Northside Valley.

Another feature of the case that was pointed to as providing its bigness was that the suspects did not cop out to the charges and were eventually sentenced to prison, even though it was the first offense for which they had been caught. Had they copped out to the charges as soon as they had been arrested and helped the detectives to clear a number of cases, it is unlikely that the case would have been seen to be as big as it was. No rearrest would have been made, no television crew would have been there to film the detectives loading up a truck with recovered property, and it is doubtful that the suspects would have been sent to prison. Without the cooperation of the suspects the case had to go to court, and this "going-to-court" aspect of the case also was taken as indicative of its importance. All in all, it was a big case in the sense that it permitted the detective to demonstrate his skills as a competent investigator (Skolnick, 1966).

A big burglary, then, derives the sense of bigness not solely from the type of burglary reported but rather from what the burglary and burglar are seen to have been all along after "all the facts are in." The "facts," in turn, receive their specific sense in the context of the case. The "fact" of a routine burglary report is later seen "really" to have been part of a series of burglaries, and at the same time is used to document a chain in that series.

For Burglary a "little" case has a texture different from a big case in several respects. If the details of the amount and nature of the property lost and the way in which the burglary is believed to have occurred point to a "routine" burglary, final judgment as to what kind of case it is will be suspended until later. Any one of the burglaries that made up the big case just described probably constituted a routine burglary. However, for a case to be seen as a little case from the outset, when the sergeant is deciding whether or not to assign a detective to work the case, a different scheme of interpretation provides the sense of the details reported. For example, the following case was received by the Burglary Detail, and while some work was done (i.e., a telephone call), the case was seen as little:

CASE 12

A woman reported that someone had taken 31 cents worth of popcorn from her home, and she named her babysitter as a possible suspect. The sergeant showed everyone the report and they all thought it was funny. A detective telephoned the "victim" and told her that he would contact the suspect and see what could be done about it. Other than that, no investigative time was spent on the case.

Another case received involved a stolen "Ding Dong," a small, cupcake-like pastry, and it, too, received no investigative efforts, for not only was the item seen to be unimportant, but it was also not the kind of thing a "real" burglar would take. Therefore, it was unlikely to constitute "one in a series" of burglaries.

Stolen Property

A characterization given to the object of most burglaries is "stolen property." That something is either "stolen" or "property" is a thoroughly accomplished sense provided through interpretive work. The victim claims that various objects have been stolen, and the objects are listed, described, and filed away by the detectives. However, the property that is claimed to have been stolen may have been hidden by the victim, who later puts in a claim to his insurance company. By checking with the sheriff's office, the insurance company can verify that the property was at least reported as stolen. Detectives realize that this may be happening on any given burglary, but their suspicions are suspended when working a case, for otherwise it would be impossible to maintain the sense of either stolen property or a burglary. A reported burglary is generally treated as bona fide, and what the victim claims as stolen property is maintained as such on a property report.

Unlike rapists, murderers, and vandals, burglars may be linked with their crime through their possession of the stolen property, at least until they dispose of it. Those who receive the stolen property are guilty of another crime (possession of stolen property), but they also serve as leads in a case, for they can tell the detectives where they got the property. Most receivers of stolen property are friends or acquaintances of the burglar, pawnshops and professional fences (cf. Klockars, 1974), or people who buy goods from burglars or fences.

Since the detectives have no control over fences or friends and acquaintances who receive stolen property directly from the burglar, they concentrate on those social outlets and receiving points where they do have some control. Pawnshops are required to have anyone who sells or pawns goods to fill out and sign a ticket describing the goods and listing his name, address, and driver's license number. By matching these tickets against stolen property, detectives are able to find some burglars. However, since, as we have pointed out, most stolen property is mass produced and hence difficult to identify, and most victims do not retain a record of their serial numbers, it is difficult to determine from the pawn tickets what items are stolen and what are not. If the same person's name shows up again and again as selling "typical stolen property," the items he sold will be checked against lists of property stolen, but even this more refined tatic rarely results in recovery. Strangers to the burglar sometimes receive stolen property in trading areas called "swap meets," "flea markets," or "penny markets"* (cf. Sundholm, 1973), generally held at drive-in theaters or open fields. In most cases they consist of people setting up tables to sell their "domestic surplus," a legitimate affair. The same settings, however, may serve as outlets for burglars who can peddle stolen property. Here, too, the police can (but rarely do) demand that receipts be given for property sold, so that if someone is found with stolen property and claims he bought it at a swap meet, the detectives can ask to see the receipt. Without such a receipt, there is little detectives can do to disprove the "buyer's" story without strong evidence to the contrary. Because the sellers at such gatherings cannot be expected to remember all the people to whom they sold their goods, or the buyers to remember from whom they bought things, the requirement of a receipt gives the detectives some measure of control. Periodic checks of the property sold at these gatherings is of little use since any of it could be found to be described as stolen. At the same time, the sellers see the inspectors coming and could hide these items until they left (Sundholm, 1973).

The requirement of record keeping at pawnshops and of receipts at swap meets has had another function in addition to being a help in identifying and locating stolen property. Some sort of receipt links both the seller and buyer with the property. If a buyer has a receipt that will tell from what seller he has bought the property, then the detectives can trace the property to the seller. In turn, the seller may have a legitimate account of

*In Europe and the Orient such gatherings are called "thieves markets."

how he came to have possession of the property. The claim that the property was purchased at a swap meet or pawnshop cannot be made without a receipt. Therefore, in those cases where detectives suspect stolen property, the receipt requirement serves to "spoil" accounts, and it becomes more difficult to have anonymous links between thieves and burglars and receivers of stolen property.

Checks and Forgery

There appear to be two basic approaches in working check and forgery cases. Cases involving stolen checks and credit cards are worked essentially in the same way as thefts and burglaries, with the exception that the stolen checks and credit cards are easier to trace back to their legitimate owners. Check cases where only fraud is involved, but no theft, burglary, or robbery was committed in obtaining the checks, are handled by the checks and forgery detective. Of the five cases I observed, four were cleared, and in all five cases eyewitnesses were available.

Theft and burglary cases involving checks are originally logged as 459 PC (burglary) or 484 PC (theft) and assigned to either the burglary or the theft detective. For example, the Burglary Detail detective I accompanied was given a report of a stolen check. He soon found that the check had been cashed at a local bank by a woman who was remembered and described by a teller. The detective located an acquaintance of the victim, but the man refused to talk with him. His behavior was taken to be indicative of knowledge of the crime and culprit, and the detective continued on this assumption. He hoped that by finding the man's circle of friends, he could clear the case. (I left the Burglary Detail before this happened, and never learned what took place.)

In another case the victim signed an affidavit claiming that someone had stolen ten checks from him and cashed them. He said that he had paid the bank for all but one of these checks. A detective who knew the victim (as a petty criminal) from a previous assignment worked the case. First, he found that the victim had moved to another address in another county. He suspected that since the victim's handwriting and that of the "forger" were the same, a false crime may have been reported. The following are notes of the conversation between the detective and the victim/suspect:

DET: Now listen, Harry, I've been working check cases for a long time, and these two signatures are the same.

SUS: No, no, I told you.

DET: Come on Harry, don't shit us, let's straighten this out.

SUS: Yeah, yeah, I want to straighten this all out.

DET: You know what forgery can get you? Harry, listen, we're trying to give you a break. Were you ever in Mountainville at a swap meet?

SUS: No, no, never been there.

DET: But, Harry, the guy who got this check said that you or the guy who gave it to him drove away in *your* car!

SUS: Oh, yeah, somebody stole my car.

DET: For a day? Oh sure Harry, did you report it to the police?

SUS: No, I didn't. . . . Larry (his brother) told me not to pay it. But Larry . . . I want to straighten this all out, look (takes out his check book), how much is it I pay you?

The suspect paid the bank in cash for the amount of the check he said had been stolen, and the detectives let him go with a warning. In this case the detectives characterized the suspect as "incredibly stupid." His stupidity was documented by his story, which included his account of his car being stolen for a day, and his failure even to try to disguise his own signature. Because of this, as well as the detective's knowledge of the suspect's history of getting into trouble and always being caught, he was not seen as a "serious" criminal. Rather, he was viewed as a bungler who occasionally tried to commit crimes. The detective did not view this as a case where his work would be accomplished by making an arrest.

However, the case does serve to illustrate a frequent problem with reported cases of forged or stolen checks. Two such cases occurred during the time I accompanied the checks and forgery detective. In one case the "victim" was believed to have written the check for the "suspect" and then changed her mind and filed an affidavit that the check was stolen. By comparing the "forged check" with a sample of the "victim's" handwriting, the detective decided that they were written by the same person. The following interview with the victim/suspect reflected this suspicion:

CASE 108

DET: Is this your personal check?

SUS: Uh huh.

DET: Did you write that check?

SUS: Nope.

DET: Did you authorize anyone to write that check?

SUS: Uh huh (shakes head).

DET: At no time?

SUS: No time. . . .

DET: I'm going to read this to you and I want you to read along with me.

SUS: O.K.

DET: This is a specified warning. It's a warning of your rights. Number one, it says you have the right to remain silent. Number two, anything you say can and will be used against you in a court of law. You have the right to talk to a lawyer and have him present with you while you are being questioned. Number four, if you cannot afford to hire a lawyer, one will be appointed to represent you before any questioning if you wish one, and that's free of charge.

SUS: Uh huh.

DET: O.K., waiver. Do you understand each of these rights I've explained to you?

SUS: Yeah.

DET: Beg your pardon?

SUS: Yeah.

DET: Will you circle "yes" and initial right above it? (Victim/suspect puts her initial next to "yes.") O.K. what I'm going to talk to you about is this check of yours. A check of Skeeter Swift.

SUS: Skeeter Swift? Huh.

DET: Right. The check is his. I also want to talk to you about its being stolen and forged.

SUS: Er, ahh, well.

DET: Having these rights in mind do you wish to talk to me now?

SUS: Uh huh, sure.

DET: O.K., will you circle "yes" and initial it please. An' over there where it says, "print name of person warned" will you print your full name?

SUS: Uh huh.

DET: O.K., where it says, "date and the time" will you put 4:20. And the date will be 5-8-73. Now "the above is true," I need your signature there. Now I'm goin' to give you a copy of it. An' here's your copy of it.

SUS: O.K.

DET: Now at any time during this conversation, you suddenly desire you no longer wish to discuss the matter with me, all you have to do is say so. O.K., now let's go back to this particular check. Now this is check number 500. Now you say you did not issue this check? Nor did you give anyone permission to write this check? Is that true?

SUS: That's true.

DET: Do you remember an affidavit of a forgery you signed?

SUS: Uh huh.

DET: That one right there?

SUS: Uh huh.

DET: Did you check the handwriting on here compared to the handwriting on here?

SUS: Yeah, I've noticed how very close it is.

DET: Very close.

SUS: Uh huh.

DET: It's so close it's unbelievable.

SUS: Uh huh.

DET: C's, the way the C's break straight down. The O's, the way you cross your T's.

SUS: Uh huh.

DET: An' then on your B's, the way your B's come up.

SUS: Mm huh.

DET: Your C's come up and drop down, come up and drop down, the same here. The A breaks off the same way. (The detective goes on to point out a number of similarities between the girl's handwriting and the handwriting on the allegedly forged check.)

SUS: I can see it. Y'know I can see your point, but I still didn't write it.

DET: You did not write this check?

SUS: No way.

The detective continued questioning the victim/suspect, but she insisted that she had not written the check. After the interview, the detective said he believed the girl to be stupid for denying an "obvious" attempt on her part and to continue claiming her innocence. Later, however, the man who had passed the check copped out to forging it, and the girl's story was retrospectively seen to have been true all along.

An interesting aspect of the interview was that the detective established from the beginning that the girl was a suspect, and he did so by reading the *suspect* her rights. The ritual of "reading the rights" serves a number of functions. Besides fulfilling the legal requirement to advise suspects of their rights before questioning, it also formalizes the seriousness of the detective's intentions and tells a person that he or she is a suspect. It is a quasi-commitment move on the part of the detective, defining his relationship with the suspect, which in this case changed from detective-victim to detective-suspect. The sense of "we don't read people their rights unless we're sure they're guilty" or "we've got the evidence" is communicated to the suspect so that he will give up and cop out. In this case the detective told the girl that he believed her to be a liar, and the fact that he read the rights to her was indicative of a commitment to his belief.

Equally interesting in this case was the use of the handwriting comparison to "prove" that the girl was lying. The sense of her lying was used to elaborate the sense that the handwriting samples were the work of the same person. The retrospective reading of the check writer as being "a pro" or a skilled forger would be used to point to differences between the handwriting samples, while the reading of the samples under the theme "she's lying" pointed to similarities.

A final case worth considering involved two acquaintances. The "victim" claimed that her friend took one of her checks and forged her signature. It is not illegal for a person to write a check-owner's signature if the owner has given his permission. The problem in this case was whether or not the girl who wrote and cashed the check had received permission to use the other girl's signature. The detective did not know which to believe, for the two girls told different stories, and neither story appeared incredible. When the detective went to see the victim a second time, he began the interview in an importantly different way:

CASE 109

DET: Now, Cindy's story differs quite a bit from yours, right now. Her contention is . . . that you also gave her permission to sign the check.

VIC: Well.

DET: You did not give her permission to sign it?

VIC: Uh uh.

DET: And your contention is still the same, that this check, the one I showed you before, to "Shoreside Body," check number 162 is in fact a forgery, and you did not sign it nor did you give anyone permission to sign it?

VIC: No.

DET: And you're willing to go to court to testify to this effect?

VIC: (Nods affirmatively)

Instead of accepting the suspect's story and beginning the interview with a reading of the rights (and thereby committing himself), the detective simply told the victim that the suspect had offered a different account. He reviewed the victim's statement with her, and she stayed with it. The questioning that followed was an attempt by the detective to find something that would lead him to believe one story or the other. At the end of the interview he appeared to believe the victim, but was still unsure.

Check cases are not only more likely to have suspects than straight burglaries; they are more likely to be formulated as involving some larceny on the part of the victim. As was pointed out, apparent burglary cases may be attempts to defraud insurance companies, but during the research period no burglary victims were ever openly suspected of having reported falsely so as to make insurance claims. However, in three of the five check cases I followed, the people who reported the crime came to be suspects. A person reporting a burglary has the same opportunity for false report as do people who report check forgeries. The difference between burglary and forgery investigations appears to be not in the "nature" of the crime or the reporting victim but, rather, in the detectives' formulation of typified acts and actors. Thus if investigators reformulated their typifications of the crimes, then no matter what the "nature" of the crime, their assumptions about victims and suspects would change.

CONCLUSION

Unlike the Juvenile and Major Crimes Details, Burglary has little variation in the cases it receives. The routine of burglary investigations is based on assumptions the detectives have about the typical burglary—namely, that there are no leads and no witnesses, and therefore it's a waste of time to work any single burglary. The detectives hope that sooner or later a burglar will be identified via one of their networks of information, and at that time can be persuaded to admit to other unsolved burglaries on which little or no investigative time has been spent. When they do get a burglary with leads or an informant, they spend real investigative efforts on it, in the hope not only of solving this one case but also, if the burglar is caught, of being able to clear several other burglaries at the same time. However, the routine method of handling what is seen as a routine burglary is simply to contact the victim and inactivate the case, waiting for the burglar to be caught in another information snare.

With forged check cases, on the other hand, there is always the possibility of an eyewitness or of something that can be developed as associative evidence to link the suspect with the bad check. Further, in view of the many "victims" of forged check cases who turn out to be suspect themselves, even if there are no apparent leads in a forgery case, the detective can begin developing information on the "victim." As a result, in the Burglary Detail check-forgery cases are seen almost always to "have" information, and burglaries are seen almost never to "have" information. As a consequence, virtually every check-forgery case is given a thorough investigation, and most burglaries only a perfunctory one, not necessarily because either type of crime intrinsically "has" more or less information, but because the detectives *assume* they do at the outset.

8

The Major Crimes Detail

On the way down to the detective's office the radio announced that there had been an armed robbery out on Hollinstead. A gas station had been hit, and I supposed that one of the detectives would be there by the time I got downtown. Nothing much had been happening in Major Crimes since they had finished up with a beach rape case other than the usual reports of obscene phone calls, disturbing the peace, and other small stuff, so I was looking forward to a little action. When I got downtown, Bill Burke was starting out to investigate the gas station robbery, so I got to go along. Normally Bill Rob would be working this one, but he had to be in court, so the sergeant gave it to Burke.

When we got to the gas station, the deputy was still there, trying to talk to the gas-station attendant. The guy was shaking, and his face was bloodless. Before he began questioning the victim, Bill asked the deputy what he had found and learned that all the victim could say was that the robber had a gun that looked like a Luger and that as the robber left, the attendant had put his hand on the getaway car.

The attendant told Bill that he couldn't leave the gas station to talk with him, so they called the man's wife to take over while he was being questioned. When she got there, after she had finished comforting her husband, Bill took the victim over to the car to interview him. Bill sat in front with the victim and I sat in back and took notes.

Bill began by explaining to the man that he understood why someone would be upset after being robbed, but it was necessary for him to regain composure so that Bill could get all the

165

*information necessary to catch the robber. The victim began
haltingly to answer the questions. Bill asked him to describe
what had happened and kept going over the story until he felt he
had every detail the victim could remember. He asked who
would know the routine, especially the fact that more cash would
be on hand on Mondays than usual. Then he questioned the
victim in detail about the robber's description. Age? Moustache
or sideburns? Hat? Coat? Buttoned or open? Color of clothes?
Describe gloves—old or new? Color? Design? Glasses? Race?
"He was Caucasian. I could tell because he had a New York
accent." (The robber had dark glasses covering his eyes and a
wool cap pulled over his head.)*

*He then went into the same detail on the getaway car. Make?
How big was the back window? Was it clean or dirty? What type
of dirt? ("It was just dirty.") How did the engine sound? ("All
VW's sound alike.") Were there any bumper stickers or decals in
the rear window? Discoloration? Luggage rack? Tail lights?
Small? Large? ("I don't remember seeing below the back window.")*

*When these questions were finished, Bill asked the victim if
he would be able to recognize the man again (he thought he
might). Then he asked about employees and former employees.
Was anyone fired lately? Is there a list of current and former
employees? Is there anyone else who would know that you'd
have $1,600 today when you usually have $25 to $75 in the
drawer? ("Anyone who worked here, I suppose.")*

*Bill knew one of the former employees from his work in
narcotics, and he knew another who had been the victim in a
similar robbery. Both were possible suspects. Bill gave the
victim some forms to fill out describing everything he had told
him in the interview and said he'd be back later to pick them up.
Then we left.*

*On the way back to the office, we drove past the house where
one of the former employees lived, hoping to find a green
Volkswagen with a handmark on the left rear fender where the
gas station attendant had touched it. We didn't find one.*

*After lunch we went back to the gas station to pick up the
forms the victim had been given to fill out, but the guy wasn't
there. The man at the station said he'd be back later, and Bill
said we'd return then. As we left, a call went out that a burglary
alarm had gone off near where we were, so we went to that.*

Later, going back into town, Bill spotted a green VW with a couple of guys in it that fit the ballpark description we had. They were going in the opposite direction, so we had to go about a block before we could turn around. We lost the car in traffic because of this move so Bill called a BOL (be on the lookout) on it. By chance Bill Rob had also suspected the car and was tailing it, but he had his radio turned off so that the suspects couldn't hear it if he had to pull up next to them, so he didn't hear the BOL. Then a black and white unit (patrol car) spotted the car in the Beachcliff area and stopped it for a field interrogation. By the time we got there the black and white unit, Bill Rob, and several foot patrolmen were on the scene.

On the left rear fender was a handprint similar to the one described by the victim, but the car's two occupants did not fit the description of the robber. However, since victims are often inaccurate in their descriptions, these two guys were close enough. After questioning them for a while, the detectives decided they were innocent and let them go, even though they recorded their license plate and checked out their registration before springing them.

We took a break for coffee and then went back to the gas station. The victim still hadn't come back, so we went back to the office. By then it was 4:30, so Howard and I called it a day and went home.

ORGANIZATION AND ROUTINES IN MAJOR CRIMES

The Major Crimes Detail was considered the elite unit in the Detective Bureau. The crimes worked by this unit were regarded as important, and, as we pointed out earlier, the status of a detective was linked to the status of the crimes he investigated. The unit was composed of four detectives and a sergeant, but one of the detectives, the coroner's investigator, was not an integral part of the unit. He would be called in on a homicide, but he would not play a central role in the search for a suspect and did not participate in the same routines as the others in the unit. Thus, in discussing the Major Crimes Detail, the coroner's detective will be excluded for the most part, and we will concentrate on the three investigators and their sergeant.

Sergeant Rogers was the youngest sergeant in the Detective

Bureau and was seen by most of the other detectives as the best man in an administrative position. He was aware of the special skills and individual temperaments of his men. Rogers did not tell his men how to carry out an investigation, but if they asked his advice about an aspect of a case, he would willingly give it. Each of the three detectives who worked under his command had special abilities which he recognized, and unless it was absolutely necessary he would never assign one man a case that was considered another man's specialty. Bill Burke specialized in homicides, Bill Rob in rapes and robberies, and Roger Fine in explosives, chemicals, and arson. These areas of abilities had been developed in special training each man had received as well as through their experience in handling cases.

The pace of the work in the Major Crimes Detail was unlike either Burglary or Juvenile in several important aspects. First, in the part of Mountainbeach under the jurisdiction of the sheriff's office, there were relatively few crimes that warranted a Major Crimes investigation. In Burglary and Juvenile there was a daily influx of new cases to be investigated by the detectives, whereas in Major Crimes, sometimes weeks would pass before a "good case" would come to their attention. (In this context a "good case" was a homicide, rape, robbery, kidnapping, or some other spectacular crime.) Second, the pace of the work differed from the other details in the amount of time that would be devoted to a single case. In Burglary and Juvenile the detectives would make only a few contacts before they would inactivate a case, whereas the Major Crimes detectives would work for days, weeks, or months on the same case even if there was only a slim chance it would be solved.

If we examined the "statistics" of the Major Crimes Detail, we would see a great number of cases being investigated. The following table represents a report submitted to the lieutenant showing the "work" received by Major Crimes over a four-month period:

CRIMES PER BEAT

MONTH	1	2	3	4	5	6	7	8
July	2	5	18	14	15	2	19	9
Aug.	8	10	13	10	14	12	13	24
Sept.	3	3	14	13	13	9	14	8
Oct.	9	9	17	15	15	8	15	10

Of all of these cases received by Major Crimes, only a few were investigated. On any given day, a number of cases considered to be "crimes against persons" would be pulled (taken out of the incoming batch of reports for reveiw) by the Major Crimes sergeant, but it was unlikely that any of the cases pulled would be investigated. For example, the following 11 cases were pulled by major crimes one day (January 24) out of a batch of about 50 cases received by the Detective Bureau:

1. 415 PC (disturbing the peace)
2. 288a PC (oral copulation—forced)
3. 415 PC, 12600 HS (firecrackers)
4. 415 PC (barking dog)
5. 23110a CVC (throwing objects from a vehicle)
6. Domestic dispute
7. 602 WIC/415 PC (juvenile disturbing the peace)
8. 597 PC (cruelty to animals—follow-up report)
9. 653m PC (obscene phone call)
10. 415 PC (loud band)
11. 245b PC (assault with a deadly weapon on peace officer: arrest).

Only one of these 11 cases would typically be investigated; to understand why, it is necessary to review discretionary patterns and the working policy in Major Crimes for choosing cases to investigate. In other studies of police dsicretion the focus has been on the situation where the crime occurred (Piliavin and Briar, 1964; Black and Reiss, 1970) or on general understandings about what is expected of the police by the community (LaFave, 1965); however, these studies have been concerned with decision making by patrol officers who are making up their minds what to do with a person who has broken the law. Almost nothing has been written on the discretionary practices employed by detectives (Pepinsky, 1975, p. 27), and we find when we do look at detectives that their discretion is based not so much on whether or not to make an arrest but on whether or not to investigate a case.

In the Major Crimes Detail, the sergeant explained that there were three categories of cases. The first consisted of crimes that would invariably be worked. Included in this category were homicide, attempted homicide, rape, robbery, kidnapping, arson (suspected arson), plus an assortment of other serious but rarely reported crimes, such as bribing an official. Second was a group of crimes that were never worked, and in general these were the bulk of the cases pulled by major crimes. The most ubiquitous of these was a 415 (disturbing the peace). This could be anything from a barking dog to a vicious family fight (known as a 415 domestic). Since the crime was against persons instead of against property, it was given to the Major Crimes Detail. Nonserious crimes that were also never worked included most vehicle violations, suspicious person reports, and other petty offenses.

The final category of offenses were those that would sometimes be investigated, depending on the characteristics of the case itself. For example, the detectives explained that obscene phone calls were often made by people who know the victim or by kids who were seen as "goofing off." Since they did not consider the harm done in these cases to be great or to have a dangerous potential, the detectives did not regard them as worth spending time with. However, every now and then they would get a persistent caller who was not a child or known to the victim. In one case, noted previously, a man called his victims and began by inquiring, "Is your pussy hairy?" This caller became identified by his opener, and he was considered to be dangerous or at least "sick." After several reports on this particular caller, Major Crimes did begin an investigation, but it was because of the special characteristics of the case, not because of the type of crime.

Similarly, investigation of battery cases would be pursued only if the victim made an effort to convince the detectives that the culprit should be brought to justice. Usually the detectives assumed that batteries were minor fights, with the victim deciding that the person who hit him should not be tracked down by the police. Assault was considered a more serious offense, but, as with batteries, the detectives assumed that after a day or so all would be forgiven. Unless the victim insisted that his assailant be brought in, the detectives would not waste their time with an investigation.

Given this priority ranking, we would expect that it would be fairly simple to predict what crimes would be investigated and which would not. In general this was the case, and in fact the sergeant sometimes gave the incoming reports to the researcher and asked him to determine which ones should be given investigative attention. It was during these occasions that I discovered how the policy actually operated and learned that categorizing cases was an ongoing accomplishment, not a static social fact (Garfinkel, 1967).

Since it was understood what cases would always be worked and which would not, with the exception of those cases involving "borderline" crimes (e.g., obscene phone calls, batteries), the decision on working a case was in the formulation of the case as being of one type or another. If a case was established to be an instance of attempted murder then it would be worked, but if it was characterized as some kind of 415 it would not be worked. This was usually an automatic procedure since the type of each crime was logged by the penal code section pertaining to the actions in question. However, sometimes the detectives would reformulate the designation of a crime after looking at the report. This could involve seeing the circumstances surrounding the crime as being suspicious or phony, or simply pointing out that the case had been improperly catalogued by the reporting officer. If the case was a phony instance of a typically worked case, the policy would be maintained, since it was consistent with the policy to work only real crimes. Similarly, if the case was seen to be improperly titled, it would be treated in terms of the reformulated title, which again would be consistent with the discretion policy. For example, we showed how a report of an attempted murder was reformulated as a 415 domestic. Other cases, as we will see, are similarly reformulated in such a way that their original designation is changed—either from more serious to less serious or vice versa. In this way, through formulations and reformulations of the reported particulars in a case, all of the work done in the detail is made understandable as being consistent with the informal policy.

Now, going back to the 11 crimes received on January 24, we can understand why only one of the crimes was worked. Most of them were 415's of one type or another, and none of these were worked. The assault on the police officer needed no investigation since the suspect was already in jail, and the cruelty to animals case was a follow-up report, so it was already being given attention by someone. The report of throwing objects from a vehicle was an unusual case to be received by Major Crimes, and since it was considered to involve essentially a litterbug, no investigation was made. This leaves only the forced oral copulation case. This was formulated as a case of "rape," was investigated, and eventually ended in an arrest and trial.

Given this "discretionary attrition" of crimes to be investigated in Major Crimes, we can understand that the statistics generated by the detail are nothing more than an artificial mechanism for satisfying bureaucratic needs through impression management (Goffman, 1959). This is not to say that the detectives are goofing off, but rather they are allocating their resources to crimes formulated as being serious enough to follow through. The criterion for the seriousness of a crime is a commonsense evaluation of "what everybody knows" is serious, and not a special evaluation by the police.

The result of the pattern of selective investigations of crimes received by the Major Crimes Detail is the pace described above, wherein they are either fully involved in an investigation or doing nothing. The only observed change in the policy occurred after the research was completed and I returned to the office on a social visit. When I asked what was happening, I was told, "Things are so slow we're working obscene phone calls." Thus, if the pace is thrown off by especially inactive periods, some of the smaller crimes that are usually not investigated are given attention. However, if things become especially busy because numerous "workable" cases are received, the detectives do not ignore some of the lesser ones that they would normally investigate, but instead just work longer hours or even enlist help from the other details.

MAJOR CRIMES AND INFORMATION RESOURCES

In order to understand the patterns of investigations in the Major Crimes Detail, it is necessary to understand the different types of investigations, for the information work is linked to the characteristics of the crimes investigated. The feature of Major Crimes that is not typically found in crimes investigated in the Burglary and Juvenile Details is that the victim is also a witness to the crime. Moreover, the victim knows at the time of the crime that a crime is being committed. About the only instance where the victim faces the criminal in crimes investigated by the other detective units involves bad check cases, but at the time the check is issued, the victim is unaware that a crime is being committed, so no special attention is given the person passing the bad check. Similarly, shoplifting apprehensions are on the basis of the victim's seeing the crime, but shoplifting itself appears very much like normal shopping behavior, and shoplifters are typically caught by store employees or security forces, so detective investigations are usually not necessary.

However, when an armed robber pulls a knife or gun in a convenience store, the clerk knows that he is being robbed and knows that the person with the gun or knife is the robber. When the detectives investigate the case, they can begin developing information on the basis of an eyewitness description of the suspect, and can link this information with other information networks in their search for the suspect. Of course this is not true with homicides, since the victim cannot talk about the killer, or in arsons, where the arsonist, like a burglar, works unobserved. Nevertheless, in most major crimes the necessary information linking the suspect with the crime is much stronger than in any other type of crime. To understand the investigative procedures and patterns, we will examine various crimes and discuss their informative linkages in society. This will explain why detectives operate in the way they do, it will also tell us about the social arrangements of information.

Homicides

During the period of research there were few homicides, and most of the data on homicide investigations were developed in interviews with the homicide detective.* However, the few homicides which did occur during the period of observation, and those which were still being investigated during the research but which happened before the research started, provided the essential forms of homicides and homicide investigations.

Homicides are of two kinds from the point of view of the detectives. There are the killings where the suspect is caught quickly, and there are those where the detectives have no initial

*Other data were collected by researchers in the same department after our research was completed, and some of this research supplied information on homicide investigations. These other researchers, Clinton Terry and David Luckenbill, knew me and we shared data with each other.

notion of who killed the victim. The former are referred to as "walk-throughs" and the latter as "whodunits." These two characterizations of killings reflect the nature of the information linking the suspect to the victim. Fortunately for the detectives, most victims and killers know one another (Wolfgang, 1961; Luckenbill, 1973). Since the detectives operate under this assumption, the realm of possible suspects is severely limited, and they can focus their investigation around those people who know the victim. Other times, even in cases where the victim and suspect do not know one another, the killer will turn himself in, and the investigation is merely a matter of "walking through" the formalities of presenting the evidence to the prosecutor.

To illustrate the different forms of investigations in terms of the information development, we will examine different kinds of "walk-throughs" and "whodunits." First we will look at a number of different "walk-throughs" and compare them with "whodunits" investigated by the detectives.

CASE 68

Two foreign consuls were invited to a hotel in Mountain-beach to receive historical artifacts from their country's revolutionary past. When they arrived to receive the artifacts, they were shot and killed by the man who had promised the items. The killer then called the sheriff's office and reported what he had done. After they had arrested the man, the detectives began investigating the case to ensure that the confession was genuine and to make a case against the confessed suspect in the event that he changed his mind about his guilt. Additional pressure was applied by the attorney general and the president of the United States, since both victims were official representatives of a foreign country, and also by the F.B.I.

In that the identity of the suspect was known from the outset, the case was considered a "walk-through," but because of the status of the victims, a great deal of work had to be done to ensure prosecution. When I questioned the homicide detective during the investigation, I asked him if this were a "walk-through," and he said, "Yes, but . . . it's not going to be all that simple." Part of the problem was establishing a motive, and until the detectives pieced together an account of the killing (Scott and Lyman, 1968), they did not know how to proceed.

The initial confusion was marked by genuine puzzlement over why the suspect, a 78-year-old man, would do such a thing. The suspect explained that he was Armenian and when he was a child the Turks had killed his family; therefore, he was getting even. Given the history of the Turk's treatment of the Armenians and the fact that the Turkish consul and vice-consel were the murder victims, this account was satisfactory. The fact that the suspect did not know his victims was accounted for by this explanation, and even though it was an unusual homicide and account, it served to tie the events together.

Another form of "walk-through" occurs when the detectives know the killer, but are unsure whether the killing is justifiable. The following case illustrates this type of investigation:

CASE 107

At a campsite, a man shot and killed a youth. During the investigation it was unclear whether the shotgun which killed the youth had gone off accidentally, had been intentionally fired in self-defense, or had been fired intentionally not in self-defense. Accounts by the witnesses were conflicting, but it was apparent that the victim had attempted to steal a camp-stove from the killer, and had returned to the campsite after having been run off by the man who ultimately killed him. Eventually the detectives decided the case was one of justifiable homicide and released the suspect.

Here again the detectives were faced with a case in which they had the homicide suspect in custody, and there was no question who did the killing. However, the victim and the killer were unknown to one another before the killing, and the circumstances surrounding the killing were equivocal. The information to be developed was not in terms of the suspect's identity but of his intentions in the context of the interaction that preceded the killing. Since the information did not center on the identity of the suspect, it was treated as a "walk-through."

The most common type of "walk-through" involves killings where the victim and killer are known to one another. One of the most common settings for this type of murder is the home of the victim and/or killer, and the following example illustrates one case investigated by the Mountainbeach detectives:

THE ROBB CASE*

At approximately six in the morning, the victim arose and started to make coffee. He returned to the living room, where he had been sleeping on the couch. Shortly thereafter an argument occurred between the victim and his wife over a banking matter. He became quite hostile and argumentative. His wife recounts that he "came swinging at me," but she was not struck. She asked him to calm down, but he continued toward her. She backed out of the kitchen and proceeded down the hall to the bedroom. Reaching the dresser, she pulled a .38 caliber revolver out of the drawer. She pointed the gun at her husband and it went off.

After the shot, the victim asked, "Why did you do that?" He turned and walked down the hall to the kitchen. She followed. He tried to sit down, but fell backward through the door onto the porch. Mrs. Robb then drove to the house of friends. She told them what happened, and they phoned the sheriff's department.

In such cases, the relationship between killer and victim serves to inform the detectives whom to look for. Detectives generally assume that some relationship exists between homicide victims and the killer and therefore typically begin homicide investigations by interviewing friends, relatives, and acquaintances of the victim. When no such link exists or when no one comes forth to confess a killing, the case is no longer seen as a "walk-through" and becomes a "whodunit." Thus, the extent to which a victim is connected to the killer in a conventional relationship suggests and defines one kind of investigation and information network.

In the detective office where this study was conducted, the homicide investigator appeared to be plagued by unusual and difficult murder cases. None of the homicides during the research period were the simple "walk-throughs" which constitute the bulk of the murders detectives investigate (illustrated in the Robb case). A number of cases still being investigated

*This example is from W. Clinton Terry III and David F. Luckenbill, "Investigating Criminal Homicides," in *Criminal Justice Process,* ed. William B. Sanders and Howard C. Daudistel (New York: Praeger, 1976), pp. 79–95. This case occurred shortly after the research reported in this study had been concluded. The name "Robb" is a pseudonym.

during the research were "whodunits." Even though one of these was "solved," the killer was never caught, and the rest of the cases were still open when the research was concluded.

The central characteristic of a "whodunit" is the lack of obvious relationship between victim and killer. Relationships serve as starting points in an investigation, and without this information, the development of information leading to a homicide suspect is extremely difficult. In the case of the killings of the two Turkish diplomats, had the killer not turned himself in, the detectives would have been unlikely to see the relationship between the old man and the two men he killed. The relationship (Armenian vs. Turks) was not a conventional one in the context of homicide investigations in Mountainbeach. Random killings of blacks in the South can be linked to such organizations as the Ku Klux Klan, and southern police detectives can "see" the obvious connection between the victim and the Klan, giving them a starting point for an investigation. But in situations where no obvious relationships exist, the detectives have to develop other connections.

One of the best examples of a whodunit occurred some 12 years before the research had begun but was "solved" during the period of research. The following excerpt from my field notes provides the elements of the case:

LOG 23*

The homicide investigator had been in San Francisco talking with some detectives there about an old case he had been looking into in his spare time. In 1961 two high school seniors, a girl and a boy, had been found shot to death in a shack near the beach. The girl's bathing suit had been cut away, her face covered with a handkerchief, and her body dumped on top of her boyfriend. Some evidence had been found, but since during the original investigation much evidence had been destroyed, there was little to go on. From the details supplied by the Mountainbeach detective, the San Francisco investigators said it sounded like the work of the "Zodiac" killer for whom they had been searching. ("Zodiac" is the name employed by a west coast killer who wrote letters to the police and newspapers boasting of his exploits, much like London's "Jack the Ripper.")

---

*Details of the information have been intentionally excluded since the case is still open and the "Zodiac" has not been caught.

Given this information, the Mountainbeach detective began reviewing the "Zodiac" cases and found a number of similarities between the beach murders and the "Zodiac" murders. Taking this set of leads, the detective was able to establish a strong case pointing to the "Zodiac" as the killer.

Since the police were never able to establish a conventional relationship between the "Zodiac" killer and his victims, they had no social map with which to trace his identity. The Mountainbeach homicide detective attempted to locate the identity of "Zodiac" through a branch of the military service, since one of the shoeprints found at the crime scene was linked to the type the military issued. However, the military is a large organization, and delimiting suspects to this population, while helpful, is not enough to isolate a single individual. Compared to the number of people who are acquaintances, friends, or relatives of a murdered individual, who may be likely suspects in a homicide investigation, the military organization is enormous. Thus, without some informative link in the more primary relationships, an investigation is opened to a larger and less manageable universe of inquiry, making the task of identifying the suspect that much more difficult.

Robberies

Robbery, as defined by the Penal Code of California (see p. 92), provides circumstances which almost necessitate some kind of identification by the victim. Unlike burglary and theft, where the culprit is typically unseen during the commission of the crime, the victim in a robbery knows that the person who is forcefully taking his money or other belongings is the criminal. As a result, the detectives can begin their investigation with questions about the robber's appearance, the timing of the crime, the route of escape, and other factors that place the detectives close to the robber's identity.

Unlike "walk-throughs" in homicide investigations, the detectives do not assume any primary relationship between the victim and the robber. Their strategies in robberies revolve around quick response to the alarm of a robbery and identification of either the robber himself or his car from the description provided by the victim. If the robber's description can be broadcast soon enough, then the patrol units can join in the search, but in these cases the investigation is more a patrol function than detective work.

If the robber is wearing some sort of mask, there is little for a detective to follow based on a witness' description. A nylon stocking worn over the head of a bank robber not only contorts the robber's face into a fiendish apparition which is unidentifiable, but it also serves to frighten a teller into turning over the money. Similarly, use of a stolen car taken only for the purpose of committing a crime leaves detectives without a vehicle to trace in the event that a witness takes note of the license-plate numbers.

For the criminal, however, a mask gives away his intentions; observation of a man with a Halloween mask, as in the famous Brinks robbery, gives an alarm to the intended victim or potential witnesses to the crime, including the police (Goffman, 1971). If a robber takes a stolen car for the purposes of misleading the police, he runs the risk of being caught for driving a stolen car before he commits the robbery. Thus, the robber's problem is to appear unidentifiable and at the same time unnoticed.

To illustrate the problem for the robber, a matter basic to dramaturgic manipulation, we will consider some of the cases where masking was used in robberies. The first case is one of poor impression management which led to a quick arrest:

CASE 60

A 16-year-old honor student was arrested for robbing a grocery store shortly after the robbery. When he committed the robbery he wore a fake beard and moustache which did not match his hair, and a customer coming into the store noticed the boy and took the license number of his car. When he was caught, he admitted the robbery and led the officers to a trash bin where he had disposed of the beard and gun, which was realistic toy model of a .38 caliber pistol. In an earlier attempt, a few days before, he wore a ski mask to rob a bar, but when he entered the bar two women laughed at him and remarked, "Here comes the phantom," which was enough to unnerve the boy.

The clumsy attempts by the 16-year-old point to the necessity for attending to the staging of public appearances which will not draw unwanted attention to oneself (Sacks, 1972). In contrast with the 16-year-old, the robber of a gas station was able to conceal his identity without appearing to be wearing a mask. He wore a navy blue watchcap over his head to cover his hair and large dark glasses to hide his eyes and part of his face, gloves to cover his hands, and a bulky jacket to hide his build. The fact that the robber chose the blue watchcap to cover his hair points to two dramaturgical insights. First, the cap is fairly common in Mountainbeach, and while another type of cap or hat may have been noticeable, no one would take a second glance at a man in a watchcap. Second, watchcaps are elastic enough to cover or encompass all different hair styles, and so a man with long hair could tuck it under the cap and look as if he had shorter hair. None of the usual identification and universe-narrowing features could be easily or accurately described because of the mask, the mask itself did not draw attention, and all of the masking devices could be easily changed.

Another concern for the detectives in their search for robbery suspects is identifying the robber's M.O. Unlike burglary investigations, where the main use of the M.O. is to identify a single person and possibly clear other unsolved cases, robbery detectives attempt to establish an M.O. in order to catch the robbers in the act. In one series of robberies described earlier, the detectives first learned that two men working either together or alone were robbing small markets. They noted that the robberies followed a temporal order based on the amount of money taken in the previous robbery. That is, if the robber or robbers got $200 in a "score" they would make their next hit four days later. From this observation the detectives concluded that the robbers were junkies who had a combined $50-a-day habit. With this information, they organized stake-outs on the basis of the takes in the robberies and the types of places robbed. Eventually, using this method, they were able to catch the robbers in the act.

This method of looking for robbers points to the use of the detectives' assumptions about social arrangements and social structure. The detectives centered their search on a possible pattern (drug addiction) that would account for both robbers' activities in society (i.e., junkies) for someone of their age and ethnic background (early 20's, Chicano). Other possibilities were not entirely ruled out, but knowing what they did, the detectives would have been surprised to find that the robbers were spending the money in any other way. The cost of living, at the time of the study and in the locale where it was carried out, did not require that much to survive, even comfortably, except for those with a legitimate life style that bordered on the upper class, or those who were supporting an expensive habit. Excluding the former possibility because of the assumptions they made about the age and ethnic background of the suspects (i.e., young Chicanos are more likely to come from a poor background and to be junkies), the detectives used the latter and eventually were able to prove their hypothesis. Obviously, there are other conclusions that might be reached, but the point is that the detectives employed sociological analysis to reach the one they did, and their need to employ knowledge of the social structure (e.g., social class distribution and opportunity) was a typical feature of their investigations.

Rapes

In rape investigations, as in robberies, the victim is the major witness. Otherwise they have few similarities, because of the problematic features of the rape laws and requirements for evidence.

Unlike most crime victims, the rape victim is accorded a deviant status in society, even more so than the rapist (Brownmiller, 1975, p. 346). Men are expected to be aggressive in sexual relations and women are expected to be passive, but not willing. The rapist's behavior is in line with male role expectations (excluding gallantry); the woman's is not. She is asked by others, either directly or through innuendo, whether she enjoyed the experience, or even encouraged it. If she did nothing in the eyes of others to encourage the rape and was obviously injured, then she may be pitied. She is still stigmatized, like the leper who is not responsible for his condition but nevertheless still has the stigma (Goffman, 1963). The status of the "innocent deviant" is accorded those like her who have been, through no fault of their own, thrown into circumstances from which they have emerged scarred—socially, psychologically, and sometimes physically. If, on the other hand, others see the victim as being in some way a cause for rape, she is seen as a "responsible deviant" and deserving of the stigma. Women who are raped while hitchhiking or while wearing an outfit that is deemed "enticing" are generally considered partially, if not wholly, responsible for what happened. They are not pitied in their stigmatization since they are believed to have "had it coming."

Whatever the type of deviant status, it is the victim, not the rapist, who suffers the most. The "innocent" and "responsible" deviant labels are *both* stigmatized statuses, and the "responsible" characterization is usually an unfair one, for hitchhiking or an enticing appearance do not constitute "asking for it." That would be like saying banks asked to be robbed because they keep money. What is important is that virtually all women's moral characters are questioned when they are raped, and, given this state of affairs, the victim attempts to minimize other's knowledge of her rape. For this reason many rapes go unreported (Ennis, 1967); when they are reported, the victims are often reluctant to go into detail or to give the detectives information that may involve others they know. As a result, rape investigations become an exercise in delicate social interaction.

For the detectives, solving a rape is a good notch for their careers since rapists are viewed as "real criminals," and their behavior is taken to be violent and dangerous. Therefore, it is important for a detective to work to solve a case of rape, regardless of what he may think of the victim's moral character. Some detectives hold sexist points of view (e.g., the victim deserved to be raped), but these attitudes are irrelevant in that they do not affect the fact that a detective's career path is paved with the successful investigation of serious crimes, and typically his career is more important than certain attitudes. During the course of the research several victims were of questionable moral character (judging from their past behavior and criminal records), but their cases were pursued the same as any other rape case. For example, in one case where the victim was attacked on the beach and raped, the detectives learned that the girl had a record of heroin use, and even though she had quit her habit, she was still considered to be less than a "good girl." Her case was nevertheless pursued until the rapist was caught and convicted. In another case, where a girl was raped by a motorcycle gang, the defense attorney pictured the victim as a "slut," and by the conventional standards of the community and from the point of view of the detectives she certainly fit the characterization. The detectives, however, spent half a year working the case until they developed evidence to find and convict the gang.

For the most part, the problems in rape cases involve establishing a case as an actual rape and getting the victim to supply the information necessary to make an investigation. These two problems are interrelated, since part of establishing a case is developing information that the case was a "righteous" (actual) rape. The following case illustrates this problem and at the same time shows how it was resolved interactionally:

CASE 113*

A patrolman I was accompanying was called to make an investigation of a reported rape. When the patrolman arrived at a nearby hospital, he found the victim, nine months pregnant, with cuts on her right cheek and left forearm. She said that a man had followed her home from a bar, raped her, and cut her on the face and arm. A vaginal smear taken at the hospital confirmed the presence of semen. The woman's ex-husband was present at the hospital, had been in the bar shortly before the victim was assaulted, and knew the name of the man who had followed her home. The patrolman went to the crime scene, found the knife the victim said had been used to cut her, and noticed blood from the wounds on the bathroom sink. After this crime-scene investigation, the patrolman, along with backup units, arrested the suspect identified by the victim and named by her ex-husband.

When he was interrogated by the detectives at the police station, the suspect admitted having had intercourse with the woman, but denied that he had raped her. His account explained the act in terms of a threat by the victim. The victim's boyfriend was in jail, and she did not want him to know she had been unfaithful to him; since the suspect was a friend of the boyfriend, she was afraid he would tell. The suspect had told the victim that if her boyfriend asked, he would tell him the truth. At this point the victim said she would call the police and claim she had been raped. Since the account by the suspect fit all the information the patrolman had developed, it was taken to be possibly true. However, the

*This case was observed in a different agency in the same state.

detectives and patrolman did not accept this explanation as final. They gave both the victim and the suspect a polygraph (lie-detector) test. The "victim" was found to be lying. After this finding the woman said she had decided to drop the charges, and the case was closed.

In this case the patrolman and everybody else (medical examiners, friends, relatives of the victim) believed the woman's account at the outset of the investigation, and she was treated with respect and understanding. Nobody assumed that a woman would cut herself or voluntarily have intercourse at her stage of pregnancy, so the authenticity of her report was not questioned until after the arrest of the suspect. Once the police had determined she was lying, the information was retrospectively reread in terms of the new understanding of the "facts" in the case. The cuts were not deep, and the blood was smeared. A self-inflicted cut by a right-handed person would be on the right side of the face but on the *left* arm, never the right.

In the initial encounters with the victim, the police never suggested that she was not telling the truth and thereby risk interactional tension. Goffman (1961, p. 20) points out that the "frame" of an encounter is broken when a party attempts to impose one perspective when another is expected to dominate. Had the detectives or investigating officers initially accused the victim of not telling the truth, they would have broken the frame of the encounter by creating interactional tension, for they would have been introducing what would have been considered an inappropriate perspective. However, the police treated the victim as genuine, and it was not until they had arrested the suspected rapist that they began questioning the validity of the woman's story.

The importance of this lies in the fact that even though the detectives did not badger the victim from the outset, they were able to arrive at the truth. Had the victim been telling the truth, the police would have assisted *their own investigation* by treating her as though she were telling the truth, for they would have minimized interactional tension. Conversely, if the police had treated the victim as though she were lying, whether she was being truthful or not, they would have hampered their investigation. A lying victim would have been alerted early to their suspicions and would have been uncooperative in relating any story the police could check out. An honest victim would be equally uncooperative, for she might fear that the police were not going to do anything about her case or that they would try and blame the assault on her. Thus, in order to maximize the information they need in a rape case, detectives must do everything possible to minimize tension, and one way of doing this is to begin an investigation by treating the victim as though she is truthful. This may appear to be a simplistic resolution to a complex dilemma, but there have been enough reports of police bumbling in rape investigations to make it seem worth considering. (See Brownmiller, 1975, pp. 343–86, for a number of examples of instances where the police perfunctorily dismiss rape victims' reports and accounts.)

In the Detective Bureau where this study was conducted, the rape investigations were carried out with a good deal of care and understanding, and the clearance rate for rape was quite high. Rape victims were never observed to be badgered unless there was a good deal of evidence to suggest that they were lying, and even then the detectives were circumspect in suggesting an alternative interpretation of the victim's story. Moreover, they were understanding when they encountered victims who lied. In one case where a victim made up a story about being raped, the detectives actually helped her cover her story. A woman who had reported a rape had done so for fear that her husband would beat her if he learned that she had voluntarily had sexual relations with another man. When the detectives learned of her lying in interviewing the suspect, a boy of 17, they confronted the "victim," who explained her fear of the husband. Since the detectives concurred with the woman's evaluation of her husband, they assisted her in concocting a story that would placate her husband, protect the boy who had been accused of rape, and not implicate her in making a false report.

By and large, however, the detectives were hoping to get an actual victim, for only with an actual victim was it possible to make a "good rip" on a rapist. Therefore, in their interaction with victims they did everything possible to relieve the stigma and offer comfort and aid. This tender concern may not have stemmed from a genuine interest in the victim's welfare, for often the detectives held a negative view of a victim's moral character; rather, their overriding interest in making the case guided them in dealing with victims. The following transcript of an interview with a rape victim provides the texture of such encounters and shows how detectives interactionally develop the information they need:

> DET: [What we need to begin] an investigation of this type would be detail. This is what helps us establish many times additional information that is very important in narrowing it down to a specific person. Because, like myself, I work mostly sex crimes out in the county and I'm quite familiar with a number of individuals involved in this type of thing.
>
> VIC: Uh huh.
>
> DET: And sometimes by talking and getting details and physical descriptions and method of operation and words spoken, we can take these and do a lot with it.
>
> VIC: O.K.
>
> DET: Number one, I want to start off with the suspect. I'm going to be asking you some questions about the suspect and try and relate the best you can. Go ahead and give your impression of the subject. He's what? A white male adult?
>
> VIC: Caucasian, yes.
>
> DET: How old would you say he was?
>
> VIC: O.K. I'd say around thirty.
>
> DET: About thirty. Would you say if you had to go one way or the other, younger or older than thirty?
>
> VIC: I'd say older.

The detective continued the interview until he had all details the victim could remember, including every detail of the assault. The explanation at the beginning of the interview provided the victim with an understanding of why the detective had to elicit these details, thereby reassuring the victim that his interest in the rape was not perverse, as some victims seemed to assume.

By narrowing the universe of possible suspects, the detectives proceeded to identify suspects as they did in any other type of case. With an eyewitness to the crime, they were able to use mug books, and since they had detailed descriptions of the rapist's M.O., they could concentrate on possible suspects whose M.O. approximated that described by the victim. This would not always lead to an arrest; in some cases I observed, the detectives came to "know" a rapist by his M.O. but were unable to name the culprit. However, in all of the cases where the detectives did catch rapists, it was only because of the information they developed in the delicate interaction between themselves and the victim.

In conclusion, it should be stressed that the deviant status accorded rape victims is by no means misunderstood by rape detectives. They are fully aware that a rape victim must be treated in terms of the ongoing situation initiated by rape assaults, and even the police criticize detective and patrol officers who are unaware of the interactive dynamics necessary to carry on an investigation. This is not a humanistic concern but, more importantly from the point of view of the detective, expedient detective work. Police-sanctioned rudeness to rape victims is merely evidence of incredible stupidity in investigative methods and social interaction.

Other Major Crimes

Rapes, robberies, and homicides constitute generic forms of crimes and investigative styles, but the Major Crimes unit was responsible for other investigations as well. If a homicide was bungled or an assault was especially vicious, the detectives sometimes characterize the case as attempted homicide. Such investigations are usually similar to "walk-throughs" since the assailant is known to the victim. At other times an attempted homicide charge would be added to "increase" the charges against a suspect in certain crimes. For example, in one case believed to be rape, the medical examination failed to reveal the presence of semen in the victim. Later, after any such evidence would have been washed away, it was found that the victim had a ruptured colon. The detectives, while treating the case as one of rape, could not use the penal code designation for rape (261 PC) because of the wording of the rape law. However, since the victim was badly beaten, the detectives could use the attempted homicide statute (217 PC). In this particular case they added armed robbery and everything else they could think of that could possibly meet the legal requirements. Thus, even though the detectives could not officially treat the assault as rape, they worked it as such using other laws.

Arson cases are worked by one detective in the Major Crimes Detail. Since a good deal of specialization is necessary to locate arson-related evidence (e.g., means used to start a fire), arsons require unique methods of investigation. Typically, the investigation will begin by establishing a case of arson through examination of the fire scene and anything that may possibly have been used to start the fire intentionally. Once this has been established, the detective attempts to learn whether the building's loss would be profitable to anyone; if so, he starts looking for information that would link the arson with the beneficiary. If there is no beneficiary among the owners of the building, the detective looks for competitors and enemies. The detective's understanding of the economic arrangements must be incorporated in the investigation, but sometimes he is looking for indications of social conflict or the covering-up of some other crime, such as burglary. So, depending on the assumptions made about the motivations behind the arson, the case could be worked like anything from a homicide to a burglary.

If the sheriff's department receives an unusual but important case, it is often assigned to the Major Crimes Detail. One such case involved the attempted bribery of a county supervisor by a land developer. The nature of the case was foreign to the detectives in that they typically do not deal with people in the "better" classes of society except as victims. In this case the man who offered the bribe appeared to be well connected, and when he was arrested they found a personal letter from Mrs. Nixon, a Secret Service confirmation of the man's reservation at a hotel in Washington, D.C., for President Nixon's inauguration, and an invitation to the inaugural ball. This took place before the Watergate scandal broke, but the full implications of what they were doing and the effect it might have on them was not lost on the detectives. After the investigation had been completed, the Major Crimes sergeant told me that he'd rather work a dozen homicides than go through a political investigation again. The most important aspect of the case was that it pointed to the esteem with which the Major Crimes unit was held in the department. Nothing about the case was typical of the normal kinds of cases the detail investigated, and since most of the work was undercover, it was much more like the kind of thing done by special investigations (i.e., vice, narcotics). Nevertheless, because the Major Crimes detectives were seen as the "best," they were assigned to the investigation.

Other crimes investigated by Major Crimes depend on their being seen as "important" in one way or another. An obscene phone caller who is persistent, an especially violent assault, or a battery case where the victim is adamant in demanding an investigation and prosecution make up a residual category of crimes worked by the detectives in Major Crimes. However, the key to understanding the work done by Major Crimes lies in the formulation of the circumstances surrounding a case, and not the mere designation of a penal code section in the initial report. To catalogue the work done by Major Crimes solely in terms of the kind of crime reported would be inaccurate, for any case is subject to massive interpretive work. Therefore, it is necessary to understand the interpretive practices whereby a case is taken to be an instance of a "case to be worked" as opposed to a "case to be ignored." Designation of the case as one or the other is contingent on the other work the detectives are doing at the time, but at some point the case has to be formulated in terms of whether or not it is to be investigated, and we cannot rely on explanations of policy, formal or informal, to account for the work done.

SUMMARY

The Major Crimes Detail is the elite investigative unit in the Detective Bureau. They investigate the kinds of cases that the public holds as stereotypical detective work, as celebrated in television serials and movies. Ironically, other than "whodunits," their work is relatively simple compared to that of the other two units. Most of their cases have an eyewitness, if not a suspect, from the outset of an investigation, and unlike the bulk of property crimes, there is a strong likelihood that they will solve any case they investigate. In terms of financial losses, small petty crimes, especially shoplifting and bad checks, are far more expensive than armed robberies but the capture of an armed robber will bring more acclaim than a hundred shoplifters and an equal number of "paper hangers." Thus, the work, while glamorous as far as the public and others in the department are concerned, does not have much objective impact on crime and criminals. However, because of the qualitative importance of their work, the Major Crimes investigators hold center stage in detective work.

9

The Reality of the Research

All sociological research occurs in the context of a set of exigencies which bear on how the research is conducted and the data are gathered. Ideally, only theoretical and methodological considerations should guide the researcher in his quest for data, but the contingencies in social life rarely afford this ideal. The researcher tries to control such contingencies through tightly constructed research designs which guide him in the direction of purely theoretical concerns; the classic experiment and questionnaire survey are two examples of highly organized research methods. However, as Arnold (1974) has aptly noted, the fact that our procedures may be neatly organized is no reason to expect the phenomenon we are studying to organize itself to coincide with the research design. The more tightly organized the methodology, the greater the likelihood that we will miss many of the unexpected and often significant aspects of social life, for these events are the most likely to be excluded from consideration in an overorganized methodology. This is not to suggest that a sloppy method is preferable to an organized method, but merely to point out that if one hopes to discover anything new, his methodology must be flexible enough to exploit the unanticipated.

Further, the researcher must be willing to see the consequences of his methodology for the phenomenon under study. It

190

is well known that the research itself can have an effect on the behavior being measured (Johnson, 1974, pp. 1–26). Second, as we have noted, the method orders what a researcher will see, and the more rigid the method, the less he sees. Moreover, the subjects sometimes attempt to "help" the researcher by giving him what he wants. Thus, if they know that the researcher's interest is in a particular area, they may reconstruct their activities to stress this area in a way that is not wholly accurate. As a result, the rigid method often creates the very reality it seeks to examine.

Third, there is an interrelationship between the research methods and the findings. Goffman once remarked that we report the "second worst thing" that happened to us in a research project, implying that researchers leave out a good deal of the actual procedures and mishaps in data collection. More pointedly, Douglas (1976) suggests that many sociologists omit certain events from their reports because full and accurate reporting would require them to admit either that some of their findings were invalid or that some of their procedures were unethical. For whatever reason, only rarely do we find candid discussions of research events. The works of Polsky (1969), Humphreys (1970), Whyte (1953), and Johnson (1974) are notable exceptions. However, it is not my purpose here to enter into an ethical condemnation of those who report only what was supposed to happen in their research projects, but rather to point out why it is important to present everything that might have a bearing on one's findings. If researchers include what happened in the collection of their data, this information can help other researchers to avoid the problems reported or to use any new tactics discovered. The problems may be specific to a research topic or area, but sometimes what is discovered during data gathering is more widely applicable. For example, in studying the police, Skolnick (1966) found that the effect of the researcher's presence decreased with time. This observation has important implications for all participant-observation studies. Other problems and tactics reported by Skolnick were more specific to research on the police.

I have therefore attempted to report everything relevant to the collection of the data, so that the reader can understand the full methodology and can assess the validity of the findings.

The Grand Alliance

During my tenure in graduate school I came to know two other students who were interested in ethnomethodology and the police. Howard Daudistel and Mike Williams had worked together on their M.A. papers in a study of the campus police. Mike was interested in police patrol and Howard in police radio communications. We had discussed the possibility of working together on a large project dealing with their interests and adding my interest in detectives, but it wasn't until Mike mentioned the possibility to one of his students, who was a sheriff's lieutenant, that we began active work together.

Initial Contacts with Police

Early in my graduate-school career, I taught sociology cours-es in the university's extension criminal-justice program. Most of my students were in law enforcement, and they constituted my first unofficial contact with police. My collaborators had also taught these classes, so all of us had some knowledge about police on a face-to-face basis. Since Howard and Mike had conducted research on the activities of the university police, they were somewhat familiar with police work as well. Thus when Mike announced that he had a contact with the sheriff's department through whom we might be able to effect a research entrance, we were extremely optimistic about our chance of being accepted.

Mike talked to the public relations officer about our interests and set up a meeting with the sheriff. Before the meeting we all got haircuts and trimmed our facial hair to neat moustaches. We decided that we would emphasize the practical aspects of our study and play down the theoretical aspects. The officers in our classes had told us that their biggest problem was paperwork, so we decided to present our research intentions as a study of paperwork. Our ethnomethodological interest in the accounts provided in the paperwork and the talk about the paperwork was of little practical concern to the police, so we never mentioned it.

Our worries, however, were not about theoretical matters. The university we attended, and particularly the sociology department, had been a center for riots and radical political activities. One student had been shot and killed by the police, and several police and sheriff's deputies had been hurt in a series of altercations. In fact, when we entered the field, a number of the sheriff's cars still had rock dents from the most recent riots, and one of the detectives with whom I spent time was still recovering from an eye wound suffered in one of the riots. Needless to say, the relationship between the sheriff's department and the university community, especially the sociology department, left much to be desired. Moreover, previous studies of the police, notably Manning's (1976) summarization of research, had found that the police were highly distrustful of outsiders. Nevertheless, our meeting with the sheriff was cordial and at its conclusion the sheriff asked us to submit a proposal outlining our plans, which we agreed to do.

At this time I began keeping a diary describing my personal reactions to various encounters and events so that later I would be able to evaluate the data gathered in terms of my state of mind. During the first meeting I had been too nervous to open my mouth, and this near-hysterical concern that things would not work out right was shared by Howard and Mike.

In subsequent meetings with the training officer, detective inspector, and lieutenant, we were able to loosen up a little and begin explaining our project and asking for advice. I had read in Joseph Wambaugh's *The New Centurions* that eye contact was important to police, so we spent a good deal of our first meeting with the detective inspector and lieutenant staring at them. They told us that a lot of studies already had been done on paperwork and were generally discouraging. Howard agreed but pointed out that very little had been done on the narrative section of the reports, in which the officers wrote a description of cases. The detectives agreed that this was important and from that point on took a more encouraging posture toward the project. They suggested that instead of beginning in the field we should begin by looking at the reports in the Records Department, so that we would have an idea of the changes that had been made in the past. This was a valuable suggestion, and we agreed to it. Later, however, we found that our access to Records was restricted.

The Proposal

To satisfy the sheriff's request for specific information about our project and also because we hoped to get a grant, we began working on a research proposal. Our initial draft had several theoretical and methodological shortcomings. The practical aspects were not sufficiently stressed and the methodology appeared to be unsystematic. We therefore reworked the proposal, drawing from Reiss' (1968) work on systematic observation and Lofland's (1971) ideas on participant observation along with other material on ethnographic methodology, so as to make our methodology more systematic, yet at the same time keep the flexibility we wanted. The problem was our feeling that until we entered the field, we would not know what to look for. Much of what we were investigating was yet to be discovered, and subsequent data collection would be built on these initial discoveries.

We decided to divide the subject of investigation into three areas of concentration. Mike would focus on patrol, Howard on communications, and I on detectives. No problems were anticipated in either patrol or communications; however, we had been told that our presence in the Narcotics Detail would be unwelcome. Since I was interested only in "regular detectives"—that is, the Juvenile, Burglary, and Major Crimes Detail—this was not a problem either.

THE RESEARCH

My research had two beginnings. In July I spent a number of days with the Juvenile Detail before taking a month off to work on another project as a research assistant. Howard had been slotted to go to the dispatch office, where he could observe the handling of incoming calls, but instead had been assigned to the complaints detective, who served more or less as the liaison officer between the sheriff's office and the D.A. Since the complaints officer was a member of the Burglary Detail (he worked checks and forgeries), Howard and I were in the same building, in contact with each other as well as with the detectives. Mike, according to plans, was out with patrol.

The first start was characterized by formal conversations and by my asking questions, mostly concerning mundane items about paperwork and investigating a case. I was suspicious that I was being "conned" and that the "real stuff" was being hidden; at the same time, I was concerned that the detectives were suspicious of me. After a short while I began to relax around the detectives, and I believe they began to do the same with me, but it is difficult to point to a specific time when this happened. It just slowly occurred until I felt comfortable in their midst.

We had to sign a waiver to relieve the department of responsibility if anything happened to us while we were doing our research. We were also given ID cards with our pictures and fingerprints on them, in accordance with a new security plan that was being instituted. Ours read "Criminal Justice Research Associate," but nobody paid much attention to the title on the tag; the tag itself was sufficient to allow us to pass without comment. After we were known, we passed without the tags.

Some of the men in the detail knew me from the class I had taught and remembered me with somewhat longer hair and a more exuberant mustache, but few comments were made about my metamorphosis. Most of the comments were joking, and a number suggested that my attitudes about the police had been changed by our class discussions and my experience with the detectives.

Having expected to find some problems related to our a priori notions about police, both good and bad, we had talked about how to approach our research. We wanted to come to understand the police point of view from the various organizational positions, but we did not want to approach the project with either a partisan "law-and-order" demeanor or a muckraking perspective. We finally decided to try to preserve an open interest, monitoring our own feelings and activities so that any data gathered could be judged in terms of "where our heads were at" at the time. Thus, the notes gathered by the uncertain, self-conscious, insecure researchers we were at the outset were markedly different from the notes of the confident, self-assured insiders we had all become by the end of the project.

The second start of my tenure in the detective division, after I returned from my work on the other project, was somewhat easier since I knew some of the detectives from before. Also, Howard had been there all along and had become familiar with the routines and accepted by the detectives as a normal feature of the office. He had even been given a number of chores, such as writing the logs and running errands for the detectives. As a result, the detectives were very much at ease around us, and it was easier to relax around them. Occasionally detectives would ask us about the project, but this gradually stopped and constituted an indicator of our acceptance.

FINDING A NICHE

In the Detective Bureau, as in other work organizations, there are officially designated places for working members. However, there are no allocated spaces for additional, nonregular people. This turned out to be a problem at first, and from time to time it was a serious one. When I began in the Juvenile Detail there was no place for me to be except "standing around." This was uncomfortable interactionally, not to mention physically. To write up notes or to wait for the detectives I was accompanying I would periodically go to the interrogation room, which was off a hallway connecting the Juvenile Detail and the Major Crimes and Burglary Details. Sometimes I would get a folding chair and sit in some corner, but usually I would get in someone's way.

This initial period with the Juvenile Detail, however, was short-lived; when the detective I was accompanying was transferred to the Burglary Detail, I went with him. The Burglary Detail had a big wooden table with a number of chairs, and I quickly made this table "my desk." For the entire period with the Burglary Detail, I never had a problem finding a place to sit.

In the Major Crimes Detail I encountered the same difficulty I had had in Juvenile. Even though Major Crimes was just across the room from Burglary, I wanted to located myself in the Major Crimes area so that I could observe the activity there. I moved a chair over by one of the desks, and one of the detectives offered me the use of his bottom drawer for my notebook and lunch. This arrangement still put me in an awkward position since I was crammed up against the detective's desk in a little nook that was not intended to allow space enough for someone to sit. (Someone later moved the chair, and so I lost even this little niche.) This period of the research was generally uncomfortable; only on the infrequent occasions when a detective was out of the office could I use one of the desks. Mostly I simply wandered around, sometimes back to the table in Burglary and sometimes to an available chair in the Major Crimes area.

This state of affairs was resolved when the whole department moved into a new building. In the new office there was a single room for all three details, with several extra desks, since there were plans to increase the manpower of the Detective Bureau. Two of the desks were available for use by Howard and me. This solved the problem of space in the office.

Whenever the detectives went out on an investigation, I sat in the back seat if there were two detectives and in the front seat if there was one. Generally I accompanied a single detective in the front seat of the detective car. When a contact was made with a victim, witness, suspect, or anyone else, I stood next to the detective. I usually said nothing other than "Hello" and "Good-bye" and would take notes during contacts. I was introduced as "Mr. Sanders," and it was generally assumed that I was another detective; since taking notes is a feature of detective work, most people thought I was "the one who took notes" while the other detective asked questions. On one occasion a victim asked if I were a "detective trainee," and the detective told her that I was "something like that," but on the whole my presence was not questioned. In fact, on only one occasion was my presence a problem, and then I had to explain my capacity as a researcher. A suspect in a child-molesting case was to be given a polygraph (lie-detector) examination, and before the examination the suspect's attorney asked about me. After I explained my purpose and showed him my ID tag, he seemed satisfied and let me sit through the preliminaries of the polygraph examination. In the field, though, finding a niche or a role was not a problem.

Taking Notes

While taking notes during an interview between the detective and someone he had contacted was not a problem, there was sometimes a problem with the detectives. If a detective said something in a normal conversation that was important to me, I would jot it down. In such instances I would be asked, "What are you writing? What are you going to say about me?" I would explain as best I could, but often I got the feeling that, even though none of the notes contained information that was in any way harmful, there would be a change in the talk whenever I took notes. At first I was especially conscious of this and whenever I wrote something down would explain what it was without being asked. I would leave my notebook open in plain sight so that anyone who wanted to read my notes could do so, or at least could see that I was not attempting to hide anything.

I kept two types of notes. I got a large, flat, black notebook in which 8 1/2- by 11-inch lined sheets were placed. It looked very much like the ones used by the detectives, and the similarity was intentional. I also had a pocket-sized notebook which I called my "BOL book." ("BOL" is an abbrieviation used by sheriff's office dispatchers for "Be on the lookout." Usually it is used when a person or car is wanted; e.g., radio call: "BOL 1973 Dodge station wagon, California license, Four Nine Three Ida Adam Nora.") I used the BOL book for writing down license numbers transmitted over the radio since it was difficult for the detective to drive and copy down information at the same time. Sometimes I would take additional notes in this book since it was easier to get at in certain situations. These notes were eventually integrated with the notes in my large notebook and usually elaborated, since there was not much space in the small notebook.

The second general type of notes that were kept were more systematic, organized almost like a questionnaire or interview schedule. These notes were made on mimeographed sheets where categorized elements of a case could be recorded by merely checking off a category. For example, the sheet included spaces for checking off whether the case was worked by Burglary, Juvenile, or Major Crimes, the code-type of the violation (e.g., Penal Code, Welfare and Institutions Code), whether it was cleared, closed, inactivated, or continued, plus other routine events which could be coded. At the bottom of the sheet was a space where I could record "what really happened" in the case, and this section was almost identical to the narrative section of the report forms used by the sheriff's office. (See the appendix for the forms used in the research.)

At first I took a number of notes and typed them at home, where they would be filled out and expanded. However, after I began to relax around the detectives and noticed that my taking notes made everyone uncomfortable, I began to take fewer notes. Occasionally I would write something down, but for a while I did not type the notes or prepare them for multiple copies as I had planned. This period of relaxed observation lasted for a month, during which I acted more as an interested companion to the detectives rather than as a researcher.

After about a month of this relaxed research, I began to take notes and to elaborate and type them on duplication masters, making logs for the notes. When I reentered the field, I began taking more notes. During the time when I was not taking notes rapport was established, I came to learn a good deal, and generally enjoyed myself. Retrospectively, the research hiatus was valuable in that the detectives got to know me during this period, and it is doubtful that I could have come to know them as well as I did if there had not been a time when I gave my full attention to sociable interaction without taking notes.

Another data-gathering device was the tape recorder. At first I used a large reel-to-reel recorder inside a briefcase with the microphone hidden in the handle. It worked fairly well, and I was able to transcribe most of the talk that was recorded. The problem was that it was bulky and heavy, and I had to turn it on before leaving the car and then operate a switch, concealed in the latch on the briefcase, to activate it. The large reels were awkward to handle, and it was difficult to locate segments for transcription. However, the detectives did not mind my taking a recorder along, even in the bulky case.

Later in the research I bought a small cassette-type recorder that fit under my arm and picked up recordings at various distances. The recorder was light and small enough to be unobtrusive and easily carried, and it made excellent recordings. About the only problem I had with it was that when we were in the car and moving, the engine noise was picked up and caused static and distortion in the tapes. Nevertheless, the tapes proved to be useful in gathering data on the encounters between detectives and various victims, witnesses, and suspects, and also allowed me to conduct interviews without having to rely on notes.

The final data-gathering tool used was a small pocket camera. My thought was to photograph physical evidence and then explain how it was bound to an account for its being seen as evidence. I also photographed events, routine work, and anything else I thought a picture would capture and preserve as potential data. The first pictures I took were of the scene of a double homicide, a room in which the detectives had gathered and photographed physical evidence. Instead of preserving only the "objective" features of the room—bullet holes, blood stains, and signs of investigative work—the photograph brought back much more. I was in the room shortly after the homicide, and the smell of blood was so strong that I thought I had a bloody nose myself. My photographs brought back the stench of blood of the two victims. Other photographs served to recall to memory numerous details of scenes and situations that I had missed in my notes. Thus, in a very real way, the photographs served as an additional set of field notes.

No one seemed to mind the camera, and I would make copies of my pictures available whenever the detectives thought they might be useful. For example, I took a picture of a ship's lantern of make identical to one that had been stolen. The theft detective wanted a picture of the "stolen lantern" to send to pawnshops, so I had a copy of the photograph made for him.

ORGANIZATION OF DATA

Typing Notes

In my diary and the field notes themselves, I frequently commented about how much I loathed typing up field notes. After eight hours of observing, it was a miserable task to come home and elaborate and type my notes. Sometimes I would fall behind and have two or three days of notes to type at once. There was no joy in it, and since many typed notes were not used in writing the final report, the pain of all that typing at times seemed useless.

About once a week I would run off the duplication masters, making ten copies. One copy would be filed chronologically under the detail where the data were collected. Another copy was placed in a loose-leaf binder for quick reference and served as a working copy. Four copies were stapled together in packs of a single log number, and two copies went to my co-researchers, one each to Howard and Mike. The remaining six copies were cross-indexed for later analysis.

Each day's typed notes were assigned a log number. Usually a day's typed notes would constitute a day's observation, but sometimes several days' observations would be typed up at one time. In the log book for field notes, the date (or dates), detail (e.g., Major Crimes, Burglary), topics, and other items that would characterize significant observations of the period and cross-references to other logs were all written down, along with the log number for the field notes. The following is an excerpt from the field-note log to illustrate its use:

DATE	DETAIL	TOPICS	REF. OTHER LOGS			LOG#
1/17/73 –1/19/73	Major Crimes	Detective meeting/ talk about leads/ change in case from 261 to 217/211 bomb film-incongruity/ 211 bank	Case 62	Tape 8	Interview 3	36

Later, when I was analyzing the data, the topics would direct me to certain field-note logs, and from the brief notations I would be able to remember a great deal more. For example, in the above log I would know that "change in case from 261 to 217/211" would be relevant to establishing a case. When a tape log and an interview log were cross-referenced, I could assume that the interview was taped and probably had something to do with one of the topics listed. By turning to the tape or interview log I could find out exactly what topics were taped. In the tape log, for instance, tape 8 was listed as "Interview with R.B. about leads and investigations."

Finally, the case log gave a title to each case that would bring back to memory the details of the case. For example, case 62 was titled "Girl Beaten," and since it probably had to do with one of the topics listed in the field-note log, it was not difficult to remember exactly what was involved in the case. Case 62 involved a change in the charge from 261 PC (rape) to 217 PC (attempted murder) and 211 PC (armed robbery), which were listed in the field-note log. If I could not remember the details of the case from its title and it appeared to be relevant to a point of analysis, I could go to the case form, filed under one of the three details. If the case form was sketchy, I would go back to the field notes for further details. When I needed still more information I could get it by going either to Records or to the detectives' files, since each case was logged with the sheriff's office log number in addition to my own log number. Generally, however, I only used the sheriff's office case number when there was a multiple clearance, long after the case in question had been worked. I would simply go through the case log, matching the sheriff's office log number with the cases that were reported cleared using the same log number.

Each day, after I had typed the field notes, everything had to be carefully logged; otherwise I would have found myself going through reams of field notes and case forms during the analysis of the data, with no idea where to find information about a case or which tape related to what case or circumstance. The logging, however, was a relief since it meant that all of the field notes for that day (or days) was completed. All of the work I had done took on a tangible character as the logs began to fill up. Besides being necessary for organizing and retrieving infromation, the logs served as benchmarks of progress, providing a psychological boost in the dreary work of organizing the information.

Field Relationships

During the research a number of relationships developed which affected the gathering of data. Besides the researcher-subject relationship, I also maintained a teacher-student relationship and/or a friend-friend relationship with several of the detectives. Each relationship, moreover, affected the others. The researcher-subject relationship varied with the individual detectives. Where I got along well on a personal level with a detective I spent a good deal of time with him as a researcher. While in the role of researcher I never felt that any detective I accompanied was a "subject." In fact, instead of doing research "on" detectives, the activity would be more accurately characterized as doing research "with" detectives. In a way, the relationship was something like a master and an apprentice, with the researcher as the apprentice.

The researcher in this role comes to take on the point of view of the subject. It is what the anthropologists call "going native," except that I was very much aware of what was happening, and instead of trying to stop it, I attempted to see why it took on the texture that it did. After a time I came to sympathize more with the detectives than with the crime victims or suspects. Sometimes victims were seen as unfortunates who had been hurt by criminals and deserved help, but often, and with increasing frequency as I came to take on the detectives' viewpoint, they were whining, ignorant, uncooperative people who did little to help the detectives, demanded impossible feats from them, and deserved what they got from the criminals. Victims demanded that the detectives recover their property or bring to justice those who had beaten or raped them, while at the same time they were hesitant about giving information so that the detectives could meet their demands. Rarely would burglary victims have a list of serial numbers which could be used to identify stolen property, yet they would indignantly decry the detectives for not recovering their televisions and stereo sets. Sometimes victims would file false reports, leading the detectives on a wild-goose chase; in such circumstances they were seen to be little better than the criminals. As for the criminals, instead of viewing them as cruelly stigmatized victims of the criminal-justice system, I came to see them as wiseass punks who thought they were somehow not subject to the conventional social mores. Since Mountainbeach had relatively few of the minorities who supply a disproportionate number of the clients of the criminal-justice system, most of the criminal suspects were white; therefore, the enforcement pattern could not be seen as guided by bigotry or prejudice. At the same time, however, none of the sociological theories concerning crime seemed to be invalid, and if anything, they were confirmed by what I saw. After seeing the effects of criminal activities on people's lives, including the criminal's, crime became maddening.

I do not claim that the viewpoint I came to take on had no effect on my data. That fact that I began to notice such things as the victim's lack of cooperation and the suspect's culpability suggests that it did indeed affect the collection of data. Moreover, the fact that I viewed the operation of detectives from their position and not that of the victim or criminal limited my perspective. However, the strictly "detective viewpoint" was tempered in that I was also attempting to test certain ethnomethodological assumptions, and the practical exigencies of collecting data on these issues forced me to pay attention to certain aspects of detective work which were irrelevant to any partisan perspective.

Another relationship between myself and certain detectives was that of teacher-student. During the fall quarter of 1972, shortly after I began my research, I was teaching a university extension course on the sociology of law, and a number of my students were detectives in the office I studied. During class I was presenting data showing that the police were enforcing laws that were serving certain interest groups at the expense of others (cf. Quinney, 1969). In this relationship, the master-apprentice relationship that existed in the field was reversed. After an evening's class I returned to the role of apprentice. While this presented no problem, it seems retrospectively that there should have been conflict in the role reversal. At no time, however, did I experience any feeling of conflict, nor did it appear that the detectives in my class did so either.

After class or work, I often went to bars with detectives and other police. During these periods a "friendship" relationship existed. Sometimes I felt like a professor socializing with his students, but generally these were nonschool, nonresearch events, simply occasions of "going drinking with some friends." The conversation dealt with detective work and schoolwork, but also with general topics of interest that had nothing to do with either situation. During these occasions the detectives and I came to know each other as people. Of course, these encounters and relationships flowed over into the research, generally having the effect of making research relationships less formal.

The final relevant relationship in the research was that between myself and the other researchers. When we began writing the proposal there were some squabbles among us, but as we entered the field and began collecting data, this ceased. At first I thought there might be some conflict between Howard and me since he was in the Detective Bureau when he was supposed to be in Communications, but this turned out to be the opposite. We were mutually supportive and it was easier for me knowing that Howard and I would be working together. We rarely saw Mike, who was with patrol when we were in the field, but occasionally we would see him in the squad room or in a patrol car.

Mike provided another important function which neither Howard nor I could reciprocate. Whenever something happened while Mike was on patrol that he knew would be investigated by the detectives, he would alert us ahead of time. For example, when the double homicide occurred, Mike called and told me about it, and I was able to get to the office in time for the investigation. Neither Howard nor I could do the same for Mike, since by the time something got to the detectives it had either been through or bypassed patrol.

Howard and I tended to view patrol as subordinate to the detectives, and as a result we saw Mike's work as less important than ours. When we got together to swap anecdotes, we always felt that Mike's were insignificant compared to ours, but Mike's position usually brought him closer to crime since patrol was first to respond to a call; therefore, he felt that his work was more interesting. For the most part we maintained good relations and whenever possible lent support to one another. In part this was due to the fact that we felt that we had become "outmembers" at the university. Whenever we discussed our adventures, outsiders would be avoided, including the professors with whom we worked. We felt they would not understand a number of the things we were talking about or would use them against the sheriff's department. If an "outsider" came in during one of our discussions we would quickly change the topic of conversation, excluding the intruder. Treating other members of the department in this way, we were very much responsible for our being "outmembers"; on the whole, we were treated well by others in the department, and they were less suspicious of us than we were of them.

THE IMPLICATIONS OF THE FINDINGS AND METHODS

A discussion of validity for a study such as this one puts the researcher in the ironic position of talking about the topic of the research. I have been looking at how detectives develop information, and now it is necessary to discuss the development of information *about* the development of information.

This study was an empirical one in that everything reported was either observed, heard, tape-recorded, photographed, read, smelled, touched, or in some other way made available to the senses. These multiple methods allowed me to cross-check the data, and all of the data were systematically and painstakingly organized and analyzed. However, the question of objectivity needs to be addressed in order to assess the truthfulness and bias-free status of the data. There are a number of reasons why it will be difficult to address the question of objectivity in the usual sense, and the following discussion will focus on the epistemological issues of objectivity as much as the objectivity in this study.

First, there was no objectivity to lose. As has been pointed out throughout this book, nothing is independent of interpretive work, and the sense of anything that is formulated as being in the world relies on assumptions, background expectancies, and a reflexively constituted context. The detectives did not merely ask for "just the facts," but instead actively developed the "facts." In the same way, there was nothing "objectively out in the world" independent of the interpretive work I put into it. Now it may be, in the truest dramaturgical sense, that something may *appear* to be objective, but this is a matter of style, not content. In another project that I have recently finished, I have a stack of computer printouts with the computer-made tables and tests of significance. The data were gathered with an observation schedule, much like a questionnaire except that rather than ask questions, the researchers *saw* what was going on. The validity and objectivity of this study are not questioned, and the comments on my computer printout findings are to the effect that everyone is glad that I'm doing "science." There are no questions as to whether or not the observations were "objective" or whether the categories are a reification of the "real world." Such questions are almost always posed when nonquantified data are presented, but since the data are seen as "hard" due to the fact that they have been digested by a computer, it is assumed they must be "objective." However, they are no more objective than the materials presented in this book. In fact, because the computer printout can tell only about the quantified data, which are a jump away from "reality" in that they are context-ignorant, the data in this book are "harder" since they are presented along with their context. Furthermore, the data here are less skewed by assumptions in that no prefabricated categories are used, whereas in the quantified study the whole often had to be broken up to "fit" the categories. Thus, instead of presenting the data in quantified studies as an unbroken process, it is necessary to break it up into pieces that can be quantified, thereby transforming the data further from the initial empirical formulation.

In conclusion, the methods employed in this study and the methods employed by detectives in criminal investigations were much the same. The constructed character of the data was both discovered and employed. At the same time that it was found that leads and evidence were context-bound and relied on massive interpretive work, this finding was "found" in the same way. Thus the topic of the research came to be used as a resource, and thereby not only was it possible to account for how detectives "gathered" empirical evidence, but at the same time it was possible to account for how these data presented in this book were "gathered." Therefore, every finding about detective investigations came to be a finding about sociological research.

Appendix

Research Forms and Logs

CASE OBSERVATION SCHEDULE

MC_____   Date Rec'd ____ Date Begin ____ Date Term. ____
BURG ____
JUV ____   TITLE: _____ LOG # ____

Patrol Report

Section	Code	Type		Case #	Dispatch Code
PC ____	HS ____	O ____	FI ____		
VC ____	CO ____	A ____	FR ____	1–73–	
WI ____	US ____	I ____	BS ____		
BP ____		FU ____			

Detective Report

Section	Code	Type		Case #	
PC ____	HS ____	O ____	FR ____		Check if
VS ____	CO ____	A ____	CU ____	1–73–	no pre-
WI ____	US ____	I ____	CP ____		vious re-
BP ____		FU ____	VS ____		port has
					been
					made

Indicate sections in narrative (A–G) which are designated DNA, UNKNOWN, NONE, AS ABOVE or are left blank.

Patrol		Detective		Disposition
A____	E____	A____	E____	Cleared ____
B____	F____	B____	F____	Closed ____
C____	G____	C____	G____	Inactivated ____
D____		D____		

Adequacy of report

Indicate both good & bad aspects of report in terms of follow-up investigation and court use.

ID Bureau: Yes ____ No ____

Items

1. suspects
2. leads
3. witnesses
4. phys. evidence
5. contacts
6. interrogations
7. outside agency
8. teletypes
9. complaint
10. communications
11. press
12. probable cause

211

Researcher ＿＿＿＿＿＿   CASE LOG

TITLE	DATE	SO CASE #	LOG #

Researcher ＿＿＿＿＿＿   FIELD-NOTE LOG

DATE	DETAIL	TOPICS	REF. OTHER LOGS			LOG #
			Case	tape	interv.	

Researcher ＿＿＿＿＿＿   TAPE LOG

DATE	DETAIL	TOPICS	REF. OTHER LOGS			TAPE #
			Case	fld.	interv.	

Researcher ＿＿＿＿＿＿   INTERVIEW LOG   Tape ＿＿
                                                            Note ＿＿

NOTE	DETAIL	TOPICS	REF. OTHER LOGS			LOG #
			Case	fld.	tape	

Bibliography

ARNOLD, DAVID O.
  1974   "Qualitative Field Methods." In *Social Science Methods: A New Introduction,* edited by Robert B. Smith. New York: Free Press.

BERGER, PETER, AND THOMAS LUCKMAN
  1966   *The Social Construction of Reality: A Treatise in the Sociology of Knowledge.* Garden City, N.Y.: Doubleday.

BITTNER, EGON
  1967   "The Police on Skid Row: A Study in Peace Keeping." *American Sociological Review* 32: 699–715.

  1970   *The Functions of Police in Modern Society.* Rockville, Md.: National Institute of Mental Health.

BLACK, DONALD J., AND ALBERT J. REISS, JR.
  1970   "Police Control of Juveniles." *American Sociological Review* 35: 63–77.

BLUMBERG, ABRAHAM
  1967   *Criminal Justice.* Chicago: Quadrangle.

BORDUA, DAVID J., AND ALBERT REISS, JR.
  1966   "Command, Control, and Charisma: Reflections on Police Bureaucracy." *American Journal of Sociology* 72 (July): 68–70.

BROWNMILLER, SUSAN
  1975   *Against Our Wills: Men, Women and Rape.* New York: Simon and Schuster.

BURKE, KENNETH
  1954   *Permanance and Change: An Anatomy of Purpose.* Indianapolis: Bobbs-Merrill.

BURNHAM, WILLIAM R.
  1975   "Modern Decision Theory and Corrections." In *Decision-making in the Criminal Justice System: Reviews and Essays,* edited by Don M. Gottfredson. Rockville, Md.: National Institute of Mental Health.

CAVAN, SHERRI
  1966   *Liquor License: An Ethnography of Bar Behavior.* Chicago: Aldine.

CONKLIN, JOHN E.
  1972   *Robbery and the Criminal Justice System.* Philadelphia: Lippincott.

COOKRIDGE, E. H.
  1966   *Set Europe Ablaze.* London: Author Baker.

COOLEY, CHARLES HORTON
  1902   *Human Nature and the Social Order.* New York: Charles Scribner's Sons.

CUMMING, ELAINE, IAN CUMMING, AND LAURA EDELL
  1965   "Policeman as Philospher, Guide and Friend." *Social Problems* 12: 276–86.

DOUGLAS, JACK
  1976   *Investigative Social Research.* Beverly Hills, Calif.: Sage.

DURKHEIM, ÉMILE
  1933   *The Division of Labor in Society.* New York: Free Press.

ENNIS, PHILLIP
  1967   "Crimes, Victims and the Police." *transaction* 4 (June): 36–44.

GARFINKEL, HAROLD
  1967   *Studies in Ethnomethodology.* Englewood Cliffs, N.J.: Prentice-Hall.

GLASER, BARNEY G., AND ANSELM L. STRAUSS
  1967   "Awareness Contexts and Social Interaction." In *Symbolic Interaction: A Reader in Social Psychology,* edited by Jerome G. Manis and N. Meltzer. Boston: Allyn Bacon.

GOFFMAN, ERVING
  1959   *The Presentation of Self in Everyday Life.* Garden City, N.Y.: Doubleday.
  1961   *Encounters.* Indianapolis.: Bobbs-Merrill.
  1963   *Stigma.* Englewood Cliffs, N.J.: Prentice-Hall.
  1967   *Interaction Ritual.* Garden City, N.Y.: Doubleday.
  1969   *Strategic Interaction.* Philadelphia: University of Pennsylvania Press.

1971   *Relations in Public.* New York: Basic Books.
1974   *Frame Analysis.* New York: Harper & Row.

GOTTFREDSON, DON M.
1975   *Decision-Making in the Criminal Justice System: Reviews and Essays.* Rockville, Md.: National Institute of Mental Health.

GURWITSCH, ARON
1964   *The Field of Consciousness.* Pittsburgh: Duquesne University Press.

HARRIS, RICHARD
1973   *The Police Academy: An Inside View.* New York: Wiley.

HUGHES, EVERETT
1958   *Men and Their Work.* New York: Free Press.

HUMPHREYS, LAUD
1970   *Tearoom Trade.* Chicago: Aldine.

JOHNSON, JOHN
1974   *Doing Field Research.* New York: Free Press.

KIDD, LT. W.R.
1940   *Police Interrogation.* New York: Basuino.

KLOCKARS, CARL
1974   *The Professional Fence.* New York: Free Press.

LaFAVE, WAYNE
1965   *Arrest: The Decision to Take a Suspect into Custody.* Boston: Little, Brown.

LEITER, KENNETH
1971   "Telling It Like It Is: A Study of Teachers' Accounts." Ph.D. dissertation, University of California, Santa Barbara.

LOFLAND, JOHN
1971   *Analyzing Social Settings.* Belmont, Calif: Wadsworth.

LUCKENBILL, DAVID
1973   "Other People's Lives." Masters thesis, University of California, Santa Barbara.

LYMAN, STANFORD, AND MARVIN B. SCOTT
1970   *A Sociology of the Absurd.* New York: Appleton-Century-Crofts.

MANNING, PETER
1971   "The Police: Mandate, Strategies and Appearances." In *Crime and Justice in American Society,* edited by Jack Douglas. Indianapolis: Bobbs-Merrill.
1976   "Observing the Police." In *The Ambivalent Force,* edited by Arthur Niederhoffer and Abraham Blumberg. Hinsdale, Ill.: Dryden Press.

MUNRO, JIM L.
  1974   *Administrative Behavior and Police Organization.* Cincin-
         nati: W.H. Anderson.

NIEDERHOFFER, ARTHUR
  1967   *Behind the Shield: The Police in Urban Society* Garden
         City, N.Y.: Doubleday.

OSTERBURG, JAMES W.
  1967   *The Crime Laboratory: Case Studies of Scientific Criminal
         Investigation:* Bloomington: Indiana University Press.

PENAL CODE OF CALIFORNIA
  1971   4th Edition. Department of General Services, Documents
         Section, Sacramento, Calif.

PEPINSKY, HAROLD
  1975   "Police Decision-making." In *Decision-making in the Crimi-
         nal Justice System,* edited by Don M. Gottfredson. Rockville,
         Md.: National Institute of Mental Health.

PILIAVIN, IRVING, AND SCOTT BRIAR
  1964   "Police Encounters with Juveniles." *American Journal* of
         Sociology 70 (Sept.): 206–14.

POLSKY, NED
  1969   *Hustlers, Beats and Others.* Garden City, N.Y.: Doubleday.

QUINNEY, RICHARD
  1969   *Crime and Justice in Society.* Boston: Little, Brown.

REISS, ALBERT J., JR.
  1968   "Stuff and Nonsense about Social Surveys and Observa-
         tions." In *Institutions and the Person,* edited by Howard S.
         Becker. Chicago: Aldine.
  1971   *The Police and the Public.* Cambridge: Harvard University
         Press.

REISS, ALBERT J., JR., AND DAVID J. BORDUA
  1967   "Environment and Organization: A Perspective on the
         Police." In *The Police: Six Sociological Essays,* edited by
         David Bordua. New York: Wiley.

ROSSI, PETER H., EMILY WAITE, CHRISTINE E. BOSE, AND RICHARD
E. BERK
  1974   "The Seriousness of Crimes: Normative Structure and Indi-
         vidual Differences." *American Sociological Review* 39
         (April): 224–37.

RUBINSTEIN, JOHNATHAN
  1973   *City Police.* New York: Ballantine.

SANDERS, WILLIAM B., AND HOWARD C. DAUDISTEL
  1974   "Detective Work." In *The Sociologist as Detective,* edited by William B. Sanders. New York: Praeger.

SACKS, HARVEY
  1972   "Notes on Police Assessment of Moral Character." In *Studies in Social Interaction,* edited by David Sudnow. New York: Free Press.

SCARR, HARRY A.
  1972   *Patterns of Burglary.* Washington, D.C.: Department of Justice.

SCHEFF, THOMAS
  1970   "On the Concepts of Identity and Social Relationship." In *Human Nature and Collective Behavior: Papers in Honor of Herbert Blummer,* edited by T. Shibutani. Englewood Cliffs, N.J.: Prentice-Hall.

SCHELLING, THOMAS
  1963   *The Strategy of Conflict.* London: Oxford University Press.

SCHUR, EDWIN, M.
  1965   *Crimes Without Victims: Deviant Behavior and Public Policy.* Englewood Cliffs, N.J.: Prentice-Hall.

SCHUTZ, ALFRED
  1971   *Collected Papers: The Problem of Social Reality,* edited and introduced by Maurice Natanson. The Hague: Martinus Nijhoff.

SCOTT, MARVIN B.
  1968   *The Racing Game.* Chicago: Aldine.

SCOTT, MARVIN B., AND STANFORD LYMAN
  1968   "Accounts." *American Sociological Review* 33: 46–62.

SKOLNICK, JEROME
  1966   *Justice Without Trial.* New York: Wiley.

SKOLNICK, JEROME, AND J. RICHARD WOODWORTH
  1967   "Bureaucracy, Information and Social Controls: A Study of a Morals Detail." In *The Police: Six Sociological Essays,* edited by David Bordua. New York: Wiley.

STINCHCOMBE, ARTHUR L.
  1963   "Police Practice, Types of Crimes and Social Location." *Americqn Journal of Sociology* 69 (September): 150–60.

STUCKEY, G. B.
  1968   *Evidence for the Law Enforcement Officer.* New York: McGraw-Hill.

SUDNOW, DAVID
1965 "Normal Crimes: Sociological Features of the Penal Code in a Public Defender Office." *Social Problems* 12: 255–76.

SUNDHOLM, CHARLES A.
1973 "Flea Markets." Unpublished paper, University of California, Davis.

SYMONDS, MARTIN
1976 "Emotional Hazards of Police Work." In *The Ambivalent Force,* edited by Arthur Niederhoffer and Abraham S. Blumberg. 2nd ed. Hinsdale, Ill.: Dryden Press.

TERRY, CLINTON, III, AND DAVID LUCKENBILL
1976 "Investigating Criminal Homicides." In *The Criminal Justice Process: A Reader,* edited by William B. Sanders and Howard C. Daudistel. New York: Praeger.

TURNER, RALPH H.
1947 "The Navy Disbursing Officer as a Bureaucrat." *American Sociological Review* 12: 342–48.

VEHICLE CODE OF CALIFORNIA
1972 Sacramento: Department of General Services. (Portions of the Welfare and Institutions Code as well as other codes also included.)

WAMBAUGH, JOSEPH
1973 *The Onion Field.* New York: Delacorte.

WEBB, EUGENE, DONALD T. CAMPBELL, RICHARD D. SCHWARTZ, AND LEE SECHREST
1966 *Unobtrusive Measures: Nonreactive Measures in the Social Sciences.* Chicago: Rand McNally.

WEBER, MAX
1949 *On Methodology of the Social Sciences.* Translated by Edward A. Shils and Henry A. Finch. New York: Free Press.

WESTLEY, WILLIAM A.
1953 "Violence and the Police." *American Journal of Sociology* 49 (July): 34–41.

WHYTE, WILLIAM F.
1953 *Street Corner Society.* Chicago: University of Chicago Press.

WIEDER, D. LAWRENCE
1970 "On Meaning by Rule." In *Understanding Everyday Life: Toward the Reconstruction of Sociological Knowledge,* edited by Jack Douglas. Chicago: Aldine.

1974   *Language and Social Reality: The Case of Telling The Convict Code.* The Hague: Mouton.

WILSON, JAMES Q.
  1968   *Varieties of Police Behavior.* Cambridge: Harvard University Press.

WILSON, THOMAS
  1970   "Conceptions of Interaction and Forms of Sociological Explanation." *American Sociological Review* 35: 697–709.

WISEMAN, JACQUELINE
  1970   *Stations of the Lost.* Englewood Cliffs, N.J.: Prentice-Hall.

WOLFGANG, MARVIN E.
  1961   "A Sociological Analysis of Criminal Homicide." *Federal Probation* 25: 48–55.

YOUNGER, ERIC E.
  1973   "A Burglar's Bag of Tricks." *Westways* (June): 41–43.

ZIMMERMAN, DON H.
  1970   "Record-keeping and the Intake Process in a Public Welfare Agency." In *On Record: Files and Dossiers in American Life,* edited by Stanton Wheeler. New York: Basic Books.

ZIMMERMAN, DON H., AND MELVIN POLLNER
  1970   "The Everyday World as Phenomenon." In *Understanding Everyday Life: Toward the Reconstruction of Sociological Knowledge,* edited by Jack Douglas. Chicago: Aldine.

Index

Index

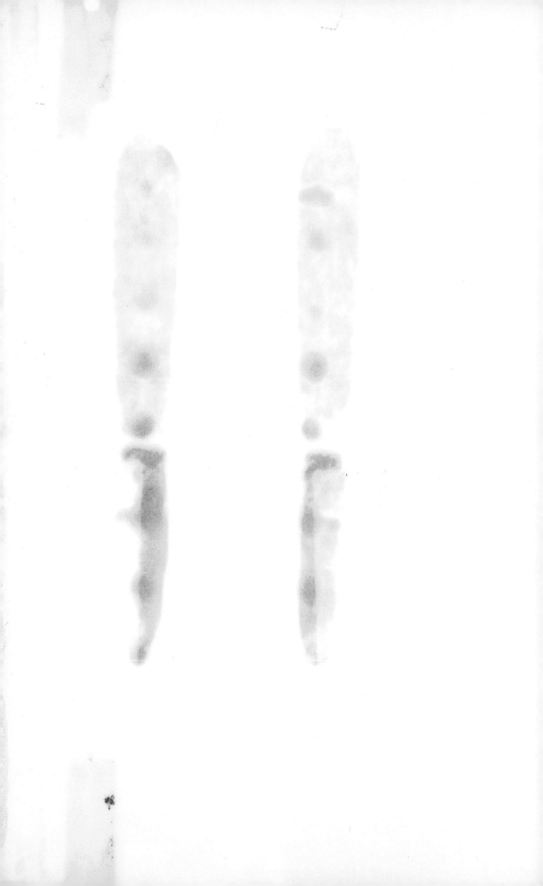